T0374922

The Pastoral Epistles
Through the Centuries

Wiley Blackwell Bible Commentaries

Series Editors: John Sawyer, Christopher Rowland, Judith Kovacs, David M. Gunn
Editorial Board: Ian Boxall, Andrew Mein, Lena-Sofia Tiemeyer
Further information about this innovative reception history series is available at
www.bbibcomm.info.

Forthcoming

The Pastoral Epistles Through the Centuries

Jay Twomey

WILEY Blackwell

Edition history: John Wiley & Sons Ltd. (hardback, 2009)

Registered Offices
John Wiley & Sons, Inc., 111 River Street, Hoboken, NJ 07030, USA
John Wiley & Sons Ltd, The Atrium, Southern Gate, Chichester, West Sussex, PO19 8SQ, UK

Editorial Office
The Atrium, Southern Gate, Chichester, West Sussex, PO19 8SQ, UK

For details of our global editorial offices, customer services, and more information about Wiley products visit us at www.wiley.com.

Wiley also publishes its books in a variety of electronic formats and by print-on-demand. Some content that appears in standard print versions of this book may not be available in other formats.

Library of Congress Cataloging-in-Publication Data

Twomey, Jay.
   The Pastoral Epistles through the centuries / Jay Twomey.
     p. cm. – (Blackwell Bible commentaries)
   Includes bibliographical references and indexes.
   ISBN 978-1-4051-2614-4 (hardcover : alk. paper) | ISBN 978-1-119-00468-4 (paperback)
1. Bible. N.T. Pastoral Epistles – Commentaries.   I. Title.
   BS2735.53.T86 2009
   227′.8307–dc22

                             2008014317

A catalogue record for this book is available from the British Library

Cover Design: Wiley
Cover Image: Wikimedia Commons

Set in 10/12.5pt Minion by SPi Global, Pondicherry, India

Printed and bound by CPI Group (UK) Ltd, Croydon, CR0 4YY

10 9 8 7 6 5 4 3 2 1

Contents

The Blackwell Bible Commentaries series, the first to be devoted primarily to the reception history of the Bible, is based on the premise that how people have interpreted, and been influenced by, a sacred text like the Bible is often as interesting and historically important as what it originally meant. The series emphasizes the influence of the Bible on literature, art, music, and film, its role in the evolution of religious beliefs and practices, and its impact on social and political developments. Drawing on work in a variety of disciplines, it is designed to provide a convenient and scholarly means of access to material until now hard to find, and a much-needed resource for all those interested in the influence of the Bible on western culture.

Until quite recently this whole dimension was for the most part neglected by biblical scholars. The goal of a commentary was primarily if not exclusively to get behind the centuries of accumulated Christian and Jewish tradition to one single meaning, normally identified with the author's original intention.

The most important and distinctive feature of the Blackwell Commentaries is that they will present readers with many different interpretations of each text, in such a way as to heighten their awareness of what a text, especially a sacred text, can mean and what it can do, what it has meant and what it has done, in the many contexts in which it operates.

The Blackwell Bible Commentaries will consider patristic, rabbinic (where relevant), and medieval exegesis as well as insights from various types of modern criticism, acquainting readers with a wide variety of interpretative techniques. As part of the history of interpretation, questions of source, date, authorship, and other historical-critical and archaeological issues will be discussed, but since these are covered extensively in existing commentaries, such references will be brief, serving to point readers in the direction of readily accessible literature where they can be followed up.

Original to this series is the consideration of the reception history of specific biblical books arranged in commentary format. The chapter-by-chapter arrangement ensures that the biblical text is always central to the discussion. Given the wide influence of the Bible and the richly varied appropriation of each biblical book, it is a difficult question which interpretations to include. While each volume will have its own distinctive point of view, the guiding principle for the series as a whole is that readers should be given a representative sampling of material from different ages, with emphasis on interpretations that have been especially influential or historically significant. Though commentators will have their preferences among the different interpretations, the material will be presented in such a way that readers can make up their own minds on the value, morality, and validity of particular interpretations.

The series encourages readers to consider how the biblical text has been interpreted down the ages and seeks to open their eyes to different uses of the Bible in contemporary culture. The aim is to write a series of scholarly commentaries that draw on all the insights of modern research to illustrate the rich interpretative potential of each biblical book.

John Sawyer
Christopher Rowland
Judith Kovacs
David M. Gunn

Acknowledgments

I would never have been able to undertake, let alone complete, this commentary without the significant support of many colleagues, friends and institutions. Thanks are due first and foremost to Judith Kovacs and Chris Rowland who shepherded me through the writing process from proposal to final revision, and who made this a much better book than it ever could have been otherwise. Thanks also to the editors at Blackwell, especially Annette Abel, for putting up with my many delays and confusions. I am grateful to the University of Cincinnati for invaluable material support. The opportunity to take an early academic leave, in addition to the travel and summer grants I received from UC's Taft Research Center and University Research Council, made all the difference in the world. Thanks as well to the Department of Classics at the University of California, Irvine, for providing me with an office and library privileges, as well as a dynamic intellectual community, during my stay there in 2006. I owe more than I can say to my many friends in the Department of English at the University of Cincinnati. Their moral support sustained me during what turned out to be some very difficult years. My parents have always been there for me; thanks to them for all that they have done throughout my academic career. Finally, I would like to thank Richard Layton, a mentor and friend, for having taught me so much not only about biblical scholarship, but also about why it matters.

Publisher's Acknowledgments

The author and publisher gratefully acknowledge the following for permission to reproduce copyright material:

"From the Corpse Woodpiles, from the Ashes". Copyright 1966 by Robert Hayden, from ANGLE OF ASCENT: New and Selected Poems by Robert Hayden. Used by permission of Liveright Publishing Corporation.

Christina Rossetti "Endure Hardness" from Rossetti, C. 1970–1990. *The Complete Poems of Christina Rossetti: A Variorum Edition*, 3 vols., ed. R. W. Crump. Baton Rouge: Louisiana State University Press. Reprinted by permission of Louisiana State University Press.

Charles Bukowski "It's strange" from Bukowski, C. 1981: *Dangling in the Tournefortia*. Santa Barbara: Black Sparrow Press. Copyright © 1981 by Charles Bukowski. Reprinted by permission of HarperCollins Publishers.

The publishers apologize for any errors or omissions in the above list and would be grateful to be notified of any corrections that should be incorporated in the next edition or reprint of this book.

Historical Overview

The three New Testament letters to Timothy and Titus, collectively known as the Pastoral Epistles, are curiously paradoxical texts when considered in terms of their reception. Unlike a major Pauline letter such as Romans, for example, the Pastoral Epistles do not feature sustained arcs of theological reflection, nor do they produce (at least not in any substantial way) the sense of a unique voice, a distinct and distinctive personality. Yet they have been essential to the development of Christian theology and have contributed significantly to the traditional portrait of Paul. Unlike 1 Corinthians or Galatians, or even Philemon, they do not give one the impression of a living community, a

The Pastoral Epistles Through the Centuries, First Edition. Jay Twomey.
© 2009 by Jay Twomey. Published 2020 by John Wiley & Sons Ltd.

charged and complex social world just behind the surface of the text. Yet the Pastoral Epistles reveal much about the social contexts of early Christianity, and they have played a tremendous role in shaping the structure, and thus the community, of the Christian church as a whole. And while they were written to and for church leaders, even a quick survey of their reception indicates the vast extent to which these letters have been appropriated and adapted for purposes quite other than pastoral care.

So, what are these letters, then, exactly? The Pastoral Epistles are a flexible, rich, if rather nebulous body of images, concepts, personal and historical references, in the form of letters addressed by Paul to his coworkers Timothy (in Ephesus) and Titus (in Crete). These two trusted friends and associates of the apostle are said to have been stationed in their respective mission cities to supervise the nascent churches there in a variety of ways. For example, they are told to choose local church leaders (1 Tim. 3; Titus 1), to perform damage control in the wake of divisive conflicts (1 Tim. 1; Titus 1; 2 Tim. 2:14), and to "present themselves" as models of pious behavior to their respective communities (2 Tim. 2:15; 1 Tim. 4:11–16; Titus 2:7–8). These instructions are contextualized in terms of typical Pauline concerns about Jewish law (1 Tim. 1:8–11) and eschatological expectations (1 Tim. 4:1; 2 Tim. 3:1; Titus 2:13), about suffering for the gospel (2 Tim. 1; 3:12) and the salvation offered to the Christian community (1 Tim. 2:3–7; Titus 3:6). Moreover, the exhortations offered to Timothy and Titus are couched in personal, indeed, touching language. Timothy and Titus are cast as Paul's own "loyal" and "beloved" children. Timothy in particular is singled out as Paul's heir (2 Tim. 2:1), is offered moral support in the form of encouraging recollections of the younger man's mother and grandmother (2 Tim. 1:5; 3:15), and is advised about his health (1 Tim. 5:23) and his young age (1 Tim. 4:12). Second Timothy, written as a last testament, also has much to say about Paul's career and his character, as he contemplates his likely execution.

The Pastoral Epistles are also, in the view of a scholarly consensus which this commentary accepts, pseudepigraphal. That is, they are post-Pauline documents, written within a generation of Paul's death, letters which seem to reflect a sense of church structure and tradition and politics quite different from what one finds in Paul's own communities (e.g., Thessalonica, Corinth, the churches in Galatia). The introductory sections within the commentary will discuss more specifically what these differences are, at least as they are construed by modern commentators. The modern refusal to grant authenticity to the Pastorals is worth considering here, though, primarily as a way of framing the reception history of these texts, for it links our moment with one of the earliest responses to the Pastorals. In the mid-second century, the "radicalized Paulinism" (Chadwick 2001: 89) of a Gnostic, or pseudo-Gnostic, theologian named Marcion led to the creation of one of the first canons of Christian scripture. Marcion, working in part from Paul's apparent rejection of the law and of Jewish ceremonial practices, believed that the God of the Hebrew Bible was a lesser, and merciless, deity, and that a higher, benevolent God who had taken pity on humanity was now offering salvation in Jesus Christ. Accordingly he compiled his "Bible" of but a handful of texts: the Gospel of Luke and several of Paul's letters, all of which he purged of any obviously Jewish material. The Pauline corpus in Marcion's canon also excluded the Pastoral Epistles; and because Marcionites eschewed the materiality of human existence (they were docetic in theology and ascetic in practice), an early father such as Tertullian could assume that Marcion left the Pastorals out intentionally because they encourage marriage and childrearing (*Praescr.* 33, ANF 3.259). Major figures in the interpretive tradition have taken Marcion, and his rigorous scriptural excisions, as a point of departure in the construction of orthodoxy over against the heresies of Gnostics. Marcion himself, it has been argued, was not a thoroughgoing Gnostic. But patristic readers could nevertheless cite him, and the threat he posed the church, in their responses to Gnostics (and Manicheans, and ascetics of all stripes). The Pastoral Epistles, apparently excluded by Marcion, become key texts in these debates. Against the "false *gnosis* [knowledge]" of the heretics (see 1 Tim. 6:20), Irenaeus, Tertullian, Origen, and others could oppose passages from the Pastorals in which Paul insists upon the goodness of material reality, or seems to repudiate the idea of a secret Gnostic–Christian teaching.

At the other end of their reception history the letters are rejected yet again, and for reasons not entirely unlike those imputed to Marcion. It is true that some nineteenth century scholars, assuming a relatively late date of composition for the Pastorals, actually suggested that the Pastor wrote these documents in response to the Marcionite heresy. Most scholars now consider the Pastoral Epistles to be earlier than Marcion, and simply reject the authenticity of these letters on the basis of their stylistic, ecclesiological, social, and theological divergence from Paul's own writings. A number of twentieth century scholars argue that the author of the Pastoral Epistles presents an institutionalized, non-charismatic, largely non-eschatological church quite different from the situation in the earliest "authentic" Christian communities. And according to this view, espoused by Rudolf Bultmann among others, "the Christianity of the Pastorals is a somewhat faded Paulinism" (Bultmann 1955: 1.185). Contemporary feminist readings of 1 and 2 Timothy and Titus can even more sharply lament the failure of these letters to maintain what some see as Paul's comparatively radical social agenda (see, for instance, the remarks of Jouette Bassler, cited throughout this commentary). While I tend to agree with the critical rejection of the Pastorals as authentic Pauline texts, nevertheless I have also to acknowledge a curious historical similarity: both the Marcionite and the modern scholarly rejection of the Pastorals mark the two ends of a single interpretive spectrum. For entirely different reasons, to be sure, readers at each pole have favored what they see as the striking newness of Paul, with his ambitious and utterly radical project – announcing a previously unheard-of salvation, in Marcion; establishing a new egalitarianism on the basis of a shared palette of spiritual gifts, in modern scholarship. They have compared the innovation of Paul to the traditionalism of the Pastor, and they have found the Pastor wanting.

The Interpretations

However, if at the beginning and the end (until now, at any rate) of their reception history the Pastorals have suffered at the hands of critics, throughout most of the rest of their history they have been cherished, troubled, exploited, read, misread as writings of the apostle Paul. It would, perhaps, be possible to write a commentary that would differentiate among the interpretive preferences most in play at different epochs of these texts' reception. One could say, in general, and with regard to the theological tradition, that: Patristic writers often use the Pastorals in the service of early Christological and Trinitarian debates; Medieval responses explore the letters' more speculative theological, mystical, dimensions; Reformation writers key in on soteriological concepts; Enlightenment thinkers focus on the political aspects of the Pastor's writings; and eighteenth and nineteenth century interpreters tend to bring elements of the Pastor's piety to the fore.

At the same time, clear interpretive traditions for these letters are difficult to establish with any precision. Major interpretive emphases return again and again across the reception history of these three letters and at some point clear historical boundaries simply break down. One can trace an Augustinian–Calvinist trajectory, on grace and predestination, from the fourth century to the present, of course; but so can one follow, from Origen to the Universalists and beyond, an insistence upon the universality of God's salvation. Additionally, writers of all periods have been invested in working out the contemporary relevance of the Pastor's ecclesiology. Just what are the duties of a bishop, for example, and how are they to be differentiated from those of deacons or elders? And which of these offices is responsible for ordaining fit Ministers of the Word? Moreover, if women are permitted to play certain roles, as deacons perhaps, or as "official" widows, then what are the limits of their authority? The Pastorals don't really provide precise guidance in these matters. These epistles also take a strict line on theological opponents, speculative troublemakers whose challenges to doctrinal authority seem to put the faith itself at risk. Readers through the centuries have consistently adapted the Pastor's critical invective for their own purposes. Ancient readers, as noted above, tended to pit the Pastor against Gnostic heretics, like Marcion or Valentinus. In later centuries, the names may change but the status of the opponents remains the same, so that Reformation writers, for instance, can cast "Papists" as the purveyors of false knowledge and harmful teachings, and a nineteenth century Anglican such as Matthew Arnold can refer to middle-class Protestant "Dissenters" as precisely those people the Pastor castigates in his epistles. And Paul's relationship to Timothy has been developed in consistent ways across diverse periods. The fatherly care he shows for his "son in the faith" becomes for a great many readers a touching reminder of the ideal of pastoral care.

I have tried to pursue such major arcs of interpretive interest wherever, and whenever, they might lead. The goal of my approach is not the construction of a univocal tradition, however. Readers will see that this commentary foregrounds a great diversity of responses, and draws attention to especially creative counter-readings, often by non-traditional figures, that trouble common and traditional understandings of these letters. If I continue to refer to "the tradition," I do so because it seems an easy shorthand for the multiplicity and complexity of what are nevertheless interconnected readings. Moreover, despite my interest in pushing the idea of reception study to its extreme limits, I do return again and again to certain key figures who, and a couple of major themes which, can provide this commentary with an overall sense of coherence. A word or two about some of these readers and themes may be helpful at this point.

Significant interpreters

John Chrysostom, whose name means "golden-mouth," probably wrote and delivered his homily series on the Pastoral Epistles in late fourth century Antioch, where he served as a priest before becoming the bishop of Constantinople in 398. The Antiochene school of interpretation favored literal over allegorical readings, and Chrysostom's homiletic treatment of the Pastor's letters evinces this emphasis on the historical, biographical, and factual. Because of this, and because his sermons were preached for the instruction of a socially complex congregation in an important urban center, Chrysostom's reading of the Pastoral Epistles often have a very concrete dimension to them which allows us to glimpse, ever so fleetingly, something of the everyday lives of his original audience. The Pastor's exhortations to slaves, for example, give Chrysostom the opportunity to address both slaves and slave owners in his audience (Mayer and Allen 2000: 35). Although in no way does Chrysostom challenge slavery as an institution, he nevertheless seems to subordinate, rhetorically at least, masters to slaves, while acknowledging the unnaturalness of slavery itself (see at 1 Tim. 6:1–2) – a curious balancing act, in which one is tempted to read a responsive awareness of tensions in the church not unlike those Paul seems to have faced in his day (e.g., 1 Cor. 7:21). Chrysostom also responds relatively personally to the Paul of the Pastorals, especially to the language of Paul's suffering and commitment from 2 Timothy. Incidentally, Chrysostom is but one of many figures cited in *The Pastoral Epistles Through the Centuries* who wrote complete treatments of these letters. Others whose work I draw upon frequently include Theodoret of Cyrus, Thomas Aquinas, Erasmus, John Calvin, and John Wesley, not to mention modern academic commentators such as Dibelius and Conzelmann (abbreviated D-C herein), Jouette Bassler, and Philip Towner.

Augustine (354–430) was also a major figure in the early reception history of the Pastorals. Augustine began his career as a student of literature and philosophy, albeit one who quested religiously for truth. Baptized by Ambrose of Milan (338–97), Augustine was ordained a priest in Hippo Regius, in North Africa, in 391, and was elevated to the episcopacy within a few years. As Bishop of Hippo, Augustine, a prolific writer and acute thinker, was central to most of the theological debates of the late fourth and early fifth centuries; and he drew upon the Pastorals in all of his most significant theological works. For instance, in his struggles with the Pelagians about the essential role of God's grace in stimulating the faith that leads to salvation, Augustine can productively cite 1 Timothy 1:13 ("I was formerly a blasphemer, a persecutor, and a man of violence. But I received mercy because I had acted ignorantly in unbelief.") to show that nothing human beings do independently of God can produce the faith requisite for salvation. Pelagius held just the opposite view, that human beings are granted reason by God's grace, and that they freely choose the paths their lives will take, thus earning their salvation or damnation by their own lights. For Augustine, however, the fact that God would choose Paul, a confessed "blasphemer," and indeed the "chief of sinners" (1 Tim. 1:13, 15), and utterly transform him apropos of nothing he himself had done, is proof positive that without the gift of grace, salvation is simply not possible. Augustine's reading of this and similar biblical texts had a profound effect upon the theology of the Christian west, although it wasn't until the Reformation (see the many relevant citations from Luther and Calvin in the commentary) that the Augustinian notion of grace came fully into its own.

Thomas Aquinas (1225–74) is cited frequently in this commentary as well, in part because he also produced a full-length commentary on the Pastorals, but also because his Aristotelian version of Augustinian thought is so characteristic of medieval scholasticism. Thomas' major work, the *Summa Theologica*, is a vast and systematic exposition of all the major points of Christian theology. Scripture serves not only as a source of proofs in the *Summa*, but as the very inspiration for reflection (cosmological, theological, philosophical, ethical) itself. One of the most significant uses Thomas makes of the Pastorals, although it seems quite uncharacteristic of the more sensitive and speculative dimensions of his thought, is in justifying the execution of heretics on the basis of Titus 3:10–11 ("After a first and second admonition, have nothing more to do with anyone who causes divisions, since you know that such a person is perverted and sinful, being self-condemned."). If civil law calls for the death of forgers and other relatively petty criminals, he asks, then how much more should the church insist upon the eradication of those who corrupt the faith?

Luther's (1483–1546) readings of the Pastorals are lively and forceful, and appear with some frequency in this volume, as do Erasmus' (1466–1536) reform-minded Catholic *Paraphrases*. But the central voice of the Protestant era cited here is that of John Calvin (1509–64). I chose Calvin quite simply because his wonderfully insightful exegesis of the Pastorals, frequently produced in support of his theory of predestination, eventually had the more significant impact on theology and literature in the American tradition, which I have tried to emphasize to some extent (for example, by citing the works of Jonathan Edwards). Calvin's commentaries on these letters were written in the early-to-mid 1550s, in Geneva, which he had helped transform into a functioning Protestant society, governed in part by a council of ministers and lay people whose function was to police the moral and religious life of the city. Despite the rigor of Calvin's theology, his commentaries on the Pastorals reveal a good deal of exegetical complexity vis-à-vis central Calvinist questions about the efficacy of grace over works, for example. Noting that 1 Timothy 4:7 advocates a "training in godliness" along the lines of the "physical training" of the athlete, Calvin acknowledges that for some believers what he would consider essentially useless works were, if performed in the right state of mind, useful aids to the religious life.

Other figures are discussed in the commentary with some regularity as well. Among them, perhaps the most interesting are: John Wesley (1703–91), representing an important strand of eighteenth century piety; and Søren Kierkegaard (1813–55), whose religious musings are rooted equally in Lutheran piety and an early philosophical existentialism.

Areas of Interpretive Interest

Another way of producing a sense of continuity across the complex, frequently bewildering array of interpretive responses collected in a commentary such as this is to foreground types of readings that recur throughout the tradition. I use several basic categories to link similar kinds of material across the three letters, the most important of which are entitled: "Women," "The Church," "Theological Speculation," and "The Opponents," each of which is outlined below. Other, less frequent categories will include material on epistolary conventions (e.g., "The Thanksgiving") and the Pastor's depictions of Paul ("Paul") and his correspondents ("Timothy").

Women

Given my own background in contemporary literary and critical theory, and my investment in feminist, queer, and cultural studies approaches to the Bible, I tend to want to foreground readings which "trouble" the texts. Indeed, I was initially attracted to the Pastorals after having discovered how the seventeenth century Mexican nun, poet, and proto-feminist Sor Juana Inés de la Cruz dispatched what many would consider the Pastor's misogyny (see examples of her critical readings at 1 Tim. 2:12 and Titus 1:12). That she had to do so is indicative of the ways in which these letters construct gender, and thus patriarchal power, for later readers; and the way she responds to the texts, rendering them more rather than less empowering for women, is indicative of a widespread tendency among interpreters to read particular verses, in various ways, against the grain.

The Pastoral Epistles rank among the New Testament's most problematic texts for women. Although the Pastor's patriarchal attitude is certainly unacceptable for many today, and for many twentieth and twenty-first century Christian women in particular, readers in all periods have frequently relied upon his strictures to enforce rigid limits on women's full participation in the religious life of their communities. Perhaps this lamentable fact is only to be expected. Still, a reception history of the Pastoral Epistles can be quite intriguing not only because it allows one to trace the role of these texts in the history of Christian attitudes toward women, but also because it shows the ways in which the Christian tradition itself has registered its occasional discomfort with such attitudes. Women like Teresa of Avila, Sor Juana, Margaret Fell, Anne Hutchinson, and Charlotte Brontë, for example, join forces with literary characters such Chaucer's Wife of Bath and historical figures whose own voices are all but lost to us, like Jerome's Marcella, collectively (if diversely) to respond to a key plank in western Christianity's traditionally patriarchal platform.

Even when the commentary treats the reception of passages unrelated to the Pastor's view of women, it does, whenever possible, feature the readings of women. Thus, for example, in considering the responses to the statement in Titus 1:11 that opponents "must be silenced," we encounter the words of two seventeenth century Quakers, Katharine Evans and Sarah Chevers, who had been imprisoned by the Inquisition, and whose understanding of the Pastor's view of his opponents inspired their own resistance to coercion. Later in the same letter, an excerpt from Jeanette Winterson's semi-autobiographical novel *Oranges are Not the Only Fruit* reads the Pastor's ambiguous concern for purity through the lens of a youthful, religious, lesbianism. Readings by men which similarly recontextualize verses from the Pastorals in more or less overtly feminist ways are also given special attention (see for example the excerpt from Donald Barthelme's novel, *The Dead Father*, at 2 Tim. 3:6–7).

Interestingly, even some of the tradition's most conservative readers have occasionally deployed unexpectedly pro-feminist tactics. For example, although Jerome may be among the last of the fathers one would turn to for thoughts on gender equality, he nevertheless notes, approvingly, that his student Marcella would, when teaching men, give "her own opinion not as her own but as from . . . [a man]. . . . For she knew that the apostle had said: 'I suffer not a woman to teach,' and she would not seem to inflict a wrong upon the male sex" (*Ep.* 2.6, NPNF2 6.256). From this it is but a short step to the exegetical ingenuity of Sor Juana who, claiming Jerome as an influence, argues that 1 Timothy 2:11 "is more in favor than against women, since it requires them to study, and while they study it is clear that they need to be silent" ("Reply to Sor Filotea," 2005: 282). Clearly, if to differing degrees, both feel they must respect the scriptural injunction; yet both also find ways of keeping to the Pastoral letter, while subverting its spirit. Other men and women develop different strategies, sometimes historicizing a passage in order to limit its contemporary valence, sometimes (as in the case of Teresa of Avila at Titus 2:5) claiming to have a divine dispensation which frees them from the Pastor's restrictions.

In a way that could, conceivably, dovetail with these efforts, even as they concern other issues altogether, major and minor figures in the reception history of the Pastorals will sometimes read gender-specific verses in gender-neutral ways. I suggest that these readings "democratize" the verses in question because they broaden their scope to include both men and women. Thus, when Augustine takes "widow" in 1 Timothy 5:6 ("the widow who lives for pleasure is dead even while she lives") to mean any and all believers regardless of gender, and even the church itself, he democratizes, generalizes the verse. Such democratizing tactics, of course, are limited neither to readings of these letters nor to issues relevant to women's religious agency (see some of the readings of "slave" at 1 Tim. 6:1, for instance). I draw attention to them partly to show the range of tools available within traditional readers' exegetical toolboxes, but also subtly to hint that efforts to read the Pastor, or any biblical text, against the grain for emancipatory purposes are authorized and legitimated by a rich history of precedents.

There are certain passages concerning women in the Pastorals, however, which merit consideration in terms of the early development of church offices. These will be addressed in the commentary under the next heading.

The church

The second major area of interest pursued in this commentary concerns church order, construed in the broadest possible sense to include everything from ethical and social prerequisites for church office to the kinds of behaviors expected of members of the communities which Timothy and Titus are striving to consolidate. The commentary treats the construction of social status and socio-political categories from a variety of perspectives in order to trouble the normative claims readers of the Pastorals have made through the centuries. For instance, the Pastoral Epistles are perhaps best known in church circles for what they have to say about the development of leadership positions in early Christianity; consequently affirmations of these offices are given pride of place when church offices are at issue. First Timothy 3 and Titus 2 include information about bishops, elders (presbyters), and deacons which readers through the centuries have both adopted and puzzled over. With regard to the most significant office, that of bishop, the latest edition of the Catholic Church's Code of Canon Law, for instance, seems very clearly to build upon the Pastor's requirements that bishops be capable of teaching, be of a certain age and standing, and be able to foster the harmonious spiritual development of the community. Indeed, the extent to which this recent restatement of the Pastor's basic qualifications has held steady through time is truly remarkable; language similar to the Pastor's (and the Vatican's) can be found in the fourth century *Apostolic Constitutions* as well as in an eleventh century communal letter by the Christian community of Noyon and

Tournai (in present-day Belgium) discussing their selection of a candidate for the episcopacy. But if the Pastor's thoughts on church office have created a relatively stable tradition of ecclesiastical thought, they have also informed radical reformers (like Milton), who find in their contemporary political contexts sufficient grounds for rejecting episcopal authority, and thus for rereading the Pastor as source of anti-episcopal rhetoric. In Milton's view, since the Pastor never makes a clear distinction between bishop and presbyter, the later historical development of the episcopacy is a deviation from the biblical rule.

Another area of productive tension concerns the question of clerical celibacy. That bishops, in the Pastor's view, ought to be married men (the most basic reading of "the husband of one wife," 1 Tim. 3:2), complicated the valorization of celibacy in early theological tradition. As a result, Augustine and others have recourse to allegorical renderings of this verse, in order not to allow that bishops could marry. Later readers, notably the reformers, find such allegorical interpretations less than compelling, and consequently turn the Pastor's comments on marriage and church office (deacons and elders, too, are required to be married) into polemical proof-texts in their battles with their ecclesiastical and theological opponents.

Despite the Pastor's interest in limiting the active religious roles women might play in his community, he is thought by a diverse range of readers through the centuries to have instituted an office of deaconesses (on the basis of 1 Tim. 3:11). Chrysostom, for instance, explained that the Pastor "was referring to those [women] having the dignity of the diaconate" and not to wives or "women in general"; and Theodore of Mopsuestia believed that the women of this verse were "to exercise the same office as the [male] deacons" (in Wijngaards 2002: 169, 178). Even Thomas Aquinas, although ultimately opposed to women holding office, has to acknowledge that it was quite possible to read the text in support of a diaconate of women (Thomas Aquinas 2007: 43).

But church office is simply one among many issues pertaining to the organization of religious life in the Pastor's communities. Another has to do with the appropriate behavior of individual believers, including slaves. The New Testament does not reject slavery as an institution, and so it should come as no surprise that the Pastorals do not either. This rather benign historical contextualization, however, cannot begin to account for the various ways in which nineteenth century American anti-abolitionists, for instance, used passages like 1 Timothy 6:1–2 and Titus 2:9–10 in support of slavery. James Shannon, for example, a president of the University of Missouri in the 1850s, sought biblical warrant for his pro-slavery agenda, and found it in 1 Timothy 6:1–5, which text led him to assume "that they had some abolition *ignoramuses* even in Paul's day; and that inspired Apostle pronounced them '*men of corrupt minds,* and *destitute of the truth,*' and commanded Christians to withdraw from their society" (Shannon 1855: 14). Abolitionists during this period similarly tried to bolster their cause with biblical citations, but the Pastoral Epistles made it all but impossible to do so convincingly. The Pastor's exhortations to slaves have also been generalized as advice to servants (Luther) and, recently, to workers generally (Nelson 2005: 143). Others, however, like the poet Wanda Coleman, cite the Pastor's "yoke" imagery only to reject it in favor of a vision of revolutionary change.

This commentary also includes, under "The Church": material concerning ritual and liturgy; what we would consider today as church–state relations; the problem of apostolic succession; and other issues.

The opponents

For the historically minded scholar of the Pastorals, the identity and program of the Pastor's opponents are a maddening conundrum since we are given almost no information about them at all. We do learn something about the Pastor himself, though, namely that he prefers not to engage his opponents directly, but rather by means of invective. And it is fascinating to note how, again and again, readers of these letters simply adapt the Pastor's criticisms of his opponents to reflect their own perspectives. Theodoret, for instance, takes up the Pastor's reference to an opponent named Alexander the coppersmith (1 Tim. 1:20; 2 Tim. 4:14) to mark, it would seem, a clearer distinction between the artisanal class and the educated elite: he is "a man of no sort of distinction at all, – no nobility of birth, no eloquence of speech, who never led a political party nor an army in the field; who never played the man in fight, but plied from day to day his ignominious craft, and won fame for nothing but his mad violence against Saint Paul" (NPNF2 3.160). Thomas Aquinas, reading Titus 3:10, was fully aware that the Pastor does not encourage the church to condemn an opponent without first trying, by admonishments, to change him. But "after that, if he is yet stubborn, the Church no longer hoping for his conversion, looks to the salvation of others, by excommunicating him and separating him from the Church, and furthermore delivers him to the secular tribunal to be exterminated thereby from the world by death" (ST SS Q[11] A[3]). Luther and Calvin consistently collapse the boundaries between their reforming moment and the Pastor's conflicts by casting the "Papists" as the opponents described in these epistles. Cotton Mather cites 2 Tim. 3:1 both to insist upon the apocalyptic signs of his times and to justify the persecution of witches in New England (Mather 1693: 23). Not all readers could so easily endorse the Pastor's approach to opposition, however. In the early twentieth century, Karl Barth acknowledged that part of the "fight of faith" was stopping the mouths of theological opponents. However, contrary to most other readings of Titus 1:11, Barth argued that "[t]he ministry of the Word can in no wise be understood as a fight of one party against a counter party" (1936: 87–8).

Theological speculation

Although they tend not to engage very extensively in theological reflection, these letters nevertheless do include some of the New Testament's most intriguing language regarding what the Pastor calls the "mystery" of God. It is quite possible that the Pastor's theological considerations include material he has borrowed from liturgical formulae, early hymns, and the like, but readers have found his imagery inspiring no matter what its original source may have been. Negative theologians, such as Pseudo-Dionysius, eagerly took up the image of a God who "dwells in unapproachable light" (1 Tim. 6:16), and spoke of "the divine darkness . . . where God is said to live. And if it is invisible because of a superabundant clarity, if it cannot be approached because of the outpouring of its transcendent gift of light, yet it is here that is found everyone worthy to know God and to look upon him" (*Epistle* 5, 1987: 265). Other readers adapt other passages – those involving concepts of God's eternal consistency (2 Tim. 2:13), for instance, or Christ's preexistence (2 Tim. 1:9) and divinity (Titus 2:13) – as the basis for their own speculative projects. The Pastorals have also been an important source of soteriological reflection in the tradition. According to 1 Timothy 2:4, God "desires everyone to be saved." This verse, with its hopeful universalism, poses particular problems for theologies of predestination. Augustine and Calvin had thus to argue that the "all" of "all men" was simply a reference to categories, hence to all *kinds* of men. Further narrowing the idea of God's universal call to salvation, Augustine even altered the verse so that it would better support his position. God teaches all those who are saved, he claimed, "*all such* to come to Christ, for He wills all such to be saved, and to come to the knowledge of the truth" (*De praed. sanct.* 14, NPNF1 5.505). Everyone else is, of course, lost. The contrary view, that "all" indeed means "all men," receives a variety of endorsements throughout the centuries as well. The Wesleys, for instance, insist in an eighteenth century hymn that "not one of all that fell / but may Thy favour find" (Hymn 15, *Poetical Works* 1868: 3.90).

The Commentary

Beyond the thematic foci helping to organize this commentary is the canonical structure of the Pastorals themselves. As with the other commentaries in this series, *The Pastoral Epistles Through the Centuries* explores the reception of these texts in generally sequential (that is, verse by verse) and chronological order. However, there are many passages in this three-letter corpus, and especially in 1 Timothy and Titus, which significantly overlap. In order to avoid repetition, therefore, I have decided to cross-reference similar material whenever possible. Generally texts are cross-referenced at the first instance of a concept's appearance. For example, readings of Titus 3:1, concerning attitudes toward the ruling authorities, are discussed at 1 Timothy 2:1–2, where we encounter the same ideas. 1 Timothy is a longer letter, certainly, containing six chapters to 2 Timothy's four and Titus' three, and this in itself justifies the greater attention afforded it. But the cross-referencing, and the consequent need to deal early on with problems in the scholarship on these letters, undoubtedly adds to the burden 1 Timothy is asked to bear in this commentary. On occasion the cross-referencing is delayed if the readings at a later occurrence of an idea or motif are generally more interesting or robust; so, for example, the "good fight" language of 1 Timothy 6:12 (and 1:18) is discussed at 2 Timothy 4:6–7.

I begin the major sections within each chapter of the commentary with a survey of contemporary scholarly perspectives. I am not thereby privileging as wholly accurate or even as more fully adequate what are, in essence, simply additional readings in the reception of these texts. Still, since many of my readers may be largely unfamiliar with the Pastorals, I thought it important to introduce the letters in the way readers would be most likely to discover them on their own: by looking into modern commentaries, or perhaps by picking up a collection of recent scholarly essays. The reader is, of course, invited to begin with these introductory sections, or not, as he or she sees fit.

The chronological order of readings is, with perhaps one or two brief exceptions, maintained throughout. Since thematic concerns naturally take precedence over strict chronological presentation, the commentary is not always especially rigorous with regard to the priority of citations within a particular period. Readers will also see that in a commentary such as this chronological ordering is a micro-, rather than a macro-, organizational tool. That is to say, discrete sets of readings, in response to specific verses, are grouped together in what are essentially miniature units, within which citations are arranged, generally, in the order of their composition. Over the course of a given chapter, however, there will be several such units, and thus each chapter as a whole bears constant witness to the ebb and flow of time – of interpretive time, that is.

To help the reader navigate through these units, the commentary makes use of two types of section headings. A major thematic unit is headed by a title (using one or the other of the categories discussed above) in bold font. The cross-referencing is given alongside this title, to indicate either that material from other letters will be discussed in this section, or simply that one can find similar ideas elsewhere in the Pastorals, or both. There follow a number of smaller sub-sections detailing the reception history of specific passages, and each of these is headed by an italicized full verse or partial excerpt from the passage. On occasion the content of these subsections is subdivided into kinds of readings (e.g., theological, political, literary), but usually no very clear distinctions are made between one mode of reception and another.

This commentary draws largely upon the New Revised Standard Version of the Pastoral Epistles, but will frequently, especially in discussing readings which cite from the letters themselves, defer to the King James or other translations. At the end of the volume readers will find a biographical glossary, which provides very basic information on most of the figures named in the commentary. This section is followed by a bibliography and index. Please note that the bibliography begins with a list of the abbreviations used throughout the book and concludes with information about the various websites referenced in the commentary.

1 Timothy 1

This first letter of the Pastorals corpus begins with the Pastor, or "Paul," describing the situation Timothy must correct in Ephesus: some members of the Christian community are teaching "a different doctrine," and are engaging in theological speculation based upon material from the Hebrew Bible, especially the genealogies and the law. "Paul" remembers his former life as a "persecutor" of the church, and considers his own transformation a model to which others might look for inspiration. The chapter concludes with comments about two individuals, Hymenaeus and Alexander, whom "Paul" has apparently excommunicated for their misdeeds.

The Pastoral Epistles Through the Centuries, First Edition. Jay Twomey.
© 2009 by Jay Twomey. Published 2020 by John Wiley & Sons Ltd.

The Salutation (1:1–2; 2 Tim. 1–2; Titus 1:1–4)

All modern commentators note that the superscription, addressee, and salutation portions of the Pastoral Epistles differ in important ways from those of the undisputed Pauline letters. The Pastoral Epistles, like Romans and Galatians, are not of corporate authorship, and like Philemon, are addressed to specific individuals (although Philemon is also addressed to "the church in your house"; Philem. 2). Unlike any letters in the Pauline corpus, however, 1 Timothy and Titus link Paul's apostleship to divine "commandment" and not to God's "will," suggesting perhaps that the Pastor thinks of Paul as having been commissioned for his task (Bassler 1996: 36). Each of the Pastorals also alters Paul's typical salutation formula, "Grace to you and Peace from *God our Father and the Lord Jesus Christ*," by adding "mercy" (1 and 2 Tim.), and by switching Paul's possessive pronoun from before "Father" to before "Lord": "God the Father and Jesus *Christ our Lord*" ("*our* Savior" in Titus 1:4). Bassler, thinking of 1 Timothy 1:2 in terms of 1 Timothy 6:13 ("God who gives life to all things"), proposes that the Pastor may have been indicating that while God is universally the father of all, Christ Jesus is the lord only of believers (1996: 36; cf. 1 Tim. 4:10).

One similarity is that neither 1 Timothy nor the authentic Paulines speak of Christ as savior (with the exception of Phil. 3:20). The Pastor uses the designation frequently of Christ and God both, or of Christ only (Titus 2:13), elsewhere, but not of Christ here. Towner, a proponent of Pauline authorship of the Pastorals, argues that the differences in usage reflect differences in intention. 1 Timothy "suppresses" the use of savior for Christ, he argues, because one of the aims of the letter is to foreground Jesus' humanity (e.g., as at 2:5, 2006: 63, 97).

Grace, mercy, and peace (v. 1)

Differences such as those mentioned above can often mark the Pastorals as non-Pauline for the modern reader. But others in the tradition, like Calvin, have noted them as well. It is unusual, first of all, according to Calvin, that "Paul" pronounces himself an apostle in a letter written to Timothy alone. Who less than Timothy needs to be told of Paul's apostolic status? "Paul," then, must have had the others in mind, the opponents, "who were not so willing to give him a hearing, or so ready to accept what he said." Possibly "Paul" expected this letter, like his others, to be read aloud in public service. More problematic is the fact that God is savior instead of Christ, which minimizes, if it doesn't eliminate, the traditional Christological weight of this term. The problem can be solved, though, if one assumes that God, having given Christ to the world, is the ultimate source of the salvation that comes through Jesus (*Commentary*, Calvin 1964: 187). Still less acceptable to Calvin was the Pastor's "grace, mercy, and peace." Not only does "Paul" here deviate from his other letters, but also he does not observe "the exact order of the words for he has put first 'grace' which ought to come second, since it is from mercy that grace flows. It is because He is merciful that God first receives us into His grace, and then goes on loving us" (188). Calvin simply concludes that there must have been some good, logical reason for the change, without suggesting what that reason was.

My loyal child in the faith (v. 2)

Even though Calvin may have had his concerns with 1 Timothy's opening verses, one should not assume from this that he seriously questioned the letter's authenticity. Readers have traditionally been quite comfortable with the Pastor's "Paul," and have taken a special pleasure in remarking upon "Paul's" relationship with Timothy, his own "son in the faith," his "dearly beloved son" (v. 2; 2 Tim. 1:2, KJV), and with Titus, his "loyal child in the faith we share" (Titus 1:4). Chrysostom, typical of a general tendency among interpreters, comments upon the poignancy of the personal affection "Paul" has for Timothy and Titus, while indicating that their faith qualifies "Paul's" paternity in significant ways:

> Not merely his "son," but, "dearly beloved"; since it is possible for sons not to be beloved. Not such, he means, art thou; I call thee not merely a son, but a "dearly beloved son" . . . where love does not arise from nature, it must arise from the merit of the object. Those who are born of us, are loved not only on account of their virtue, but from the force of nature; but when those who are of the faith are beloved, it is on account of nothing but their merit, for what else can it be?

Chrysostom adds, with a vaguely comic inconsistency, that Paul "never acted from partiality," but that nonetheless he felt he had to call Timothy "beloved son" to allay fears about his delay (1 Tim. 4:13; 2 Tim. 2:4; 4:6–9) in returning to Ephesus (*Hom. 1 Tim.*, NPNF1 13.476; cf. Theodoret, *Comm. 1 Tim.*, 2001: 2.252).

Recent readers have similarly found the relationship between "Paul" and his sons significant, but often in more intensely personal terms (see also Chrysostom at 2 Tim. 4:7). Ellen White appreciates the tender "love" this father feels for his son (*Acts of The Apostles*, 1911: 204), while Ceslas Spicq, in his commentary, imagines Timothy's devotion to his spiritual father "Paul" as akin to the attraction of "a heavenly body which revolves around a great star" (1969: 1.49–50).

The Opponents: Speculators (1:3–7; 4:1–5, 7; Titus 3:9)

The opening salvo of the letters, this attack upon and warnings about the "vain janglings" (KJV) of "certain people," provides very little concrete information. The references to "myths and genealogies," "old wives' tales," "stupid controversies," especially in conjunction with an interest in the law, suggests, as most recent commentators agree, some combination of a rather ill-defined early Gnostic speculative reading of the Hebrew scriptures (D-C 1972: 17), and the creative, more or less self-consciously Jewish practice of midrash (in which the Pastor himself also engages, Collins 2002: 74; Hanson 1982: 30). The Pastor's message seems to be that speculation is tantamount to teaching false doctrines, to heterodoxy. For some commentators, this is simply one among many indications that the Pastor is no theologian, that he has "a rooted mistrust of all speculative thinking" (Easton 1948: 22), or even that in combating his opponents, he is in fact attempting to stifle a group of truly "creative theologians" (Donelson 1986: 124). Others are more sympathetic to the Pastor's situation, suggesting that the enormous religious confusion of Ephesus and Crete is driving the Pastor's comments (Keck and Furnish 1984: 141). Although some scholars have admirably attempted to paint a full portrait of the opposition facing the Pastor in Ephesus (e.g., Towner 1989), the vagueness of the Pastorals with regard to these opponents is probably as indicative of generalized polemical aims and the pseudepigraphal impulse as it is a response to actual opponents in Ephesus (D-C 1972: 66; Bauer 1971: 89; Donelson 1986: 124; Bassler 1996: 29).

Myths and genealogies (vv. 3–4)

As will become evident in this volume, readers of these letters frequently draw upon the Pastor's tendentious presentation of his opponents either to spar with opponents of their own, or to comment on their own historical moments. Athanasius accuses the Arians of both building upon the kind of false teachings seen in Timothy's Ephesus and Titus' Crete, and even surpassing them "in impiety" (*Hist. Ar.* 8.66, NPNF2 4.294). Other early patristic writers clearly considered the work of these speculative genealogists to be Gnostic in nature (e.g., Irenaeus AH 1.1, ANF 1.315). Still others assumed that the genealogies in question were Jewish and argued, with Ignatius, that such reflection was a denial of grace (*Magnesians* 8, ANF 1.62). Augustine treats Faustus similarly, suggesting that he "fulfills" the message of 2 Timothy 4:3–4 about believers with "itching ears" rejecting the truth in favor of myths (*C. Faust.* 2.4, NPNF1 4.157). John Milton, himself a latter-day Arian and anti-clerical radical, borrows from these passages to mock the use of scripture and church history supporting episcopal hierarchy in the Church of England. His posthumous opponent, Lancelot Andrewes, is said to "enforce" his position "with much ostentation of endlesse genealogies, as if he were the man that St. *Paul* forewarns us of in *Timothy*" (*Reason of Church Government, Complete Prose* 1.774). He might have added, had he had the benefit of citing Erasmus' *Paraphrases* on 1 Timothy 1:4, that the "gift of evangelical salvation" does not "trickle . . . down to us through the corporal branches of family trees" (1993: 7).

Chaucer's Parson, although not engaged directly in polemic, hints at the contemporary relevance of the Pastor's criticism of "myths and genealogies" when, in the Prologue to his tale/sermon, he explains:

> thou getest fable noon ytoold for me,
> For Paul, that writeth unto Tymothee,
> Repreveth hem that weyven soothfastnesse
> and tellen fables, and swich wrecchednesse.
> Why sholde I sowen draf out of my fest,
> When I may sowen whete, if that me lest?
>   (X [I] 31–36, 1987: 287)

The Parson seems implicitly to condemn the tales preceding his own as wretched insofar as they mix truth and "fables," understood here not as fictions, but as lies – or perhaps, as Calvin will say, "trifles," not wholly untrue, but simply "foolish and unprofitable" (*Commentary* 1964: 189). Indeed, many, like the Parson, find in the Pastor's advice to Timothy a rejection of figurative language as unsuitable for religious discourse. John Bunyan's "Apology" to his *Pilgrim's Progress* reflects upon this attitude, but defensively. Bunyan, citing also from 1 Timothy 6:3 (cf. 2 Tim. 1:13; Titus 2:8), explains:

> Sound words I know Timothy is to use,
> And old Wives Fables he is to refuse . . .

Certain of his friends having discouraged the publication of his book on the grounds that "such a stile as this" will only obscure the meaning, Bunyan says he was initially reluctant to proceed. He quite slyly notes, however, that:

> ... grave Paul him no where doth forbid
> The use of Parables; in which lay hid
> That Gold, those Pearls, and precious stones that were
> Worth digging for [Matt. 13:46], and that with greatest care.

And he goes on to argue, in a traditional vein, that even the Bible "in many places, / Hath semblance with this method," granting to his allegory the imprimatur of "holy Writ" (2003: 7).

Speculations rather than the divine training (v. 4)

The anti-speculative thrust of the Pastoral Epistles is more of a problem for recent commentators than for others in the tradition. Earlier figures in the tradition seem to feel that the Pastor was well within his rights to foreclose debates of this kind. Chrysostom judges that "he who questions cannot believe," rhetorically effecting the impossibility of religiously motivated inquiry. Nevertheless, he seems also to recognize that theological questions not only ought to be acceptable, but in fact are legitimated by Jesus himself, who said: "seek and you shall find" (Matt. 7:7, KJV) and "search the scriptures" (John 5:39). He is forced, then, to circumscribe the very idea of questioning within a tighter compass: "the seeking there [i.e., in the Gospel passages just cited] is meant of prayer and vehement desire, and He bids 'search the Scriptures,' not to introduce the labors of questioning, but to end them, that we may ascertain and settle their true meaning, not that we may be ever questioning, but that we may have done with it" (*Hom. 1 Tim.*, NPNF1 13.410). As long as questioning is more or less equivalent to a careful and faithful exegesis, it is acceptable. Moreover, faith of this sort must be acknowledged not merely as a restriction placed by "Paul" upon Christian intellectual freedom, but as foundational to everyday life too. Without faith, he writes, "everything is subverted. And why do I speak of it in heavenly things? We shall find upon examination that earthly things depend upon it no less. For without this there would be no trade nor contracts, nor anything of the sort. And if it be so necessary here in things that are false, how much more" in those heavenly things, which are true and eternal (*Hom. 1 Tim.*, NPNF1 13.411). Faith, not money, makes the world go around.

Calvin uses 1 Timothy 1:4 as an opportunity to disparage scholastic debates, but he, more than Chrysostom, also wants to allow space for theological disputes. Accordingly he decides that "Paul" in this passage "judges of doctrine by the fruit"; questions leading to "edification" and not to "unprofitable disputes" are perfectly acceptable (*Commentary* 1964: 190).

The end of the commandment (v. 5)

The Pastor everywhere indicates that questioning the faith is not only unprofitable for faith and "contrary to the sound teaching" (v. 10), but unethical as well, for by asking questions and engaging in disputes his opponents have "deviated" from "the end of the commandment [which] is charity out of a pure heart, and of a good conscience, and of a faith unfeigned" (v. 5, KJV). This verse is frequently cited by Augustine in any number of contexts. For example: Adam and Eve loved God with precisely this love (*caritas*) prior to the Fall (*De civ. Dei* 14.26, 2000: 474); "[F]aithful women who are married [and without children], and virgins dedicated to God," whose dedication and devotion derive from "the end of the commandment," charity, are to be understood "spiritually" as "mothers of Christ" (*De virg.* 6, NPNF1 3.419); and indeed this love, like proper attire at the wedding in the parable (Matt. 22:11), is the love that distinguishes true Christians in community from others who, although they may participate in communities of their own, have only fruitlessness and vanity to show for it (*Serm.* 40.6, NPNF1 6.394). Augustine also, and perhaps most significantly, takes "the commandment" to refer to "all the divine precepts" of the "law and the prophets," the "Gospels and the apostles," concluding that "every commandment has love for its aim" (*Enchiridion* 121, NPNF1 3.275).

The verse is not simply indicative of the paramount importance of love in Christian life, however. It also provides Augustine and others a way out of an exegetical bind. Aquinas, for instance, notes a tension between "the great commandment" (Matt. 22:36–40, KJV), which enjoins love of God and love of neighbor, and Paul in Romans 13:9, who seems to suggest that the single most important commandment is to "love your neighbor as yourself," apparently to the exclusion of the love of God. The solution proposed by Aquinas, with the help of 1 Timothy 1:5, is to understand that "every law aims at establishing friendship [*amicitiam*], either between man and man, or between man and God. Wherefore the whole Law is comprised in this one commandment, 'Thou shalt love thy neighbor as thyself,' as expressing the end of all commandments: because love of one's neighbor includes love of God, when we love our neighbor for God's sake" (ST FS Q[99] A[1]).

Calvin, on the other hand, finds the verse puzzling, a problem in itself, for "we have to begin with faith," rather than love; the resolution is simply to parse the verse's theological grammar, as it were, which then can seem to posit faith as the cause of an effect like love (*Commentary* 1964: 191). Kierkegaard too finds the priority of love unusual, but unlike Calvin he feels that "a good conscience" rather than "sincere faith" is the ground for the other two elements in the verse ("Love is a Matter of Conscience," *Writings* 16.138).

His poignant reflection upon love, however, gives the latter a lyrical if not a logical primacy: "a pure heart is not a free heart . . . a pure heart is first and last a bound heart. For this reason it is not as delightful to speak about" as freedom in love. "The heart, if it is to be pure, must without limit be bound to God. . . . The free heart has no history; when it gave itself away, it gained its history of love, happy or unhappy. But the heart infinitely bound to God has a prior history . . . the one and only history of love, the first and the last"; every other kind of love one experiences "is only an interlude, a contribution to this" other love (148–49).

A wonderful literary echo of 1 Timothy 1:5 is to be found in Cervantes' satirical *Dialogue of the Dogs*. Two dogs, named Scipio and Berganza, are discussing their experiences with philosophical wit, when the former complains:

> The Lords of this world are very different from the Lord of heaven. When the former take a servant they firstly scrutinize his lineage, then they test his skill, take a good look at his appearance, and even want to know what clothes he possesses. To enter God's service, on the other hand, the poorest is the richest and the humblest comes from the most distinguished line. As long as he's willing to serve him with a pure heart his name's written in the wage ledger and the rewards are so rich in quantity and proportion that they surpass his wildest dreams.

After this Berganza, possibly recognizing the echo from 1 Timothy, complains that his friend is preaching, to which Scipio replies "I agree, and so I'll be silent" (1998: 260).

The Opponents: On the Law (1:8–11)

In castigating opponents, the Pastor relies upon stock forms of slander, such as the vice list here associated with "the lawless," to cast as broad a net as possible, making his criticisms potentially viable for any number of circumstances across a relatively generous span of time (cf. 2 Tim. 3:1–5). The specific vices enumerated are less important than the overall effect. Indeed, as Collins suggests, "it is often quite useless to try to distinguish one vice from another" (2002: 30; cf. Karris 1973).

Efforts have been made to read this vice list in terms of the Decalogue, given both its contextualization in a discussion of the law and the consonance of some of its terms with material from Exodus 20:1–18; but the overall imprecision of the connections between the two has led some modern commentators, like Towner, to conclude that "correspondence is rather to be found in the impression of opposition to God" than between the commandments and all the vices listed here (2006: 125). Commentators also note that the Pastor's reflections on the law are quite radically distinct from Paul's own. In fact, it is difficult to find in these remarks any theological content at all, as if the Jewish law were merely a set of penalties for criminal behavior and were not at the heart of a covenantal relationship with God. Although v. 8 begins with an echo of Romans (7:12, 16), Paul's argument that "the law . . . disclose[s] the paradoxical situation of man without faith" is entirely absent (D-C 1972: 22; cf. Hanson 1982: 58–59; Bassler 1996: 41–42).

The law is good (vv. 8–9)

Still, something of a paradox remains in the idea that the law can be used legitimately, by the faithful, even though it is meant exclusively for the lawless. This odd tension has given rise to creatively productive speculation. Clement of Alexandria agrees with the Pastor "that the law was not made for the sake of the good" (*Str.* 4.3, ANF 2.411). The reason is not moral, however, but psychological in that "when you take away the cause of fear, sin, you have taken away fear; and much more, punishment, when you have taken away that which gives rise to lust." The faithful, or in this case the truly philosophical soul (he has Socrates in mind), has been purged of that which the law governs, even if it is still true that the law "by menacing with fear, work[s] love" and thus is good (410).

A similar idea holds for Augustine as well, according to whom the righteous man "lawfully uses the law, when he applies it to alarm the unrighteous" (*De spir. et litt.* 16, NPNF1 5.89). The righteous man ultimately owes his salvation to God's unmerited grace, but the law may nevertheless prompt the unrighteous to "flee for refuge to the grace that justifies" (90). Augustine also deploys allegory in his reading of the Gospel of John (chapters 11–12) to untangle the Pastor's paradox. Lazarus, he writes, represents those who are "dead under that stone, guilty under the law. For you know that the law, which was given to the Jews, was inscribed on stone. And all the guilty are under the law [whereas] the right-living are in harmony with the law. The law is not laid on a righteous man" (*Jo. ev. tr.* 49.22, NPNF1 7.277). The righteous man, thus, can use the law legitimately, but does not experience its crushing, mortal force.

A related, and quite common, understanding of the legitimacy of the law can be found in Bernard of Clairvaux. In Bernard's view, the righteous do indeed need the law too, but the difference between sinners and saints is that "the law . . . is not imposed on [the latter] against their will, but freely given to them when they are willing, and inspired by goodness" (*On Loving God,* 1987: 203). The righteous have the goodness intended by the law already in their hearts. That this is so leads Francis de Sales to imagine how things must stand with "the Blessed in Paradise . . . since from their enjoyment of the sovereign beauty and goodness of the well-beloved, a most sweet yet inevitable necessity in their spirits of loving eternally the most holy divinity, flows and proceeds"; he concludes from this that "we shall love God in heaven . . . not as being tied and obliged by the law, but as being allured and ravished by the joy which this object, so perfectly worthy of love, shall yield to our hearts" (*Treatise on the Love of God*, 1971: 413).

Slave traders (v. 10)

The reference to "men-stealers" (KJV) or "slave traders" in v. 10 has been extremely significant, especially during periods when slavery was legal and practiced by Christians (cf. 1 Tim. 6:1). John Wesley, linking in criminality "most traders in negroes, procurers of servants for America, and all who list soldiers by lies, tricks, or incitements," argues that men-stealers are "the worst of all thieves, in comparison of whom Highwaymen and house-breakers are innocent!" (*Explanatory Notes* 1850: 439). We should note that although Wesley unfortunately indicts only *most* slavers here, he was certainly opposed to all slavery. The American abolitionist George Cheever seizes upon 1 Timothy 1:10 and declares that "a more tremendous passage against slavery does not exist than this"; if Christians followed Paul's instructions, Cheever feels, "slavery would be abolished from our land" (in Harrill 2000: 157). Harriet Beecher Stowe notes an even more egregious hypocrisy in an appendix to her anti-slavery novel, *Dred: A Tale of the Great Dismal Swamp*. The Presbyterian *Book of Discipline* from 1793, which she reproduces, cites this verse as biblical proof for the injustice of slavery. According to Stowe, however, the 1816 version of the same document suppresses the reference to 1 Timothy, and the 1818 text, although coming out strongly against the institution of slavery, renders the slave trade slightly less reprehensible to good Christian souls by insisting that slaves are not yet ready to be freed (Stowe 1856: 2.362).

"Paul" (1:12–17; Titus 3:3–4)

The Pastoral Epistles can sometimes take a broad view of sin and of the possibilities for redemption (cf. 2 Tim. 2:25). In fact, one commentator even suggests that the Pastor may evoke, by describing "Paul's" sinful past, the current sins of his opponents in Ephesus in order to hold out hope for "a future act of divine mercy for the present blasphemers as well" (Bassler 1996: 44). Paul offers himself as the perfect model of repentance and conversion, proving, in Lewis Donelson's wonderful expression, that "today's blasphemers are tomorrow's good Christians" (1986: 103). It is possible to read Titus 3:3–4 as a personal confession of Paul's as well, although more likely that text is meant as a generalized statement of sinfulness prior to conversion, "one of the most common topics in early Christian preaching" (D-C 1972: 147).

On the other hand, that "Paul" actually refers to himself as a blasphemer provides additional evidence for many scholars that 1 Timothy is not authentically Pauline (see D-C 1972: 28). Even those who hold that Paul authored these letters find this a difficult verse to deal with. Towner, for example, abruptly dispatches "blasphemer" in a meager two sentences, concluding that the term refers both to Paul's "scorn for the messianic claim about Jesus and his hostility" toward the earliest Christians (2006: 139).

Because I had acted ignorantly and in unbelief (v. 13)

Despite the difficulties of this material for modern commentators, for readers such as Augustine this passage only helps to situate "Paul," and contemporary Christians, within a complex theological and psychological context. "Paul" is in a sense like David, another great sinner, according to Augustine. The difference is that David could not claim ignorance. Nevertheless God has mercy for both David and "Paul," even if David requires the greater share (*En. ps.* 51.6, NPNF1 8.191). In Augustine's theology, however, "Paul's" former state matters not at all because "God . . . returns good for evil by His grace, which is not given according to our merits" (*De gr. et lib. arb.* 12, NPNF1 5.449). Nevertheless, the Pastor's "Paul" is not especially privileged, for all that. Indeed, in Augustine's view, young, "wholly chaste" Christian virgins have a certain advantage not available to "Paul," namely to be unable to report that their past lives ever were lives of sin (*De sancta virg.*, NPNF1 3.430). Differences and similarities between certain figures or groups and the Paul of 1 Timothy 1:13–16 have thus encouraged productive reflection upon the moral diversity of believers, even if, in general, the attitude of readers has been that God much prefers to reach out to the innocent and ignorant than to the knowing sinner.

Sinners – of whom I am the foremost (vv. 15–16)

"Paul" positions himself in the Pastorals self-consciously as an example (v. 16) or pattern for others to follow. Chrysostom resists "Paul's" own self-disclosure as the worst of sinners: he does not "condemn his own life as impure, let not this be imagined." Rather, comparing his worth to the infinite superiority of God, "Paul" necessarily comes up short. Still, he can pattern the gift of salvation for others by thus rhetorically exaggerating his own sinfulness. And to show how the patterning works, Chrysostom produces the following imaginative analogy:

> Suppose a populous city, all whose inhabitants were wicked, some more so, and some less, but all deserving of condemnation; and let one among that multitude be more deserving of punishment than all the rest, and guilty of every kind of wickedness. If it were declared that the king was willing to pardon all, it would not be so readily believed, [unless] they were to see this most wicked wretch actually pardoned. (*Hom. 1 Tim.*; NPNF1 13.420)

John Bunyan, whose *Grace Abounding to the Chief of Sinners* recounts his own, seemingly endless temptations to blasphemy, certainly assumes, unlike Chrysostom, that if "Paul" models both the hope and inner turmoil of believers like him it is precisely because "Paul" himself was so deeply sinful prior to his conversion. John and Charles Wesley, poetically inhabiting the pattern such a sinful "Paul" provides, embrace the very generous view of salvation found in the Pastoral Epistles. One may begin with an honest, if truculent, despair:

> What have I Thy grace to move?
> Beast and devil is my name;
> God I hate, and sin I love,
> Sin I love, and sin I am.

But soon enough one recognizes that:

> Jesus is the Sinners' Friend,
> Sinners Jesus came to save.

Salvation is thus possible even for the "captain" of sinners, the blackest of souls ("1 Timothy 1:15," *Poetical Works* 1868: 2.147–48).

The Opponents: Excommunication (1:18–20; 2 Tim. 2:17; 4:14–15)

The shipwreck imagery in v. 20, with roots in Greek philosophy (D-C 1972: 33), and the enigmatic figures of Hymenaeus, Alexander, and Philetus in 1 and

2 Timothy, account for some of the more creative uses of these letters. Who are these characters? What have they done to their faith? What does it mean that "Paul" will turn them over to Satan? There is no hint in Acts or the authentic Pauline letters that Paul knew men named Hymenaeus and Philetus, although their focus on the resurrection in 2 Timothy 2:18 is not dissimilar from problems Paul encountered elsewhere (1 Cor. 15:12). There is an Alexander in Acts 19:33 who emerges and disappears quite suddenly in the chaos of a dispute instigated by one Demetrius, a silversmith of Ephesus; but his identity, and his relationship with the Alexander of the Pastorals, is entirely unclear. In 1 Corinthians 5:5, Paul commands the faithful in the community to "deliver" a man guilty of incest "unto Satan for the destruction of the flesh." Precisely what that verse means is an open question (Towner 2006: 161; Martin 1995: 168–69), but in 1 Timothy 1:20, we find similar, and similarly ambiguous, language; Hymenaeus and Alexander have been "delivered unto Satan, [so] that they may learn not to blaspheme." These men are expelled from the community, clearly. Perhaps the hope is that they will do whatever they can to return, for outside the church "the avenues of social support were severed and there was no divine protection against the cosmic forces of the devil" (Bassler 1996: 47).

Shipwreck in the faith (v. 19)

The image of a shipwrecked faith has received a variety of interesting literary treatments, even in theological contexts. In a magnificently self-conscious extended simile, Basil compares the competing rhetorical and exegetical forces in the Trinitarian controversies of his day:

> . . . to some naval battle which has arisen out of time old quarrels, and is fought by men who cherish a deadly hate against one another, of long experience in naval warfare, and eager for the fight. Look, I beg you, at the picture thus raised before your eyes. See the rival fleets rushing in dread array to the attack. . . . Fancy, if you like, the ships driven to and fro by a raging tempest, while thick darkness falls from the clouds and blackens all the [scene] so that watchwords are indistinguishable in the confusion, and all distinction between friend and foe is lost. . . . From every quarter of heaven the winds beat upon one point, where both the fleets are dashed one against the other.

This vivid conclusion to his *On The Holy Spirit* creatively imagines "whole churches" as ships with their "crews and all, dashed and shattered upon the sunken reefs of disingenuous heresy, while others of the enemies of the

Spirit of Salvation have seized the helm and made shipwreck of the faith" (30, NPNF2 8.48).

John Donne connects the Paul of 2 Corinthians 11:25 with the Pastor's Hymenaeus in a prayer which contemplates the risks of backsliding into sin. In the prayer, Donne reminds God that "Thy holy *Apostle, Saint Paul*, was ship-wrackd *thrice*; & yet *stil saved*. Though the *rockes*, and the *sands*, and the *heights*, and the *shallowes*, the prosperitie, and the adversitie of this world do diversely threaten me, though mine owne *leakes* endanger mee," he petitions: "O *God*, let mee neuer put my selfe *aboard* with *Hymeneus*, nor *make shipwracke of faith, and a good Conscience*" (*Devotions* 23, "Prayer," 1624: 629–30).

The metaphor becomes at once more sophisticated and intimate in Kier-kegaard's appropriation of it. He depicts the body as a ship and asks "whether there are any spikes that in particular can be said to hold the ship's structure together, I do not know, but this I do know – that this faith is the divine joint in a human being and that if it holds it makes him the proudest sailing ship, but if it is loosened it makes a wreck of him." The faith of which he speaks is specifically "faith in God's love" and a person who gives it up "is suffering the shipwreck of eternity's joy of living" ("Gospel of Sufferings," *Writings*: 15.269).

Hymenaeus and Alexander (v. 20)

Readers have commented upon both the theological positions, and the char-acters, of these men. Athanasius, conflating different Pastoral passages (v. 20 and 2 Tim. 2:17–18), considered both Hymenaeus and Alexander, along with the Sadducees, to have "scoffed at the mystery of the resurrection"; and because they dared to engage in theological speculation Athanasius casts them both as spiritual heirs of Satan (*Ep.* 2.5, NPNF2 4.511). Augustine worries about an apparent similarity between the heresy of 2 Timothy 2:18 and Jesus' proclama-tion in John 5:25 that "the hour is coming, and now is, when the dead . . . shall live" (KJV). However, he feels that in the Gospel Jesus, unlike Hymenaeus and Philetus, was not speaking of bodies, but minds, thus preserving the futurity of the promised physical resurrection (*Jo. ev. tr.* 19.14, NPNF1 7.128). In Erasmus' *Paraphrases*, which is vaguely sympathetic to these shadowy heretics of Ephesus, the idea behind the past resurrection is that "we are somehow reborn and given new life in the children who resemble us" (1993: 47).

Even if readers cannot say precisely what these men are guilty of, still many find quite creative ways to slander their imagined characters. Alexander is, in Theodoret's *Eranistes*, "a man of no sort of distinction at all, – no nobility of birth, no eloquence of speech, who never led a political party nor an army in the field; who never played the man in fight, but plied from day to day his ignominious craft, and won fame for nothing but his mad violence against Saint Paul" (Prol., NPNF2 3.160; Robert Hill, in a fitting metacommentary on Theodoret's elitism, points up the inappropriateness of such a "snobbish remark about manual workers from a successor to a band of artisans assembled by a carpenter," in Theodoret 2001: 2.248). Ralph Waldo Emerson comments that contemporaries who challenged the New Testament text, specifically nineteenth century German biblical scholars, were like these opponents in 1 and 2 Timothy. "Historical speculators" undermine the faith just as surely as do heretics, according to Emerson, and they create a situation in which "every drunkard in his cups, and every voluptuary in his brothel will loll out his tongue at the resurrection from the dead . . . the unassailable virtues and the traditionary greatness of Christianity." He feared that in fact all morals would collapse as a result of their "attack," and that the resulting breach would "let in the ghastly reality of things" (*Sermons*, 1989: 4.259–60). In the sermon of another nineteenth century American minister, Alexander and Hymenaeus are also a corrupting social force. However, James Axley, an itinerant Methodist frontier preacher, rugged and perhaps illiterate, couldn't have been more different from Emerson. In his reading of, or rather midrash on, the relevant verses, Axley has "Paul" convince the community to beat its brandy stills into "bells and stewkettles." Alexander, one of the foremost still-makers, joins "Paul" by becoming a "class-leader" in this "new society," and everything proceeds wonderfully until the next peach harvest, when there are so many peaches, of such good quality, that Alexander begins building stills again, and the townsfolk renew their brewing and drinking of brandy. When "Paul" finds out he expels both Alexander and his partner Hymenaeus. The latter pair has the last laugh, however, because they immediately "flew off the handle and joined the [New Light] Schismatics" (in Finley 1854: 238–40).

The character of Alexander in particular is parodied and impugned in Thomas Hardy's Alec d'Urberville, who seems in fact to have gotten his first name from the Pastor's Alexander. After seducing and ruining Tess, d'Urberville finds religion and becomes an itinerant minister, only to abandon his faith as soon as Tess reenters his life later in the novel. He jokingly invokes the names of Hymenaeus and Alexander to explain his own inconstancy (*Tess of the D'Urbervilles*, 1998: 319).

Whom I have turned over to Satan (v. 20)

Whoever these men are, and whatever they have done, "Paul" reminds Timothy that he has "turned" them "over to Satan, so that they may learn not to blaspheme" (v. 20). Augustine, ventriloquizing Pelagius, asks if such a disciplinary procedure could really work; consigning sinners to Satan to cure them of sin seems rather like fighting fire with fire. In response Augustine uses analogies from medicine to the effect that poisons are sometimes used to heal poisonings, that the "heats of fevers are sometimes subdued by certain medicinal warmths" and that therefore it is not impossible that exposure to Satan may be spiritually salutary (*De nat. et grat.* 32, NPNF1 5.132).

But perhaps the more important question asks whether or not it is legitimate to consider a relationship between God and Satan for the maintenance of a spiritually healthy community. Using Job's testing by Satan as a paradigmatic case, both Tertullian (*De fuga* 9.2, ANF 4.117) and Chrysostom (*Hom. 1 Tim.*, NPNF1 13.425) argue that the devil in fact does operate at the behest of God for the sake of the elect. The principle, in Tertullian's formulation, is that "righteousness may be perfected in injustice, as strength is perfected in weakness"; and the devil, since he serves at the pleasure not only of God but also of God's servants, is indeed weak, having no power he can use on his own (*De fuga* 9.2, ANF 4.117–18).

The Pastor urges both Timothy and the community at Ephesus to offer up prayers for the pagan ruling authorities. Such prayers are useful in that they may help to secure peace and stability for the church. But the Pastor suggests a secondary interest as well: perhaps by means of prayer and, one assumes, good relations with the non-Christian world, others will be brought to salvation. He then reproduces a hymn, according to which Christ is the "mediator between God and humankind," before turning once again to the subject of prayer. When the community gathers, he tells Timothy, it is to gather and pray in peace. Women especially are to behave according to proper social mores. They are to remain silent and respectful of the community's men. Their subordinate role is a result of Eve's sin, the Pastor explains, although women are not entirely lost as they will

The Pastoral Epistles Through the Centuries, First Edition. Jay Twomey.
© 2009 by Jay Twomey. Published 2020 by John Wiley & Sons Ltd.

be able to redeem themselves by bearing and raising good Christian children.

The Church: Politics (2:1–2; Titus 3:1)

The relationship between church and state in the New Testament presents interesting problems of interpretation, not the least of which is what one might mean by "church" and "state" in the New Testament period (Ritter 2006: 524–27). Paul in Romans 13, and John of Patmos in Revelation 13, for example, offer two radically distinct approaches to the problem, and reveal between them something of the complexity of these early positions. The question of the extent to which the church ought to participate in the civic life of the state was also posed from the outside, for "the Christian refusal to acknowledge the gods by whose favour the empire enjoyed" security and prosperity, "or to take an oath by the genius of the emperor, provoked distrust and fear" (Chadwick 2001: 110). Defending Christianity against charges that adherence to the new religion could, and in fact did, bring about "political catastrophe" (Ritter 2006: 534), both apologists and polemicists in the tradition could draw upon the language of 1 Timothy 2 and Titus 3 in support of their vision of the church's position vis-à-vis the civic order (Collins 2002: 51).

Supplications, prayers, intercessions and thanksgivings (v. 1)

Readers have often been puzzled by the Pastor's fourfold exhortation that Christians pray for those in authority. Many, as a result, have tried to discern the differences among the terms the Pastor uses in v. 1. John Cassian, in the context of reflections upon prayer in the monastic life, maintains that each kind of prayer is individually useful in itself, and that sometimes the distinctions between each type are subordinated to the overall intensity of the prayerful effort. Nevertheless, he also links each to a specific stage in the life of the religious individual:

> [T]he first seems to belong more especially to beginners, who are still troubled by the stings and recollection of their sins; the second to those who have already attained some loftiness of mind in their spiritual progress and the quest of virtue; the third to those who fulfill the completion of their vows by their works, and are so stimulated to intercede for others also through the consideration of their

weakness, and the earnestness of their love; the fourth to those who have already torn from their hearts the guilty thorns of conscience, and thus being now free from care can contemplate with a pure mind the beneficence of God and His compassions. (*Conf.* 9.15, NPNF2 11.392)

Schleiermacher draws upon this verse in his thinking about prayer as the nexus of divine and human will in the church. Prayer tends toward the magical, he opines, especially when individuals or groups seek to influence the deity in their favor. But prayers, such as these from 1 Timothy 2:1, expressing the spirit of the collectivity of Christians, are a different matter: "if the church's need has been rightly apprehended, and if the dominating presentiment has arisen out of the Church's whole consciousness of its own inner condition and outward circumstances, then the prayer is charged with the full truth . . . its content cannot but be fulfilled." The reason has less to do with the response of God to prayerful petition, however, than to the fact that the whole body of the church, as "a perfect reflection of Christ," would presumably ask only for that which Christ himself had already willed (*The Christian Faith*, 1963: 2.672).

Prayers for kings (vv. 1–2)

Tertullian argues that Christians who pray for the well-being of the emperor do so both because of texts like 1 Timothy 2:1–2 (and Titus 3:1, "remind them to be subject to rulers and authorities, to be obedient, to be ready for every good work") and because they sincerely desire "the complete stability of the empire." Tertullian also assumes, perhaps on the basis of 2 Thessalonians 2:6–8, that Rome serves as a stay against the impending apocalyptic *eschaton*, and thus that a prayer for her stability was really a prayer for the continued exis-tence of all social and political structures (*Apol.* 32, ANF 3.42–43). Similarly, Calvin, commenting on Titus 3:1, feels that "since [magistrates and kings] have been appointed for the preservation of human life, he who desires their removal or shakes off their yoke, is an enemy of equity and justice and so devoid of all humanity" (*Commentary* 1964: 337). Cotton Mather, writing well before the American Revolution, complains that "our Setting Light by Excellent Magistrates, has been the Scandalous Crime of our Country; and for that Crime whole Colonies may come to Smart under the Revenges of God." Interestingly, Mather's comment on Titus 3:1 is made in the context of a work entitled *A Family Well-Ordered*, and resonates, as we shall see, with some interpretations of 1 Timothy 3:5 in its further claim that "Rulers are Parents" (1699: 70).

A quiet and peaceable life (v. 2)

There may be limits, however, to one's duty to earthly rulers. Origen, in response to Celsus' insistence that all people should serve their leaders, even to the point of fighting in their armies, argues that "none fight better for the king than we [Christians] do." But he draws an intriguing parallel between pagan priests and Christians in prayer in order to deny that Christians must fight in the armed forces: neither kind of religious person is drafted into the military, but both perform an invaluable service by praying for the king. Therefore, he continues, "we do not indeed fight under him [i.e., the king], although he require it; but we fight on his behalf, forming a special army – an army of piety – by offering our prayers to God" in the battle against those demonic forces which "stir up war, and lead to the violation of oaths, and disturb the peace" in the first place (*C. Cels.* 8.73, ANF 4.668–69; cf. Theodoret, *Comm. 1 Tim.*, 2001: 2.213). In a variation upon this view, Chrysostom, who similarly agrees that warfare is incompatible with Christian piety, transmutes the impetus behind the "quiet and peaceable life" of v. 2 from the actual conditions of social order to the spiritual dimensions of the soul. War can't harm us, Chrysostom affirms, unless by war we mean the inner strife at work "when the body is at variance with the soul, and raises up evil desires"; then and only then, he seems to suggest, are quiet and peace truly at risk. He also fears that a general peace would benefit sinners as well as saints, and thus felt that "Paul" added "in all godliness and honesty" as a limiting factor – not any peace is intended, but a specifically Christian peace (*Hom. 1 Tim.*, NPNF1 13.429).

By contrast with the foregoing concerns about warfare, Luther, in his *Lectures on Titus* 3:1, apparently has few worries about organized violence or, for that matter, judicial executions, whenever such are required "by the authority of the prince" (*Works* 29.73) – although the polemical context of this comment, in which the calling of lay people is emphasized over the work of Catholic clerics exempt from such public service (60), may militate against any easy appreciation of Luther's meaning.

Right and acceptable (v. 5)

Despite such basic differences, for most readers there is little difficulty in endorsing these verses, even if the endorsement is sometimes qualified by ambiguous reflections upon the religious and moral quality of leaders. Tertullian thus explains that Titus 3:1 holds for believers "within the limits of discipline, so long as we keep ourselves separate from idolatry" (*De idol.* 15,

ANF 3.71). Luther also warns that "it happens that some men administer the government unjustly," and suggests that there are certain very limited contexts in which disobedience may be sanctioned – for example, when the government tries to turn Christians against other Christians (*Lectures on Titus*, *Works* 29.73). And Erasmus, who assumes in his reading of Titus 3:1 that "Paul" envisioned something of a necessary opposition between church and state, writes that "every order which does not in any way diminish our godliness has to be obeyed. They take away our wealth; the treasury of godliness increases. They drive us into exile; Christ is everywhere" (*Paraphrases* 1993: 64).

Others, however, prefer a greater, and more politically charged, clarity. Milton acknowledges "Paul's" instructions "that prayers should be made for kings . . . but he had instructed before that prayers should be made for the people. . . . When Paul makes mention of Nero, he calls him not a king but a 'lion,' that is a savage beast, out of whose mouth he rejoices that he was snatched. . . . And so for kings, not for beasts, 'we should pray, so that we may lead a peaceful and quiet life'. . . . You see that it is not so much of kings here, as of peace, piety and respectability too that account should be taken" (*The Tenure of Kings and Magistrates* 3, 1991: 120). In the twentieth century, Hans Urs von Balthasar reads this verse in conjunction with 1 Timothy 1:9 ("the law is not made for the righteous"). The authority in question in 1 Timothy 2, then, exists for the wicked. Even in the best of times law and government are of dubious merit for the Christian since "nowhere in the New Testament does the slightest ray of divine glory fall upon the structures of the state" (*The Glory of The Lord*, 1989: 7.502). The problem is that we do not inhabit the best of times; the state is no longer the neutral force imagined by Romans 13, but the evil and corrupt power of Revelation (503).

Theological Speculation: Christ as Mediator (2:4–6)

In his commentary on the Pastoral Epistles, A. T. Hanson remarks that the "noble statement of the universality of God's love" expressed in v. 4 (God "desires everyone to be saved") "runs directly counter to the strict predestinarian tradition in Christianity which Augustine so emphatically championed, and Calvin, eleven hundred years later, reaffirmed. Consequently both Augustine and Calvin had to evade the obvious meaning of these words by saying that it means God chooses his elect from all classes of men" (1982: 68). Whether the meaning is obvious or not, the universality of the Pastor's soteriological vision is most definitely an issue with which readers of these letters have had to contend, amid "intense heart-searching and controversy," down the centuries (Kelly 1981: 62).

The Pastor also refers to Christ as mediator in the hymn of vv. 5–6. The New Testament refers to Christ as a mediator between the human and the divine only here and in Hebrews (8:6; 9:15; 12:24). The model for mediation seems to be Moses, both as the mediator of the covenant (cf. Gal. 3:19–20, where the usage is ambiguously negative; D-C 1972: 42; *pace* Kelly 1981: 63), and more generally as the intermediary between an utterly transcendent God and human-ity (Davies 1996: 15). Hanson argues that the Pastor is actually drawing upon the Septuagint version of Job 9:33 ("I wish there were our mediator and reprover," 1968: 57; "daysman," KJV; "umpire," NRSV; "arbiter," JPS), and thus that this verse is to be taken, if not exactly as an answer to Job, then as indic-ative of the author's belief that Job 9:33 contains "a prophecy of Christ's redemp-tion" (62).

Everyone (v. 4)

The Augustinian–Calvinist perspective, which, it should be noted, has other New Testament resources to draw upon (notably Rom. 9:15–24), holds, as Hanson noted, that "everyone" really refers to the fact that God draws his elect from among all kinds of people, from all stations of life. In one of Augustine's last writings, the Pastor's global vision of salvation is reinterpreted in this way:

> [T]he "word of the cross is foolishness to them that perish; but unto them that are saved it is the power of God" [1 Cor. 1:18]. God teaches all such to come to Christ, for He wills all such to be saved, and to come to the knowledge of the truth. (*De praed. sanct.* 14, NPNF1 5.505)

As Gene Fendt notes, in Augustine's "tendentious" version of this verse, God "wills all *such* to be saved" [*hos enim* omnes vult salvos fieri] (2001: 221), essentially limiting salvation to such as are chosen already.

In a very different context, Thomas Hobbes argues as well for the Augus-tinian position, but recognizes the need to provide a "more intelligible and reasonable interpretation" of relevant biblical texts than those produced by "the Schoolmen" (*Questions Concerning Liberty, Necessity, and Chance*, 1994: 5.12). The idea that "God will have all men to be saved" (KJV), he reasons, does not refer to God's "will internal" but his "will revealed," that is, to scripture. For Hobbes, it is important to remember that there are instances in the Bible when God's revealed will differs from his own hidden "decree and purpose" (for example, God reveals to Abraham his desire that Isaac be sacrificed, but his internal will was that Isaac be spared). The same discrepancy is apparently at work in 1 Timothy 2:4, Hobbes claims; all the text really means is that God reveals his will in the form of commandments to humanity which ostensibly provide access to eternal life, but the efficacy of which is always subordinated to God's inner counsel (13). In this case, the divine will is in fact that salvation has not been reserved for all.

The alternative perspective is nicely expressed by Jacob Arminius, who complains that the doctrine of predestination "hinders public prayers from being offered to God in a becoming and suitable manner, that is, with faith, and in confidence that they will be profitable to all the hearers of the word"; and since "the apostle" "commands" that prayers be offered for all alike, in view of the universality of salvation, it is clear that "predestination is in open hostility to the ministry of the gospel" (*Writings* 1956: 1.233). The Wesleys, later Arminians, agree, hymning:

> Thou wouldst have all men come to Thee,
> Saviour of the human race.
> . . .
> Thee every soul may see,
> Thy saving grace may prove,
> Confirm the merciful decree
> Of universal love.

Further on in the same poem, as part of an ingeniously subversive reading of Romans 9:21 ("Hath not the potter power over the clay, of the same lump to make one vessel unto honour, and another unto dishonour," KJV), a text which has served as a touchstone for proponents of predestination, the Wesleys continue:

> Lo! in Thy hand I lay,
> And wait Thy will to prove;
> My Potter, stamp on me, Thy clay,
> Thy only stamp of love.
> (Hymn 15, *Poetical Works*
> 1868: 3.90)

The vessel made for dishonor, or damnation, here becomes, in the light of 1 Timothy 2:4, the bearer of God's love, rather more akin to the sentiment of 2 Corinthians 1:20–22 (God "hath also sealed us, and given the earnest of the Spirit in our hearts") than that of the passage about God the potter in Romans.

The mediator (v. 5)

For most readers of this passage through the centuries, the mediator serves as the link between a sinful humanity and God. But the manner in which that mediation works has been conceived in a diversity of ways. Irenaeus, for example, sees Christ's mediatory role in his restoring the "friendship" between humanity and God. In sin, humanity transgressed, becoming God's enemies, and Christ, by undoing disobedience with obedience, returns both parties to amity, while also allowing human beings to commune obediently with the divine (AH 3.18.7, 4.17.1, ANF 1.448, 554; on the human–divine "friendship" effected by the mediator, cf. Theodoret, *Comm. 1 Tim.*, 2001: 214; on the role of the mediator in bonding humans to God, cf. Gregory of Nyssa, *C. Eun.* 2.12, NPNF2 5.122).

Augustine enjoys toying with the rhetorical possibilities which this passage opens up for him. He considers Christ's mediation as that which places him "between the mortal sinners and the immortal Just One – mortal with men, just with God" (*Conf.* 10.43, NPNF1 1.162). It also functions to bring humanity, lost in the diversity of experiences, "in many distractions amid many things," toward the oneness of God (*Conf.* 11.29, NPNF1 1.174). Conceiving of sin itself as something of a negative form of mediation, Augustine suggests that between us and God there are two media, even if one is rather a barrier, a "separating wall," than a shared zone of interaction: "there is a separating medium, and, on the other hand, there is a reconciling Mediator. The separating medium is sin, the reconciling Mediator is the Lord Jesus Christ" (*Jo. ev. tr.* 61.8, NPNF1 7.231). Figures like Symeon the New Theologian could believe that the mediatory role of religious authorities is analogous to that of Christ. In response to a perceived crisis of morality among the monks of his order, Symeon asks: "do you think it is a small thing to draw near the light unapproachable [1 Tim. 6:16] and become a mediator between God and man?" (*Catechetical Discourses* 18.10, 1980: 216). Calvin (*Institutes* 3.20.20) and Wesley (*Explanatory Notes* 1850: 540), however, insist upon the singularity of Christ as the mediator, denying that humans or institutions can intercede as sufficiently with God on behalf of sinners.

Women: Silence in the Church (2:8–14)

This passage, one of the most troubling in the Pastorals, if not the New Testament as a whole, deserves a volume of commentary unto itself. Through the centuries the Pastor's denial of a significant aspect of women's religious agency, namely the ability to participate actively and independently in community worship, has both reassured and rankled readers. Many major figures in the tradition have, clearly, embraced the circumscribed role for women which the Pastoral Epistles envision. In fact, it has been argued that a text such as 1 Corinthians 14:34–35 is quite possibly an interpolation by the Pastor or someone sharing his views (D-C 1972: 47; Hanson 1982: 72). Thus, even the canon of the New Testament itself may bear witness to the great influence exerted by the Pastor's misogyny. On the other hand, it would be a mistake to assume that the Pastor's perspective was entirely definitive, or that it is only recently that critics have questioned the Pastor's gender politics. As Rosemary Ruether asserts, "Christian women have probably dissented from these arguments since the beginning of Christianity" (Ruether 1990: 1). The apocryphal *Acts of Paul and Thecla* have frequently been taken as an indication of precisely this kind of alternative attitude within early Christianity, one according to which women had a good deal more agency than even Paul might have allowed (MacDonald 1983; cf. Kidd 1990: 186).

Needless to say, many in the tradition have assumed that the Pastor, or "Paul," was in fact speaking for all Christians at all times, and this because he grounds women's subordinate status in the Genesis account of Eve's tardiness at creation, as well as in her transgression. If Eve-as-woman, secondary and more sinful by contrast with Adam-as-man, takes upon herself the role of teacher, she is yet again transgressing, this time "the fundamental order of things" altogether (Verner 1983: 170).

The discussion of children introduces an interpretive problem, for there is a shift from the singular to the plural in v. 15: from "she shall be saved" to "if they continue." Although the matter is far from clear, modern commentators frequently assume that both the "they" and the "she" refer to the women in the community, and explain that the singular "she" arises because Eve (or "the woman") in the previous sentence is singular (Collins 2002: 76).

Prayer without anger (v. 8)

The Pastor begins this section by advocating prayer in harmony and undisputed faith ("without wrath and doubting," KJV; "without anger or argument," NRSV). The fact that men are to "lift up holy hands" in praying suggests to Cassiodorus that one is to pray in the form of the cross (*Ex. ps.* 62.5, 1991: 2.85–86). The absence of a specific localization for prayerful gathering provides many readers with evidence of Christianity's evolution from what was taken to be its more limited Jewish origins. Jews were allowed to pray only in

Jerusalem, according to such commentators, but "Paul" and "the practices of grace" (Theodoret, *Comm. 1 Tim.*, 2001: 2.215) legitimate the use of all earthly space for prayer (Chrysostom, *Hom. 1 Tim.*, NPNF1 13.432).

Although, in context, this verse seems to envision a congregation of men at prayer, without the women, Origen considers this text especially (although not pleasantly) applicable to women. In his view, the Pastor is here concerned to teach that a praying woman must "[banish] from her governing mind everything that would remind her of incontinent and womanish ways" (*De orat.* 4.1, 1979: 98; cf. Erasmus *Paraphrases*, 1993: 16).

Women should dress themselves modestly (v. 9)

Women are told to dress themselves modestly, in the good works of their godliness. Tertullian is clearly inspired by verses such as this in his work *On The Apparel of Women*, which begins by advising woman as a class "to go about in humble garb, and rather to affect meanness of appearance, walking about as Eve mourning and repentant, in order that by every garb of penitence she might the more fully expiate that which she derives from Eve, – the ignominy, I mean, of the first sin, and the odium (attaching to her as the cause) of human perdition" (1.1, ANF 4.14). For many readers, the desire for sartorial splendor is characteristically feminine, and leads to a certain confusion in both men and women: as Chrysostom puts it, "we can no longer distinguish harlots and virgins" (*Hom. 1 Tim.*, NPNF1 13.434).

However, there is a great deal of complexity among readers regarding just what the Pastor's prohibition might mean for contemporary believers. Clement of Alexandria understands such restrictions within the general economy of Christian life. So, for instance, all believers should wear simple homespun, and avoid clothing purchased in the marketplace. Interestingly, however, he does allow cosmetics and alluring dress in the case of women who were unfortunate in having unchaste husbands, men who would seek pleasure elsewhere if their wives did not make themselves attractive. This exception, however, is meant only as a temporary measure, until wanton husbands can be weaned from luxury to the pleasures of a simply and holy life (*Paed.* 3.11, ANF 2.285).

In part because v. 9, beginning "also," seems to link the instructions for men in prayer to what is said here about women's dress, other commentators, while not entirely mitigating the negative tenor of 1 Timothy 2, expand the injunction to men as well. According to the popular eighteenth century commentary, *The Family Expositor*, the late sixteenth, early seventeenth century exegete, Estius, had even observed "that this Discourse concludes with yet stronger Force against Foppery in Men" (in Doddridge 1739–56: 5.450). John Wesley goes the next step and simply democratizes the verses as they are, declaring that "you cannot be clear before God unless you throw aside all needless ornaments, in utter defiance of that tyrant of fools, fashion; unless you seek only to be adorned with good works, as men and women professing godliness" ("On Obedience to Pastors," *Works*: 7.116; cf. "On Dress," *Works*: 7.15–26).

Among literary treatments, perhaps Chaucer's feisty Wife of Bath provides the most striking repudiation of the Pastor's scandalized feelings about women's clothing:

> Thou sayest also, if that we make us gay
> With clothing and with precious array,
> That it is peril of our chastity.
> And yet, – with sorrow! – thou enforcest thee,
> And say'st these words in the apostles name:
> 'In habit made with chastity and shame
> ye women shall apparel you,' quoth he,
> 'And not in tressed hair and gay perrie,
> as pearlës, nor with gold, nor clothes rich.'

Her response to the Pastor is nothing short of definitive rejection:

> After thy text nor after thy rubrich
> I will not work as muchel as a gnat.
> (3 [D] 337–47, 1987: 109)

Silence with full submission (vv. 11–12)

The heart of the Pastor's perspective on women, however, is really in the verses which follow. The logic of later Christian misogyny, derived from this text, is given perfect expression in a reading of Chrysostom's: "the woman taught once and ruined all. On this account therefore [Paul] saith, let her not teach. But what is it to other women, that she suffered this? It certainly concerns them; for the sex is weak and fickle, and he is speaking of the sex collectively. For he says not Eve, but 'the woman,' which is the common name of the whole sex, not her proper name" (*Hom. 1 Tim.*, NPNF1 13.436). Chrysostom is aware that Paul, in Romans 5, blames Adam, and not Eve, for the presence of sin in the world, and hence accuses Adam, not Eve, of transgressing in the garden. However, he mitigates the thorniness of this problem by generalizing, and then gendering, the Pauline typology of Romans 5:14, according to which Adam is "the figure of him that was to come" (KJV). If this is true of Adam-as-Christ, it must also hold for Eve-as-woman, and hence "the female sex transgressed, and not the male" (436).

Augustine also finds the contrast between Romans and 1 Timothy troubling; but he is able to maintain the subordination of women by insisting, with the Pastor's language in mind, that Adam "was not deceived" because he was fully aware of what he was doing. In a reading of Genesis 3 that becomes nearly canonical thanks to Milton's *Paradise Lost* (9.998–99), Augustine argues that Eve was indeed deceived because she "accepted as true what the serpent told her, but the man could not bear to be severed from his only companion, even though this involved a partnership with sin. He was not on this account less culpable, but sinned with his eyes wide open" (*De civ. Dei* 14.11, 2000: 459). Clearly, the desire to restrict women's religious lives is scripturally difficult to sustain with any success. Augustine's scruple about the tension between Romans and 1 Timothy is repeated later in Aquinas, but with reference to other biblical texts, namely Proverbs 31 and Judges 4–5. With regard to the former text, Aquinas says that Lemuel's mother teaches her son in private, which is not in fact proscribed by "Paul" but, to some extent, encouraged (cf. Titus 2:3; 2 Timothy 1:5). With regard to the latter, Deborah is not considered exemplary because her "teaching [was] through the spirit of prophecy, and the grace of the Holy Spirit does not discern between man and woman" (Thomas Aquinas 2007: 32).

A much more striking instance of the same rationale is to be found in Thomas' reflection on whether or not the Virgin Mary had received the fullness of grace. Replying to the idea that because Mary never taught or worked miracles in her lifetime she must not have experienced grace to the fullest, Thomas claims, in deference to the Pastor, that "there is no doubt that the Blessed Virgin received in a high degree both the gift of wisdom and the grace of miracles and even of prophecy, just as Christ had them. But she did not so receive them, as to put them and such like graces to every use, as did Christ: but accordingly as it befitted her condition of life. . . . [S]he had not the use of wisdom as to teaching: since this befitted not the female sex" (ST TP Q[27] A[5]). So not even the Mother of God is allowed to teach (compare Sor Juana at Titus 1:12).

However, even for some traditional figures, experience often produces the need for a careful consideration of the question of women's religious roles. Jerome, for instance, praising his former student Marcella, needs to explain how a woman who taught scripture to others could nevertheless be justified on the Pastor's terms. Marcella, who had debated exegetical issues with Jerome, was so gifted that the latter deigned not to describe her intellectual acumen fully to others for fear that in doing so he would "exceed the bounds of men's belief" (*Ep.* 2.6, NPNF2 6.255). He is able to reassure any critics, however, that when Marcella was later consulted by men, including priests, on "obscure and doubtful points" of interpretation, she would give "her own opinion not as her own but as from me or some one else [i.e., another man], thus admitting that what she taught she had herself learned from others. For she knew that the apostle had said: 'I suffer not a woman to teach,' and she would not seem to inflict a wrong upon the male sex" (ibid.: 256). One is tempted to hear in such remarks a consonance with Luther's theological anthropology, which holds that "the husband differs from the wife in no other respect than in sex; otherwise the woman is altogether a man" (in Clark 1977: 166). While this most certainly does not mean, in practice, that women are equal to men, it still allows Luther to grant some flexibility to women teachers in certain circumstances. For example, "if it happened . . . that no man could be secured for [a teaching] office, then a woman might step up and preach to others as best she could; but in no other instance" ("Sermon for Pentecost Tuesday," *Sermons* 2000: 3.375).

The relative ambiguity of these otherwise proscriptive readings disappears entirely when we turn to a figure like John Knox, according to whom the Pastor is writing of "women in general, excepting none; affirming that she may usurp authority above no man." Because Knox's vituperation arises in response to the ascension of women, particularly Mary Tudor and Mary Stewart, to positions of royal power, the upshot of his interpretation is "that woman by the law of God, and by the interpretation of the Holy Ghost, is utterly forbidden to occupy the place of God in the offices aforesaid, which he has assigned to man, whom he has appointed and ordained his lieutenant in earth, secluding from that honour and dignity all women" (*First Blast of the Trumpet*, 1994: 13, 14). Since Mary Queen of Scots, and then Elizabeth I, were politically in support of the Protestants, Knox's vehement denunciation of "the monstrous regiment of women" (3) eventually proved embarrassing. He would later explain, although without retracting his opinion, that his "book was written most especially against that wicked Jezebel of England," the Catholic Mary Tudor (xvi).

Let a woman learn . . . and teach (v. 12)

As noted above, however, one can trace another critical and even proto-feminist tradition of readings. The seventeenth century Mexican nun, Sor Juana Inés de la Cruz, in a fascinating commentary on a variety of scriptures pertaining to women's religious life, engages with this text selectively in order to subvert its intended meaning. Responding to a bishop's criticism of her literary and exegetical work, Sor Juana suggests that 1 Timothy 2:11 "is more in favor of than

Figure 1   A contemporary rendering of the negative impact of this verse upon women's religious agency. *Source*: russellsteapot.com/know-your-bible/

against women, as it says that they should learn, and while they are learning, obviously, they must needs keep quiet." She goes on to say that women are not forbidden in these texts from writing, for otherwise the church would have had to repudiate important women such as Sts. Gertrude and Teresa, Brigitta of Sweden, and others. Therefore, women can in fact "teach by writing," even if the pulpit is forbidden them ("Reply to Sor Filotea," 2005: 282–83). By means of such exegetical sleights-of-hand, restriction becomes possibility.

Other women have chosen to limit strictly the Pastor's normative valence to a specific historical moment. Margaret Fell, a seventeenth century founder of Quakerism, for instance, suggests that "Paul" is merely concerned with the disruptions caused by certain "undecent and unreverent Women" in his community. Certainly he did not mean that "such as have the Power and Spirit of the Lord Jesus poured upon them, and have the Message of the Lord Jesus given unto them," are not to speak the Word ("Women's Speaking Justified," 1989: 12; cf. Schüssler Fiorenza 1992: 23–24, for additional examples of such "revisionist" tactics). Like many others, Fell recognizes, and affirms, the active roles women play in key texts from both the Hebrew Bible and New Testament. She also extends this list, brilliantly, to include the woman clothed with the sun from Revelation 12, in which image "the Church of Christ is a Woman, and those that speak against the Woman's speaking, speak against the Church of Christ, and the Seed of the Woman, which Seed is Christ; that is to say, Those that speak against the Power of the Lord, and the Spirit of the Lord speaking in a Woman, simply, by reason of her Sex, or because she is a Woman, not regarding the Seed, and Spirit, and Power that speaks in her; such speak against Christ, and his Church, and are of the Seed of the Serpent, wherein lodgest the Enmity" (4). The oblique reference to Eve's transgression may have been meant to undermine 1 Timothy 2:14 as well. Charlotte Brontë could almost have had Margaret Fell in mind when she has a female character in her novel *Shirley* respond to a pointed question, posed by a man, about how she would "account for" the Pastor's words:

> Hem! I – I account for them in this way: he wrote that chapter for a particular congregation of Christians, under peculiar circumstances; and besides, I dare say, if I could read the original Greek, I should find that many of the words have been wrongly translated, perhaps misapprehended altogether. It would be possible, I doubt not, with a little ingenuity, to give the passage quite a contrary turn; to make it say, 'Let the woman speak out whenever she sees fit to make an objection'; – 'it is permitted to a woman to teach and to exercise authority as much as may be. Man, meantime, cannot do better than hold his peace,' and so on. (1979: 370–71)

John Wesley bypasses these verses rather nimbly, stopping only long enough to indicate that v. 12 refers to "public teaching" (*Explanatory Notes* 1850: 541). But Wesley is elsewhere outspoken on the important public roles women could play, telling the women of his congregation: "You, as well as men, are rational creatures. You, like them, were made in the image of God; you are equally candidates for immortality; you too are called of God, as you have time, to 'do good unto all men [Gal 6:10].' Be 'not disobedient to the heavenly calling [Heb. 3:1]' " ("On Visiting the Sick," *Works* 7.126). Moreover, he is a cautious but active supporter of women's preaching, despite biblical prohibitions and contemporary attitudes to the contrary (Collins 1996). Wesley's Methodist tradition currently supports the ordination of women, even to the office of bishop. The United Methodist church explains on its website that, although 1 Timothy seems to imply "a wholesale prohibition" against women's preaching, a careful reconstruction of the historical context shows that "what Paul resisted was a woman 'running ahead' of the development of the church at that time and presuming a role of 'authority' not yet universalized in the Body of Christ" (Harper).

Saved through childbearing (v. 15)

That Eve represents for every woman the "ancient weakness of her sex" (Erasmus *Paraphrases*, 1993: 17) does not mean that women have no hope, however. The Pastor amends his rather stark view of women with the proviso that, "notwithstanding" all this, a woman "shall be saved in child-bearing, if they continue in faith and charity and holiness with sobriety" (KJV). Typical of many readings of this verse is that of Augustine, who takes it for granted "that the woman having been brought into the transgression by being deceived, is brought to salvation by child-bearing." He argues, however, that "those things which are called good works are, as it were, the sons of our life, according to that sense of life in which it answers to the question, What is a man's life? that is, How does he act in these temporal things? . . . and because these good works are chiefly performed in the way of offices of mercy, while works of mercy are of no profit, either to Pagans, or to Jews who do not believe in Christ, or to any heretics or schismatics whatsoever in whom faith and charity and sober holiness are not found" (*De Trin.* 12.7, NPNF1 3.159; cf. Gregory of Nyssa *De virg.* 13, NPNF2 5.359).

Many readers, however, see the children as actual children. The onus, then, is on the woman to raise her children to be good Christians. Salvation is hers if she can achieve this end. Chrysostom's image of women who "have trained up wrestlers for the service of Christ" is a colorful, but representative reading of the verse in these terms (*Hom. 1 Tim.*, NPNF1 13.436; cf. Jerome C. *Jov.* 1.27, NPNF 2-06: 367; Erasmus *Paraphrases* 1993: 18). Calvin understands the verse to pertain to pregnancy and childbirth itself: "a woman who considers the condition God has assigned to her as a calling and submits to it, not refusing to bear the distaste of food, the illness, the difficulty, or rather the fearful anguish associated with childbirth or anything else that is her duty – God is better pleased with her than if she were to make some great display of heroic virtues and refuse to accept the vocation given her by God" (*Commentary* 1964: 219).

In *Ulysses*, James Joyce, thinking also of 1 Timothy 6:12 or 2 Timothy 4:7, imagines with Victorian flair the postpartum exaltation of Mina Purefoy. This aptly named woman has "fought the good fight" (on which expression, see at 2 Tim. 4:7) of childbirth, "and now she was very very happy. Those who have passed on, who have gone before, are happy too as they gaze down and smile upon the touching scene. Reverently they look at her as she reclines there with the motherlight in her eyes, that longing hunger for baby fingers (a pretty sight it is to see), in the first bloom of her new motherhood, breathing a silent prayer of thanksgiving to One above, the Universal Husband" (1986: 343). Although her salvation is not assured, the language of the passage hints that, at least from a certain social perspective, Mina Purefoy has acquitted her maternal function successfully, and that God will reward her for it abundantly.

The Pastor now turns his attention to church offices. Bishops and deacons are to be moral, upstanding citizens, husbands and fathers whose skill at managing their households is indicative of their leadership abilities more generally. The Pastor may also envision an office of deaconess too. "Paul" then tells Timothy that he hopes to visit him in Ephesus soon, but suggests that he will likely be delayed. The chapter closes with a Christological hymn in celebration of the "mystery of our religion."

The Church: Bishops and Deacons (3:1–13; 5:1, 17; Titus 1:5–9)

Modern discussions of the Pastoral Epistles note that these texts seem to depart significantly from the Pauline letters on the question of official church

The Pastoral Epistles Through the Centuries, First Edition. Jay Twomey.
© 2009 by Jay Twomey. Published 2020 by John Wiley & Sons Ltd.

structures. Although Paul does mention bishops and deacons in Philippians 1:1, his intentions behind the use of these terms remain entirely unclear, for in the other authentic letters there is no trace of these offices. The Pastor, however, mentions at least three offices, those of bishop (or overseer), deacon (or server), and presbyter (or elder), and establishes guidelines for the selection and qualifications of the officeholders. Dibelius and Conzelmann feel that there is no way to tell how or if leadership in the Pastor's community was organized hierarchically (1972: 56). The Pastor's descriptions of the different church offices mentioned in these letters are quite general, and provide almost no sense of the distinctive obligations entailed by each position, suggesting a certain indistinguishability among these roles (D-C 1972: 56; Collins 2002: 331; Hall 2006: 417). It is possible, however, that bishops, whatever their specific functions – teaching and managing among them – may have been appointed from among the ranks of elders (Collins 2002: 328), and that some elders were paid and granted a certain degree of job security (329; Collins refers to 1 Tim. 5:17–19 as "something akin to the elders' . . . bill of rights"). Moreover, even if the Pastor does not clearly differentiate among these offices, still it seems as though, especially given his sense of the church as "the household of God" (1 Tim. 3:15), he has in mind the traditional power structures of the Greco-Roman household, with the paterfamilias providing oversight and keeping order, assisted by a variety of inferior servers (Verner 1983). Reginald Kidd reads the "noble task" of 3:1 in fiscal terms. The wealthiest Christians may have felt, in accordance with the wider social order of the Hellenistic world, that they would accrue honor and positions of authority for themselves in the community by means of their beneficence. In Kidd's view, the Pastor writes 1 Timothy, among other reasons, to counter this tendency.

An ambiguity develops with v. 11, which may indicate that women could serve as deacons in the Pastor's communities. Towner, like other recent scholars, believes that probably they could, but maintains, sensibly in light of 1 Timothy 2:11–15, that the Pastor's deaconesses were "probably under at least a temporary restriction from teaching and holding authority" (2006: 265–66 n. 28).

Whoever aspires to the office of a bishop desires a noble task (vv. 1–6)

As hinted above, the Pastor's instructions regarding church offices have signaled for some modern readers a historical shift in early Christianity – away from the charismatic communities of Paul's day to the institutionalization of Christian practice and faith. Nevertheless, through the centuries these letters' comments on bishops, deacons, and presbyters have exerted a tremendous influence, out of all proportion to their value otherwise, on the development of the church. 1 Timothy 3 begins by outlining the requisite qualities of a bishop. Ancient Christian literature sometimes touched upon precisely the same issues raised by the Pastor here, and indeed throughout the Pastoral corpus. For instance, Ignatius, the late first century bishop of Antioch, and martyr, wrote that bishops should be respected leaders, capable of producing unanimity and worthy of respect, even if they are still young men (Eph. 2:2; 6:1; Magnesians 3:1). In later Patristic writings, discussions of the importance and qualifications of the bishop are given shape and impetus largely by the Pastor's language. Origen, in discussing the "rafters" of the Song of Songs (1:17), cites the "noble task" ("good work," KJV) of 1 Timothy 3:1 and the "apt teacher" of v. 2: "and I think that those who faithfully discharge the office of a bishop in the Church may fitly be called the rafters, by which the whole building is sustained and protected. . . . Moreover, the rafters are said to be of cypress, which tree possesses a greater strength and a sweetness of smell; and that denotes a bishop as being at once sound in good works and fragrant with the grace of teaching" (*Cant.* 3.3; in Cunningham 1985: 27). Cyprian, exploiting the ambiguity of *didaktikon* in v. 2 (which can refer to "apt" teaching or learning), commented of the bishop in 1 Timothy 3 that "he who is meek and mild in the patience of learning is teachable. For bishops ought not only to teach, but also to learn because he who grows daily and profits by learning better things teaches better" (*Ep.* 74.10; in Cunningham 1985: 36; cf. Gratian's twelfth century *Decretum*, 18.5, according to which bishops must attend ecclesiastical synods in order "to teach or be taught what is useful for correction" [2 Tim. 3:16]). The fourth century *Apostolic Constitutions* reflects nearly all of the qualities outlined by the Pastor, but in a revised form which brings out an ethical dimension only implied in the New Testament text:

> A bishop must be no accepter of persons [Acts 10:34; Rom. 2:11]; neither revering nor flattering a rich man contrary to what is right, nor overlooking nor domineering over a poor man. . . . Let a bishop be frugal . . . ever in a sober frame, and disposed to instruct and admonish the ignorant; and let him not be costly in his diet, a pamperer of himself, given to pleasure or fond delicacies. Let him be patient and gentle in his admonitions, well instructed himself, meditating in and diligently studying the Lord's books, and reading them frequently. (2.2.5; in Cunningham 1985: 39)

Echoes of the instructions to Timothy and Titus ring throughout this passage (see for example, the advice for peaceful admonitions in 2 Tim. 2:23–25), even as it seems slightly at odds, at the end, with the Pastor's almost wholly negative reading of the law in 1 Timothy 1:9.

By the medieval period, the Pastor's list of episcopal qualities, especially as it is clarified and to a certain extend codified by such texts as Gregory the Great's late sixth century *Pastoral Care*, becomes a standard description of one of the most powerful political posts of the age. Indeed, even lay congregants could, when speaking of their bishop, simply take the paradigm offered by 1 Timothy 3 for granted. Upon the election of one bishop to replace another who had recently passed away, for instance, the mid-eleventh century Christian community of Noyon and Tournai (in present-day Belgium) wrote in a communal letter announcing their choice that:

> We elected him just as apostolic and canonical authority commands: [he is] catholic in faith, by nature wise, teachable, patient, temperate of mores, of chaste life, sober, humble, expressive, merciful, lettered, educated in God's law, circumspect in the meanings of the scriptures, trained in ecclesiastical doctrines, and orthodox according to the ways and tradition of scriptures . . . , hospitable, modest, a good manager of his household, not a neophyte, a man of good character, one who has followed ecclesiastical tradition at every step, who has administered good works to all and right reason to the satisfaction of all who have asked for it. (in Ott and Jones 2007: 2)

Contemporary bodies of church law (the Catholic Church's Code of Canon Law, or the Canons of the Church of England) draw upon centuries of legal thought in fixing the duties and requisite characteristics of the bishop, and it is interesting to see how little has changed over the course of time. In the text cited above, for example, we find moral qualities mentioned along with pedagogical skill and academic training as essential considerations in the selection of a bishop. The Catholic canon treating of the qualifications for bishops (Canon 378) insists that the candidate for the office be:

1. outstanding in solid faith, good morals, piety, zeal for souls, wisdom, prudence, and human virtues, and endowed with other qualities which make him suitable to fulfill the office in question;
2. of good reputation;
3. at least thirty-five years old;
4. ordained to the presbyterate for at least five years;
5. in possession of a doctorate or at least a licentiate in sacred scripture, theology, or canon law from an institute of higher studies approved by the Apostolic See, or at least truly expert in the same disciplines (in Beal, Coriden, and Green 2000: 516).

As the episcopacy became ever more fully implicated in state power (see Carleton 2001: 7–42; Robinson 1991: 288–305), calls for the reform or abolition of the episcopacy became common. By Milton's day, radical discontent with extensive (and not infrequently corrupt) episcopal authority led English reformers to hark back to the pre-Constantinian church, to an age prior to state–church power structures, in thinking about the proper way of implementing the instructions of 1 Timothy 3. For Milton, according to one scholar's paraphrase, not only was the Pope the Antichrist, "but . . . bishops were more antichristian than the Pope" (Hill 1977: 105). Indeed, there is no biblical justification for the bishopric, Milton held, the bishop being simply another name for presbyter. Timothy and Titus, contrary to the common impression that they were bishops, "had rather the viceregency of an apostleship committed to them, then [sic] the ordinary charge of a Bishoprick, as being men of an extraordinary calling" (*Of Prelatical Episcopacy, Complete Prose* 1.626). In the eighteenth century, Milton's righteous anger is seconded by Voltaire's bitingly satirical portrait of the episcopacy. Voltaire's *Philosophical Dictionary* provides an anecdote about one "Samuel Ornik, native of Basle" in the entry "Bishop." Ornik finds nothing but crass materialism and religious ignorance in the bishops he encounters. The entry concludes when Ornik tells a bishop he has met:

> "[D]o you not know that there were no cardinals in the time of Jesus Christ and St. John?" – "Is it possible!" exclaimed the Italian prelate. – "Nothing is more true: you have read it in the Gospel." – "I have never read it," replied the bishop; "I know only the office of Our Lady," – "I tell you there were neither cardinals nor bishops; and when there were bishops, the priests were almost their equals, as St. Jerome, in several places, assures us [e.g., *Ep.* 69.3, NPNF2 6.143, in reference to the Pastorals]." – "Holy Virgin!" said the Italian, "I knew nothing about it; and what of the popes?" – "There were no popes either." – The good bishop crossed himself, thinking he was with the evil one; and leaped from the side of his companion. (Voltaire 1843: 212)

In the nineteenth century, American Presbyterian theologian Albert Barnes published a tract in the Miltonian vein, denying the biblical grounds for an episcopal church polity. Focusing on Titus and Timothy as potential biblical exemplars of episcopacy, Barnes ingeniously insists upon their temporary stays in Crete and Ephesus. Timothy, for instance, was given the role of a temporary overseer until Paul arrived (1 Tim. 4:13), or during a period in which Paul's arrival might be delayed (1 Tim. 3:14–15) – there was, in other words, nothing permanent in the appointment (Barnes 1835: 47; for similar arguments about Titus see p. 66).

A rather different, and traditional view, of course, is that there were bishops, or at any rate individuals who functioned as bishops, in the New Testament, and that Timothy and Titus were among their company. Early readers attest to this position (see, for instance, Eusebius, *Church History* 3.4, NPNF2 1.136; Chrysostom, *Homily* 1 *in Philippians*, NPNF1 13.184; Theodoret 2001: 217). And this view is still current. US Catholic bishops, for instance, understand the advice to Timothy in 1 Timothy 6:20 ("guard what has been entrusted to you") as indicative of Timothy's supervisory role, that is, his episcopal function, and thus of the primary work of the diocesan bishop (in Carey 1998: 333).

For some in the tradition, reflection upon 1 Timothy 3:1 could, in fact, be quite intensely personal. For example, Augustine, who was initially compelled into the clergy against his will, writes in the *Confessions* of the difficulties he had as a child when forced to study. Looking back upon that period, he could say, with a certain degree of ambivalence, "no one doth well against his will, even though what he doth, be well. Yet neither did they well who forced me, but what was well came to me from Thee, my God" (*Conf.* 1.12, NPNF1 1.50–51). However, he would eventually come to find the use of force a pragmatic expedient in manning vacant ecclesiastical positions. Although "the Apostle" may have insisted upon the "goodness" of the episcopal office, Augustine eventually, perhaps because of his own experience of compulsion into the priesthood, recognizes that "in order to make the office of a bishop be accepted by many men, they are seized against their will, subjected to importunate persuasion, shut up and detained in custody, and made to suffer so many things which they dislike, until a willingness to undertake the good work is found in them" (*Ep.* 173.2, NPNF1 1.544). In writing to a man he had detained for precisely this purpose, in fact, Augustine says, as if by way of apology, that "it becomes one of your disposition to devote to Christ that which is in you by His own gift"; for this reason, he continues, "we have given orders that this letter be not read to you until those to whom you are necessary hold you in actual possession. For we hold you in the bond of spiritual love, because to us also you are very necessary as a colleague" (*Ep.* 69.2, NPNF1 1.326).

Obviously this is not the whole story, though, for some, Augustine included, have worried about precisely the opposite as well, namely that the bishopric would attract greedy candidates seeking worldly authority, or honor, by means of a title which is, much more humbly, much less glamorously, simply "the title of a work" (*De civ. Dei.* 19.19, 2000: 698). Milton, railing against this problem, which he considered to be general, complained that "[s]o long agoe out of date is that old *true saying* . . . [of 1 Tim. 3:1]: for now commonly he who desires to be a minister, looks not at the work but at the wages . . . what can be planer Simonie?" (*Considerations Touching the Likeliest Means to Remove Hirelings out of the Church*, *Complete Prose* 7.315).

However, the list of social and ethical qualifications for church office is often considered sufficient protection against the abuse of power. Perhaps it is true, as Chrysostom notes, that the Pastor did not insist upon moral qualities equivalent to those of Paul or Jesus himself. How could he have done so since "plainly . . . few could be found of such a character, and there was need of many bishops" (*Hom. 1 Tim.*, NPNF1 13.438). Nevertheless, for someone like Irenaeus, it would go without saying that the early church chose the very best of men as successors to carry the gospel into the future (AH 3.3.1, ANF 1.415). And indeed it is possible to see in the Pastor's virtue list the basic requirements for any good Christian's life. Basil, for instance, drawing extensively upon virtue lists of the Pastorals and elsewhere, explains that "many things . . . set forth by inspired Scripture [are] . . . binding upon all who are anxious to please God" (*Ep.* 22, NPNF2 8.128). Bernard of Clairvaux, without reference to any church office, describes the peacemaker, he who "wins the souls of many others" while being in calm and sure possession of his own, as the one seeking the "good work" of the Pastor's bishop (*On Conversion*, 1987: 90).

Married only once (v. 2)

The Pastor himself relies upon one set of qualifications in particular, those pertaining to the domestic situation of the bishop and other church officials, as in themselves capable of ensuring quality leadership. One specific pair of qualifications stands out in the history of interpretation as paramount: the bishop must have been "married only once" (NRSV), or "the husband of one wife" (KJV), and must rule his house well (1 Tim. 3:2, 4–5, 12; cf. Titus 1:6). Although there is significant disagreement as to what the Pastor may have meant – is he worrying about polygamy (as in Calvin, *Commentary* 1964: 224), or is he endorsing serial monogamy (as in Theodoret, *Comm. 1 Tim.*, 2001: 2.218)? – readers have most frequently assumed that the marital and familial status of bishops and deacons (as well as widows in 1 Tim. 5:9) is important because it is indicative of their true moral fiber.

Needless to say, these verses have also been a serious point of contention between those who support clerical celibacy, and those who feel that religious leaders should marry if they so choose. The former camp tends to read these verses allegorically. In Augustine's view, the Pastor seems to have had in mind an ecclesiology even more than a requirement for office: "As the many wives of the old Fathers signified our future Churches out of all nations made subject unto one husband, Christ: so our chief-priest, the husband of one wife, signifies unity out of all nations, made subject unto one husband, Christ" (*De bono conjug.* 21, NPNF1 3.408). The medieval church could even conceive of the bishop's ring as a wedding band, signifying materially this spiritual, allegorically grounded, marital bond (Robinson 1991: 258). The reformers would agree with early figures like Jerome (*Ep.* 69.5, NPNF2 6.144) that such readings distort the simple meaning of the passage. Calvin even called them "childish nonsense" (*Commentary* 1964: 223), and Luther, not to be outdone, asks in his *Lectures on Titus*: "are these [and similar readings] not shocking and obvious monstrosities?" (*Lectures on Titus, Works* 29.18). Luther also notes that the Pastorals themselves condemn false teachers who forbid marriage (cf. 1 Tim. 4:3), for "the text clearly states that marriage is a creation of God"; therefore, one cannot prohibit anyone from marrying, let alone a bishop, for "it is not permissible to establish human traditions contrary to that which has been ordained by God" (20).

The issue of marital status and its attendant virtues, however, is not all the Pastor has in mind. According to him, a man "must manage his own household well" before he can "take care of God's church" (v. 5). This means governing not only his children (v. 4) and managing the property, but controlling his wife and slaves as well. This was not an uncommon classical topos (cf. Chrysostom, *Hom. 1 Tim.*, NPNF1 13.439; D-C 1972: 53). Nevertheless, the idea that the quality of one's household management was indicative of one's skills at governance struck a chord among Christian readers of these texts, who sometimes felt, with their classical forebears, that the equation was self-evident. Pseudo-Dionysius developed the notion into a bureaucratic hierarchy of leadership abilities: "the one who commands himself will command another. The one who commands another will command a household. The commander of a household will command a city, and the commander of a city will command a nation" (*Epistle* 8, 1987: 275–76). For Erasmus, "the home is nothing but a miniature state" (*Paraphrases*, 1993: 20).

Cervantes, in *Don Quixote*, picks up this general theme when a duchess, who has offered to make good on Don Quixote's pledge to reward Sancho with an island, remarks playfully that Sancho must be mad to follow a mad knight: "And that being so, people will disapprove . . . if [I] give the said Sancho an island to govern; for how will he who does not know how to govern himself know how to govern others?" (1981: 613).

The similarities between home and state in the Pastor's model can be reversed as well. Horace Bushnell, in *Christian Nurture*, a theologically based handbook on the rearing of children, writes that the Pastor's domestic standard is "a very singular test, in one view, for a Christian bishop; one that passes by the matter of learning and eloquence, and church reputation, laying hold, instead, of a gift in which some very ordinary men, and not a few ordinary women, excel." The analogy with the Pastor's description of the episcopacy is just, Bushnell continues, because "what indeed is the house but a little primary bishopric under the father, taking oversight thereof?" (1876: 315).

The snare of the devil (v. 7)

Among the risks of selecting a poor candidate for bishop is that, if he does not reflect the leadership qualities of the Hellenistic world, he may "fall into reproach and the snare of the devil" (v. 7, KJV; cf. 2 Tim. 2:26). The Pastor is probably thinking in metaphorical terms, here, as Tyndale understood when he unpacked the "snare of the devil" as slander or evil speech (*Obedience of a Christian Man*, 2000: 86). On the other hand, some have thought that this verse refers more literally to a punishment like that the devil received in his expulsion from heaven (Theodoret, *Comm. 1 Tim.*, 2001: 2.219). Symeon the New Theologian, in a wonderfully creative clarification, plays on the image by extending it, this time with regard not to the opinions of outsiders, but to the passions within:

> As for those who approach this road [of monastic devotion], this way of life, with indifference and contempt, why should we mention how great is their attachment to their relatives, when one sees how they fall into every snare of the devil like senseless birds? They expose themselves to every passion, they constantly become the prey of the wicked one who "goes about roaring like a lion seeking whom he may devour [1 Peter 5:8]." (*Catechetical Discourses* 7.13, 1980: 142)

The symbology of the tempter as a bird catcher is operative in medieval painting. In Pieter Bruegel the Elder's *Winter Landscape with Skaters and Bird Trap* (Figure 2), for example, there may be no specific reference to Timothy, and certainly no commentary on the episcopacy. But "in pictorial form, the Pauline image of the great tempter in the guise of a modest bird catcher" is seen in the quietly hidden trap in the lower right corner of the painting. The bird catcher is here not even visible, except for the string he will pull on the deadfall to pin the birds, i.e., to trap the souls of the wayward (Bauer and Bauer 1984: 146).

Deacons (v. 8)

In the Pastor's text, as we noted above, deacons, bishops, and presbyters can seem to play quite similar roles, even if many readers have found it difficult, perhaps offensive, to imagine that a deacon, a "server," could in any way approximate the bishop's status. Jerome scoffs, after learning that someone has equated the two offices of deacon and bishop: "must not a mere server of tables and of widows be insane to set himself up arrogantly over men through whose prayers the body and blood of Christ are produced?" (Jerome, *Ep.* 146.1, NPNF2 6.288).

Figure 2   Pieter Bruegel the Elder's *Winter Landscape with Skaters and Bird Trap*, 1565.
Source: Les Musées Royaux des Beaux-Arts de Belgique/Bridgeman Art Library

Others, however, are fully aware of the fact that church titles, in the Pastor's usage, simply do not reflect their contemporary experience of ecclesiastical hierarchy. Wesley, for example, remarking upon the apparent distinction implied by the separate references to bishops and deacons here, asks "but where are the presbyters? Were this order essentially distinct from that of bishops, could the apostle have passed it over in silence?" (*Explanatory Notes* 1850: 542). Wesley, like others, seizes hold of this confusion to circumvent what he considered an overly restrictive, and unbiblical, hierarchical scheme. As he writes to his brother Charles, after he had begun ordaining ministers without the authority of a bishop, "[s]ome obedience I always paid to the bishops in obedience to the laws of the land. But I cannot see that I am under any obligation to obey them further than those laws require. . . . [for] I firmly believe I am a scriptural *episkopos* [bishop], as much as any man in England or in Europe" (*Works* 13.220). The letter specifically takes aim at the tradition of apostolic succession which figures from Irenaeus down to Wesley's own day endorsed (see at 2 Tim. 2:1–2).

Women likewise (v. 11)

Given the conventionally patriarchal tone of these letters, it is interesting to note that in this discussion of the requirements of deacons one can find space for a church office held by women. The Pastor seems to speak of deacon's wives in v. 11 ("women likewise must be serious"; "even so must their wives be grave" [KJV]). Some readers through the centuries have assumed that this verse grants women a quasi-independent leadership status within the church. For instance, Chrysostom explained that the Pastor "was referring to those [women] having the dignity of the diaconate" and not to wives or "women in general"; Theodore of Mopsuestia believed that the women of this verse were "to exercise the same office as the [male] deacons" (Wijngaards 2002: 169, 178); and even Thomas Aquinas, although ultimately opposed to women holding office as deacons, had to acknowledge that it was quite possible to read the text in support of a diaconate of women (Thomas Aquinas 2007: 43; see also Wijngaards 2002: 125–26). In a recent study which draws upon these and other references to women deacons, John Wijngaards argues that "if the diaconate of women was a true diaconate, if it was one valid expression of the sacrament of *holy orders* [and he feels quite strongly that it was], then women did in fact receive holy orders and the [Catholic] priesthood too is open to them" (2002: 6). Other voices, however, like that of Calvin, have historically resisted reading women into the Pastor's discussion of deacons, and have insisted that the women mentioned here are simply the obedient wives of deacons and bishops, not officeholders in their own right (Calvin, *Commentary* 1964: 229; cf. Luther, *Lectures on 1 Timothy*, *Works*: 28.299).

Theological Speculation: The Mystery (3:14–16)

In the last part of this chapter, the Pastor makes a play for epistolary verisimilitude. I hope "to come to you soon," he writes, while warning that he might be "delayed." Moments of personalia such as this (we will see many more in 2 Tim.), especially as they echo similar language in other letters (e.g., 1 Cor. 4:19; 2 Cor. 13:10) have convinced some modern readers of the Pastorals (e.g., Towner 2006; Fee 1995; Guthrie 1990; Kelly 1981) that the letters, or portions of them at any rate, are authentic Pauline texts. The position of this commentary, as was made clear in the introduction, is that they are not, and that, as Collins puts it, the Pastor's comment about "Paul's" delayed arrival, really his "indefinite absence[,] provides cover for the timely advice that he now offers in Paul's name" (Collins 2002: 101; see also at 2 Tim. 4:9–22).

The architectural imagery involved in construing the church as "the pillar and bulwark of the truth" (v. 15; cf. 2 Tim. 2:19) has echoes elsewhere in the New Testament, especially in references to major individuals of the early community (e.g., Peter, James, and John, Gal. 2:9). Given the Pastor's key idea that the church is a "household of God," many commentators have read this imagery as a metaphorical description of that social space (e.g., Bassler 1996: 73). Hanson, drawing literary parallels between our text and descriptions of Solomon's temple, on the one hand, and the pillar of cloud, on the other, concludes that "what this densely packed phrase means is that the Christian church is the true temple of God, the place where his presence is to be found" (1982: 83).

Modern commentators tend to assume that v. 16 is a fragment of a "Christ hymn" (Towner 2006: 276; cf. Bassler 1996: 77; D-C 1972: 61). Its fragmentary nature is evident from the fact that it begins with a relative pronoun, 'who,' for which there is no clear antecedent. It seems evident that the hymn must refer to Jesus, although many, the KJV translators included, either understood the passage in Trinitarian terms or had access to manuscripts which replace "who" with "God" (Bassler 1996: 75; cf. Gregory of Nyssa, *C. Eun.* 4.1, NPNF2 5.176; Chrysostom, *Hom. 1 Tim.*, NPNF1 13.442; Theodoret, *Comm. 1 Tim.*, NPNF2 3.166; Calvin, *Institutes*, 4.14.2). Bassler proposes the following reconstruction of the words preceding our text: " 'Blessed be our Lord and Savior Jesus Christ, who . . .' " (1996: 75). The "mystery" of this hymn is essentially the content of its message about Christ's incarnation, his historical ministry and the church founded in his name. It is the teaching which deacons are particularly responsible for maintaining (3:9).

Pillar and bulwark of the truth (v. 15)

The imagery of "pillar and bulwark" has been taken to refer either to the Christian teaching, and its teachers, or to the whole church itself. Irenaeus uses this text to emphasize the unbroken line of transmission bringing that truth to contemporary readers. God's "plan of salvation," he writes, was "handed down to us in the Scriptures, to be the ground and pillar of our faith"; because of this, "[i]f any one do not agree to these truths, he despises the companions of the Lord; nay more, he despises Christ Himself the Lord; yea, he despises the Father also, and stands self-condemned, resisting and opposing his own salvation, as is the case with all heretics" (AH 3.11.8, ANF 1.414–15). Naturally this implies that "the 'pillar and ground' of the Church is the Gospel and the spirit of life; it is fitting that she should have four pillars, breathing out immortality in every side, and vivifying men afresh" (428). For Origen, " 'the Church of the living God, the pillar and ground of the truth'. . . . is built upon 'the tops of the mountains,' i.e., the predictions of all the prophets, which are its foundations" (*C. Cels.* 5.33, ANF 4.557). Calvin concurs that this verse is about teaching rather than the community itself. Here "Paul" is "expounding to pastors the greatness of their office"; "the church is the pillar of the truth because by its ministry the truth is preserved and spread" (*Commentary* 1964: 231). The "Papists," on the other hand, do not belong to the church since among them "the truth not only lies buried, but is shockingly destroyed and trampled under-foot" (232).

The idea that the "pillar and ground" of truth refers, as in the letter, to the church itself, to this gathering of souls as opposed to the doctrine taught by ministers, is embraced by Augustine, who writes in praise of "[t]he Church of Christ in the Saints, the Church of Christ in those who are written in Heaven, the Church of Christ in those who to this world's temptations yield not. For they are worthy of the name of 'firmament'" (*En. ps.* 48.1, NPNF1 8.164).

The mystery of godliness (v. 16)

The highest of the Christological moments in this letter is to be found in the last verse of the current chapter: "he was revealed in flesh, vindicated in spirit, seen by angels, proclaimed among Gentiles, believed in throughout the world, taken up in glory." Calvin, as if aware of the paradox of a mystery which is also rationally expounded (D-C 1972: 41) in the form of a teaching passed on from Paul to Timothy, and from Timothy to the church leaders, writes in his sermon entitled "Great is the Mystery of Godliness":

> When we hear this word, *mystery*, let us remember two things; first, that we learn to keep under our senses, and flatter not ourselves that we have sufficient knowl-edge and ability to comprehend so vast a matter. In the second place, let us learn to climb up beyond ourselves, and reverence that majesty which passeth our understanding. (1999: 22)

For Calvin, the actual mystery is certainly "that Jesus came and joined His Godhead with our nature; which was so wretched and miserable" (ibid.). But the rhetoric of mystery functions to create the proper conditions for the appre-ciation of the teaching itself, and thus refers, at least in Calvin's view, to a species of training, not unlike that which the Pastor may have in mind in 4:7 (see chapter 4 for reflections on the Pastor's use of "godliness"). Erasmus makes sense of the utterly visible "mystery" of Christ by contrasting it with what he considered the obscure mysteries of the Jerusalem temple, where signs of the divine were symbolic at best, and where the real divinity hidden in the inner chambers were but the few could go. Christianity's mystery is different in its self-evidence and worldwide diffusion (*Paraphrases*, 1993: 23).

The hymn has several mysteries, however, in its several clauses. That "he" was "revealed in the flesh" refers, as Calvin notes, to Jesus' incarnation. That

Jesus was "vindicated in spirit" means to Theodoret that his identity was acknowledged in his production of miracles (*Comm. 1 Tim.*, 2001: 2.220). That he was "seen by angels" suggests to a number of readers that his identity, his "essence," was a secret of which only God himself was aware prior to the incarnation – "so that Angels together with us saw the Son of God, not having before seen Him. Great, truly great, was this mystery!" (Chrysostom, *Hom. 1 Tim.*, NPNF1 13.442; cf. Augustine, *De Trin.* 20, NPNF1 3.84–85; Theodoret, *Comm. 1 Tim.*, 2001: 2.221; Calvin 1964: 234). And that he was "received up into glory" means to Edward Taylor that sinners might appropriate that glory, or some of it, for themselves:

> Let some, my Lord, of thy bright Glories beams,
> Flash quickening Flames of Glory in mine eye
> T'enquicken my dull Spirits, drunke with dreams
> Of Melancholy juyce that stupify.

Taylor's plea for revelation, essentially for an enlivening of his own religious sensibility, very quickly begins to exceed the humbleness of the request. Undoubtedly he wants to awaken from spiritual dullness and torpor by the gift of "some" divine glory, but the end result will, apparently, be his transformation into a prophet along the lines of Isaiah (6:6–7):

> A Coale from thy bright Altars Glory sure
> Kissing my lips, my Lethargy will Cure.
>   (1960: 216)

Despite the apparent multiplicity of mysteries implied by the Pastor, however, Pseudo-Dionysius, who in fact purports to be writing to Timothy, insists that "Christ remains forever unchanged, even when fully and truly made one of us. . . . [he] remains forever the same amid all the workings of his divine goodness" (*Ecclesiastical Hierarchy* 4.10, 1987: 231).

Just this diversity in simplicity is taken up by American poet Robert Hayden in a poetic reflection on Christ's mysterious glory, which, as Collins notes, may refer equally to the incarnation and to post-resurrection appearances (2002: 108). For Hayden, the history of the twentieth century provides a particularly gruesome vantage point from which to understand both of these interpretive options:

> From the corpse woodpiles, from the ashes
> and staring pits of Dachau,
> Buchenwald they come –

O David, Hirschel, Eva,
cops and robbers with me once,
their faces are like yours –

From Johannesburg, from Seoul.
Their struggles are all horizons.
Their deaths encircle me.

Through target streets I run,
in light part nightmare
and part vision fleeing

What I cannot flee, and reach,
that cold cloacal cell
where He, who is man beatified

And Godly mystery,
lies chained, His pain
our anguish and our anodyne.

(1975: 116)

The suffering Christ, "Godly mystery" incarnate, is also human suffering under regimes of violence worldwide in which, it would seem, Christ is also appearing again and again and again.

The Pastor returns to his opponents again and claims that their heterodox teachings are a sign of the last days. The false teachers are encouraging ascetic practices in the Pastor's community, specifically celibacy and abstinence from certain foods. Timothy can best keep himself and the believers at Ephesus safe from these opponents if he maintains piety and keeps in mind the spiritual gift he had received in his ordination.

The Pastoral Epistles Through the Centuries, First Edition. Jay Twomey.
© 2009 by Jay Twomey. Published 2020 by John Wiley & Sons Ltd.

The Opponents: End Times (4:1–10; 2 Tim. 3:1)

Some scholars argue that for the Pastor, as for Paul, the end was nigh (Towner 1989: 64–65; Kidd 1990: 190; cf. Collins 2002: 112, 244). Others, however, feel that these letters, despite the language of latter or last days, have lost Paul's eschatological edge (Bultmann 1955: 2.183; D-C 1972: 8), and that they deploy such end-time motifs quite consciously for polemical and rhetorical effect (Donelson 1986: 184; Bassler 1996: 79). Since the Pastor does not otherwise seem anxious about, or insist upon, the eschatological urgency of present choices (as opposed to Paul in 1 Cor. 7:25–31, for example), this second interpretation may be preferable.

Generally, as we have noted, the Pastor's portraits of his opponents are vague and draw upon stock lists of vices, allowing readers to conclude little about the actual issues at stake. 1 Timothy 4:3, however, may get us closer than anything else in these letters to an understanding of those positions. The Pastor warns about false teachers who "forbid marriage and demand abstinence from foods." Based to a large extent upon this passage, several scholars have assumed that the Pastor's opponents belonged to a more ascetic, perhaps even radically democratic movement, one emphasizing women's sexual abstinence in order to free them from the social restrictions of the patriarchal home, and one perhaps more closely allied with the authentic Paul (Bassler 1996: 81; cf. MacDonald 1983: 98). If this is an adequate depiction of the opponents' position, it should come as no surprise, as Margaret MacDonald reminds us, that only women are said to be attracted to the new teaching (1988: 179). The Pastor, either because he is concerned for the safety of a church seen, from the outside, to be flouting social conventions (MacDonald 1996), or because he finds the flouting of those conventions utterly reprehensible, counters this teaching with his emphases on marriage and childbearing (2:15; 3:2, 4, 12; 5:14; Titus 1:6).

The Pastor advises Timothy that, to prepare for his difficult dealings with these opponents, he should "train [him]self in godliness" (v. 7). In Hellenistic culture, godliness [*eusebia*] referred to "reverence for the Gods," but also "a kind of piety that called forth respect for traditional values and practices," and included what Collins dubs ancient "family values" (Collins 2002: 123). Here, the Pastor contrasts godliness with the physical training of the athlete, and in so doing strikes a note common to ancient philosophical paranesis, emphasizing the superiority of intellectual over bodily exercise (D-C 1972: 68–69; Kelly 1981: 100). Commentators have often assumed, however, that this verse implicitly criticizes not, or not only, the athlete but also the Pastor's theological opponents, whose asceticism and ritualism might be considered, in some sense, a relatively misguided form of bodily training (Towner 2006: 306; Bassler 1996: 84).

In later times (v. 1, cf. 2 Tim. 3:1)

That the Pastor may have been striking an eschatological pose, however, is not a concern of many of his readers for they, too, have adapted his "in later times" in terms of their own contemporary ends, and this in at least three ways. The first and most obviously relevant reading of these verses is itself apocalyptic. Joachim de Fiore reminds his readers: what "you have read in the Apostle Paul . . . has been truly fulfilled for him and what you know has been truly foretold"; after citing 2 Timothy 3:1–5 Joachim warns his readers not to imagine some future end, because "this will not take place in the days of your grand-children or in the old age of your children, but in your own days, few and evil" (in McGinn 1979: 114, 117). Cotton Mather uses these verses both to insist upon the apocalyptic signs of his times and to justify the persecution of witches in New England (*Wonders of the Invisible World*, Mather 1693: 23). Another apocalyptic American, Hal Lindsey, who came to prominence as the author of the 1970 bestseller *The Late, Great Planet Earth*, provides nearly up-to-the-minute readings of the signs of the times on his website, *The Hal Lindsey Report*. The "perilous times" of the "last days" (KJV) predicted by the Pastor in 2 Timothy 3:1 are to be seen, Lindsey reports, in such diverse policies and phenomena as Hurricane Katrina (which struck New Orleans a devastating blow in August, 2005), US gun control laws, and the absence of prayer from public schools (Lindsey Report website).

A second, less apocalyptic, though still vaguely eschatological interpretation is exemplified by John Chrysostom, who declares in his commentary on 1 Timothy that "it is [now] . . . the last time" because the heresies and "sects" of the day are exactly what "Paul" had had in mind in v. 1. Interestingly, he is also aware that certain of the signs of the times about which the Pastor warns have come to pass, possibly, within orthodoxy itself. The "seducing spirits" of the "latter times" will forbid people from marrying, the Pastor says. Thinking about the Christian privileging of virginity, Chrysostom asks: "And do we not forbid to marry?" His answer is that "we" do not, for to encourage virginity is not to keep people from marrying, (*Hom. 1 Tim.*, NPNF1 13.444, 446). In any event, Chrysostom does not worry overmuch about the end-time implications of the verse, which are better suited to measuring the status and nature of apostasy than the approach of the *eschaton*. Pope Leo XIII also hints in his encyclical on the Holy Spirit, *Divinum Illud Munus*, although no more fretfully than Chrysostom, that given the frequency with which people resist "the truth through malice . . . those dark times seem to have come which were foretold by St. Paul" in these passages (in Carlen 1981: 2.415).

Finally, another traditional option has been to extend the Pastor's reference to the last days ("in the last days distressing times will come," 2 Tim. 3:1) indefinitely, and not just into the writer's present. As Calvin puts it, "this whole New Testament time, from the point that Christ appeared to us with the preaching of his gospel even to the Day of Judgment, is designated by 'the last hour,' 'the last times,' 'the last days.' This is done that, content with the perfection of Christ's teaching, we may learn not to fashion anything new for ourselves beyond this or to admit anything conceived of others" (*Institutes* 4.8.7, 1960: 2.1155; cf. Wesley, *Explanatory Notes* 1850: 543, who begins the age of the "latter times" with the ascension).

In addition to aiding in theological crises and conflicts wedded to some sense of eschatological urgency, these verses also support a certain defensive traditionalism, especially with regard to the higher criticism and scientific developments. Anglican poet and hymnist Charlotte Elliott laments, in a poem entitled "2 Timothy 3:1," that:

> The light of science grows more bright
> New fields of knowledge are explored;
> But heavenly truth's refulgent light
> Is so rejected or ignored,
> That few hold on their steadfast way,
> Turning from all false lights away.
>
> That finished work, that glorious plan,
> By Christ, for our salvation, wrought,
> By erring and presumptuous man
> Is deemed superfluous – set at nought!
> While human systems are believed,
> Man's doctrine as the truth received.

The poem ends with a deep sense of yearning for divine judgment, apparently upon those forces in the world working to foreground the human at the expense of the divine:

> O! hasten then those glorious days,
> When Thou wilt claim Thy dear-bought throne,
> And make this ransomed world Thine own.
> (1871: 203–04)

Adventist founder Ellen White, similarly invested in the coming end, argued with reference to these passages that "Satan has undermined faith in the Bible

... direct[ing] men to other sources for light and power," sources such as "criticism and speculation concerning the Scriptures." For White this "opened the way for spiritism and theosophy – those modernized forms of ancient heathenism" (*Desire of the Ages*, 2005: 257–58). Billy Graham likewise argues that Satanic "deceivers with intellectual arguments [about the Bible] which sound like the epitome of scholarship are beguiling many" (*How to Be Born Again*, 1977: 61).

Demanding abstinence from foods (v. 3)

The "teachings of demons" (v. 1) which the Pastor has in his sights, however, are fairly specific: his opponents are forbidding marriage and enjoining "abstinence from foods which God created to be received with Thanksgiving by those who believe and know the truth" (v. 3). Earlier we noted some readings of the Pastor's opponents' radical emphasis on celibacy and the rejection of marriage (see at 1 Tim. 3:2). Here we will focus on the ascetic abstinence from foods. Augustine found in this verse support for his theological insistence upon the nature of good, the goodness of being itself. Everything created by God, everything that has being, even the forbidden fruit, is good, it is just that some goods are better than others. For example, God's will that Adam and Eve not eat from the tree of the knowledge of good and evil is better than the inherent goodness of the tree and its fruit. This does not mean that the tree or its fruit were evil, however. "God did not plant an evil tree in Paradise," Augustine argued on the basis of this verse, "but He Himself was better who prohibited its being touched" (*De nat. boni* 34, NPNF1 4.358). Others in the tradition agree, and like Augustine are thus required to relegate evil to the will of the creature (Catherine of Siena, *Dialogue* 150, 1980: 318).

Nonetheless, this passage poses at least two problems. First, if everything created by God is good and is to be received as such by the faithful, how is one to understand the dietary laws of the Hebrew Bible? And second, what about legitimate Christian asceticism, temporary fasts for instance, which seem to be rendered moot by the Pastor here? The first problem can be solved with recourse to typology. Augustine, reading 1 Timothy 4:4 alongside Titus 1:15 ("unto the pure all things are pure"), marks an epistemological difference between the real nature of things and their representation: "[t]he apostle speaks of the natures of the things, while the Old Testament calls some animals unclean, not in their nature, but symbolically, on account of the prefigurative character of that dispensation. For instance, a pig and a lamb are both clean in their nature, for every creature of God is good; but symbolically, a lamb is clean, and a pig unclean" (*C. Faust.* 6.7, NPNF1 4.171). Swine was forbidden not because it is evil in itself, but only for its figurative associations. As an animal that does not chew the cud it typifies the human fool who fails to learn the lessons of the faith. Augustine argues that "to recall, in quiet repose, some useful instruction from the stomach of memory to the mouth of reflection, is a kind of spiritual rumination. The animals above mentioned are a symbol of those people who do not do this. And the prohibition of the flesh of these animals is a warning against this fault" (ibid.).

The second problem has elicited a less creative, if more complicated, solution. A variety of figures in the history of this passage's interpretation essentially argue for a compromise between a position like that of the Pastor's opponents and the position of the Pastor himself. That is, rejecting certain foods for a time is acceptable so long as one does not make the mistake of assuming that one rejects them because they are inherently evil. In Cyril of Jerusalem's exhortation, believers should "abstain not as from things abominable . . . but as being good things disregard them for the sake of better spiritual things" (*Catechetical Lectures* 4.27, NPNF2 7.24). And John Cassian writes that it is simply the intentions of those who fast that matter. If we fast because we consider food or certain foods sinful, we "shall not only gain no advantage by our abstinence but shall actually contract grievous guilt and fall into the sin of impiety" (*Conf.* 3.21.13, NPNF2 11.508). In a peculiar variant of this idea, Jerome suggests a fusion of scripture and medical advice in his reading of 1 Timothy 4:4–5. Certainly he could not gainsay "Paul;" but in his view, one he shared with Galen, moderation in the consumption of food is nevertheless in order since "neither the fiery Etna nor the country of Vulcan, nor Vesuvius, nor Olympus, burns with such violent heat as the youthful marrow of those who are flushed with wine and filled with food" (*Ep.* 54.9, NPNF2 6.105). Jerome's use of this passage links the Pastor's rejection of food abstinence to questions of sexuality – although not so as to link what is said about food to a rebuttal of the opponents' view of marriage. Indeed, Jerome's entire purpose in this text is to convince a young widow to remain unmarried. After disparaging the passions, and warning of all the pitfalls of marriage, he concludes his missive with the uplifting advice: "[t]hink every day that you must die, and you will then never think of marrying again" (*Ep.* 54.18, 109).

Old wives' tales (v. 7)

The Pastor, evoking the dismissive rhetoric conventional in philosophical debates (D-C 1972: 68), declares that certain kinds of interpretations among his opponents are merely the stories old women tell themselves and their children or grandchildren in idle hours. Irenaeus labels as "old wives tales" the complicated logics of Gnosticism (AH 1.16.3, ANF 1.341), and Minucius Felix, a contemporary of Tertullian, rejects pagan mythic narratives in the same terms (*Octavius* 20, ANF 4.184). The very same accusations were apparently tossed about by opponents of Christianity as well. Origen reports that Celsus sneeringly rejected the Genesis 2 account of creation as an old wives' tale (*C. Cels.* 4.36, ANF 4.513). Augustine speaks not of opponents, exactly, but those "lovers of this world" who, until they recognize the emptiness, the vanity, of worldly pursuits, resist the "salutary admonitions" of wisdom, "and regard them as old wives' fables" (*Ep.* 203, NPNF1 1.558). Many readers throughout the tradition have simply borrowed this language for their own purposes, as they frequently do with the Pastor's criticisms of his opponents. The expression "old wives' tale" became common in English usage with Tyndale's translation of the New Testament in 1526 (Knowles 2005: 508).

Although the derogatory import of this verse is simply conventional, having nothing in particular to do with women's narratives per se, modern readers have sometimes taken it to be misogynistic in its general usage. As feminist theorist and critic Tania Modleski puts it, in explaining the title of her study, *Old Wives' Tales: And Other Women's Stories*:

> I wanted to suggest [by choosing this title] that many of the stories told by women are always already discredited by the larger culture. . . . feminism can help grant legitimacy to women's tales. . . . [O]n the other hand, feminism obviously ought not to affirm women's accounts simply because they are women's, for sometimes the stories women tell qua wives, like the ones invoked by Clarence Thomas' wife, are intended to discredit other women's stories and to shore up patriarchy. (1998: 8)

Train yourself in godliness (vv. 7–8)

To ready himself for his ministerial combat, Timothy is told to "train yourself in godliness." The Pastor acknowledges the importance of other kinds of training too, even as he insists upon the paramount importance of godliness. But the idea of a training which has something in common with physical exercise (v. 8) has struck some readers as odd. Calvin specifies that the Pastor does not have in mind "hunting or racing or digging or wrestling or manual labor," but rather "all outward actions undertaken for the sake of religion, such as vigils, long fasts, lying on the ground, and such like," by those who would purchase works at the cost of grace. However, in allowing that physical training is at least slightly profitable (it "is of some value" rather than "none at all"), the Pastor provides a certain leeway within the tradition for external practice in the service of godliness. Thus Calvin recognizes that the support provided by religious ritual and ascetic practice did at one time inspire individuals who, in all good faith, must have believed "that there was some divine or angelical perfection in their austere rule of life." Had they not held to the efficacy of such things, he continues, "they would never have practiced [them] . . . with such ardor" (*Commentary* 1964: 243). The religious individuals envisioned here were the hermits, monks, and nuns of ancient Christianity; and although Calvin doesn't immediately connect their eremitic impulse with that of John the Baptist, the logic of his commentary leads him to John, and to compare John to Jesus, in order to reassert his basic point about "physical training": "Christ did not follow as ascetic a way of life as John the Baptist, and yet He was not for that reason any whit inferior" (244).

Whether or not readers find the athletic analogy appropriate, they have still had to wrestle with the meaning of *eusebia*. English translators have rendered *eusebia* in the Pastorals as "godliness," "piety" (KJV), "religion" (NEB), and, in its occurrences elsewhere in the New Testament, Acts 3:12 for example, as "holiness" (KJV), and "virtue" (Wycliffe). Some interpreters adopt a decidedly intellectual understanding of the word. Athanasius considers "training in godliness" to be, or at least to involve, meditation (*Ep.* 11.7, NPNF2 4.535). For Clement of Alexandria, godliness is that "knowledge of the truth" (2 Tim. 2:25) which Jesus sent the Paraclete to teach. It is our ability to become like God and, because of this, God becomes our most apt instructor (*Protr.* 9, ANF 2.196). In another sense, godliness itself "is instruction, being the learning of the service of God, and training in the knowledge of the truth, and right guidance which leads to heaven." Clement extrapolates upon this sense of an education in godliness by means of a number of creative images, one of which combines the hazards of being "shipwrecked in the faith" [1 Tim. 1:19] with a pedagogical spirit:

> [J]ust as the helmsman does not always yield to the winds, but sometimes, turning the prow towards them, opposes the whole force of the hurricanes; so the Instructor [i.e., Christ] never yields to the blasts that blow in this world, nor commits the child to them like a vessel to make shipwreck on a wild and licentious course of life; but, wafted on by the favouring breeze of the Spirit of truth, stoutly holds on to the child's helm, – his ears, I mean, – until He bring him safe to anchor in the haven of heaven. (*Paed.* 1.7, ANF 2.223)

In Calvin's view, the word "godliness" designates "the spiritual worship of God which is found only in a pure conscience." As in Clement, it also means in some sense becoming like God, even if God's absolute sovereignty and humanity's total depravity in Calvinism foreclose the possibility of union. Once one "attains to" godliness, in fact, one achieves a certain parity with God's will for believers, for after this "God requires no more of us" (*Commentary* 1964: 243–44).

Each of these readings reflects upon piety as the attitude proper to faith. Social and political implications of *eusebia*, however, have also been foregrounded. John Cassian, for example, considers "*eusebia*" to be "the actual perfection of love, which has the promise of the life that now is and of that which is to come." A solid training in love is necessary in a world of "inequalities and differences of conditions . . . brought about by the wickedness of men; viz., of those who have grasped and kept for their own use (without however using them) those things which were granted to all by the Creator of all alike [1 Tim. 4:4–5]" (*Conf.* 1.10, NPNF2 11.299). Thomas Aquinas understands that the concept is ultimately concerned with the stability of the social order, and that it implies allegiance to the state (cf. Hanson 1982: 90–91); hence his rendering of "*eusebia*" as a kind of religious patriotism, involving proper respect for fatherland and family. The point, he says, is that God is the ultimate father, and that all Christians come from the same country (Thomas Aquinas 2007: 53).

1 Timothy 5

Turning his attention a second time to members of the community, and specifically to officeholders, the Pastor describes a category of women he calls "real widows" who can apply for public assistance from the church only if they are above a certain age and, if they can provide evidence of their moral worth. Elders are discussed as well, as are procedures for adjudicating charges made against them. Timothy, apparently of a weak disposition, is advised at the chapter's end to drink a little wine in addition to water. It will help his stomach, the Pastor tells him.

The Pastoral Epistles Through the Centuries, First Edition. Jay Twomey.
© 2009 by Jay Twomey. Published 2020 by John Wiley & Sons Ltd.

Women: Widows (5:1–10)

The material in this chapter deals largely with a group that seems to have been causing problems for the Pastor: widows. Elders are mentioned too, and the chapter as a whole closes with another of "Paul's" personal touches, but it is widows who absorb the Pastor's concern, and who therefore predominate in the readings of chapter 5 down through the centuries. The references to "honor," which can mean either honor or payment/material aid (v. 3; cf. v. 17 below), and the taking of widows "into the number," or enrolling them (v. 9, KJV), have led to questions about the possibility of a remunerated order or office of widows. That such orders played an important role in slightly later Christian society is clear (Bassler 1996: 92; Penn 2001). Although the evidence from the Pastorals is uncertain, most modern commentators feel that an office of widows is at least strongly implied by our text, a conclusion supported by the similarities among requirements for bishops and deacons, in chapter 3, and widows in chapter 5.

Controversy arises in the scholarship when it comes to deciding upon the Pastor's attitude toward widows. As we have seen, in chapters 2 and 4, one of the Pastor's goals is to curtail women's religious agency. With this in mind, feminist commentators argue that the Pastoral Epistles know of a community of women for whom the order of widows granted a certain freedom: from the restrictions of the patriarchal household and for active participation in religious life. Taking into consideration the Pastor's generally critical attitude here, and the ways in which he severely restricts that category of official widows to women over 60 who have none to care for them (vv. 8–9), these scholars assume, sensibly enough, that 1 Timothy 5 intends to "decimate the office" and reassert strict male control over the church (MacDonald 1983: 75; cf. Beattie 2005: 104; D'Angelo 2003: 275). Even sympathetic interpreters can be perplexed that the Pastor would pick "this genuinely elderly age," which few in "a small Christian congregation" would be likely to reach (Towner 2006: 346). Others argue that the situation of heresy in Ephesus, which may have affected or involved the widows quite directly, and the difficulties of caring for an increasingly complicated order, or office, of widows (some of whom, the young ones, were sometimes interested in remarrying [v. 11]), required the Pastor to take certain necessary, if still restrictive, measures (Hanson 1982: 96–100; MacDonald 1996: 157–62; Towner 2006: 332–60) for the good of the community.

Younger widows are not to be enrolled because, given "their sensual desires" (v. 11), they will likely violate "their first pledge" (v. 12). Commentators have often assumed that "first faith" (KJV) here means a vow of celibacy, indicative of a special office of widows (Kelly 1981: 117; D-C 1972: 75; Davies 1996: 41; Bassler 1996: 97). Collins (2002: 141) and Towner (2006: 352) are not convinced that a pledge is in view (it is unlikely that widows over 60 would be required to take such a pledge, Towner feels), but rather that the Pastor, like the Paul of 1 Corinthians 7, feared young women would remarry outside the church. Knight is surely right, however, in arguing that "introducing . . . a nonbelieving husband into the text miss[es] the inherent contrast in the text itself" between young enrolled widows and young non-enrolled widows. The latter can remarry without prejudice or judgment (1992: 226). Couldn't they also marry an outsider?

Do not speak harshly to an older man (v. 1)

The passage begins not with widows, however, but with a few brief comments to Timothy regarding his parenetic style. He is to treat the aged and the young, both, with familial respect, as parents and siblings, even when "rebuking" (KJV) or "speaking harshly to" (NRSV) them. Augustine cites these verses in his study of the rhetorical models found in scripture which can and should be practiced by ministers. He argues, drawing upon Cicero, that there are three basic styles of oratory – the subdued, the temperate, and the majestic. In Augustine's view, the Pastor in these verses is advocating the use of the temperate style (*De doc. Chr.* 4.19.38, NPNF1 2.587, 588). Chrysostom similarly considers the opening verses of chapter 5 in rhetorical terms, but his concern is more exclusive to questions of audience. Older people, he says, will be offended if you rebuke them. Younger men, naturally high in spirits, are likely to respond with agitation to criticism, so moderate your exhortations in light of this. Younger women are a special case, not because of any attitudinal propensities of their own, but rather because associating with them in the course of your ordinary duties can, unfortunately, arouse suspicion in others. Therefore, "Paul" emphasizes that younger women must be approached "in all purity" so that your dealings with them "should give no ground for suspicion, no shadow of pretext, to those who wish to calumniate" (*Hom. 1 Tim.*, NPNF1 13.450).

Honor widows who are really widows (v. 3)

The fourth century *Apostolic Constitutions* reiterated the Pastor's language about widows and women in general, adding only that widows cared for by the church constitute an "order" (*Apostolic Constitutions* 3.1.1, ANF 7.426). The order of widows here seems only to refer to the official list of those women cared for by the community, for the *Apostolic Constitutions* do not grant widows any special authority. Indeed, widows must seek the permission of the deacon (or deaconess) even to leave the house to dine with others (3.1.7, ANF 7.429). They are allowed to pray at home for those who have given them alms, however (3.1.13, ANF 7.430).

It is clear that those who belong to this order, or class, are women who have no one to care for them. The language of the text in v. 4, however, is rather confusing. Does "let them learn first to show piety at home" (KJV) refer to the children or grandchildren of a widow, whose care for their older relative will relieve the community of the burden of paying for her upkeep? This seems to be the most sensible reading, and it is followed by most commentators. However, many traditional readers, along with the NRSV, have assumed that the subject of the sentence does not change, that is, that widowed women who still have family to care for cannot be enrolled as "widows indeed" unless they "learn their religious duty to their own family" first. Theodoret, who considers the situation mutually beneficial to the women and their family members, believes that such widows "should make a return to them [i.e., to their younger relatives] for the care they received from their own parents . . . and receive in return care at their hands" (*Comm. 1 Tim.*, 2001: 2.224; cf. Chrysostom, *Hom. 1 Tim.*, NPNF1 13.450). Luther, who agrees with this reading, also deploys the Pastor's exhortation about widows in a passage of anti-Catholic polemic: "This passage says much against the pope and the monks ever since the time of Jerome, who boasted about their life in the desert and belittled the authority of parents and the religious training of children. . . . [t]his is a very strong passage against the monastic life and its plan" (*Lectures on 1 Timothy, Works* 28.335).

In an interesting modern twist on this same generally conservative reading, religious groups will sometimes refer to 1 Timothy 5:8 to castigate women who work outside of the home, or at least will decry the circumstances that might lead them to do so. See for example the following representative comments posted on a website called LadiesAgainstFeminism.com:

> Christians should be confronting [this] issue squarely, because Scripture does. Women are never, ever to be left defenseless and without support. Men are not allowed an "easy out," either. Scripture is clear: if we do not support widows and orphans, we have abandoned "pure and undefiled religion" (James 1:27). The early church had a daily distribution for women who needed support (those who lacked families to take care of them – see Acts 6:1 and I Timothy 5:3–16). We can't expect the secular world to protect women and children, but the fact that Christian women now feel pressured to get careers to support themselves in case their husbands leave them or die is a horrible reflection on the church and

Christian households in general. We really don't take Scripture seriously when it says that a man who refuses to provide for the widows in his own family is "worse than an infidel" (I Tim. 5:8). We sweep those uncomfortable passages under the rug, and then we have no answers when the world comes knocking.

Other individuals and groups have used the same language from 1 Timothy to combat the Equal Rights Amendment to the US Constitution, first proposed in 1972 but never ratified (Matthews 1993: 140). These recent uses of the text recognize the contrast established by the Pastor between families that support their own widows, and families that do not. The latter are to be condemned for failing to live up to the Pastor's "family values."

They are similarly blameworthy in Thomas Aquinas's view both because Christians who know better incur more guilt for sin than pagans, but also for more strictly theological reasons. Thomas cites this verse in replying to an objection, in the *Summa*, that there is no "order of charity," that is, no differences in the degrees of love one owes to others at different removes from oneself (family members v. coreligionists v. strangers, etc.). He argues, on the contrary, that there are theologically valid distinctions to be made. Indeed, 1 Timothy 5:8 specifically implies, he claims, "that we ought to love most those of our neighbors who are more virtuous or more closely united to us" before we love, say, irreligious family members or friends (SS Q[44] A[8]).

The widow who lives for pleasure is dead (v. 6)

The Pastor also establishes, this time to the individual widow's potential discredit, a difference between the widow who, in her piety, "continues in supplications and prayers night and day" (v. 5), and the widow who "lives for pleasure," for the latter are dead while alive (v. 6). This verse allows Chrysostom a particularly galling invective against women, who are imagined, thanks to the simple binary of self-sacrificing piety v. pleasure provided by the Pastor, to have only two options available to them: obscene luxury or charity for the poor.

> Hear this, ye women, that pass your time in revels and intemperance, and who neglect the poor, pining and perishing with hunger, whilst you are destroying yourself with continual luxury. Thus you are the causes of two deaths, of those who are dying of want, and of your own, both through ill measure. But if out of your fullness you tempered their want, you would save two lives. . . . Consider what comes of food, into what it is changed. . . . The increase of luxury is but the multiplication of dung! (*Hom. 1 Tim.*, NPNF1 13.452).

The moral issue involved here, however, is easily generalizable to all believers, men and women, and was frequently read by Augustine in this gender-neutral way. In the *Confessions*, it is true, Augustine singled out his mother Monica as the model of Pastoral widowhood (*Conf.* 9.22, NPNF1 1.137). But in citing this verse, one of his favorites from the Pastorals, he more typically tries to apply this description of widowhood to all Christians. For example, in defending the doctrine of the immortality of the soul he writes that the soul and the body each have their own peculiar lives and deaths: "Dying, to thy flesh, is the losing of its life: dying to thy soul, is the losing of its life. The life of thy flesh is thy soul: the life of thy soul is thy God. As the flesh dies in losing the soul, which is its life, so the soul dieth in losing God, who is its life. Of a certainty, then, the soul is immortal. Manifestly immortal, for it liveth even when dead. For what the apostle said of the luxurious widow, may also be said of the soul if it has lost its God, 'she is dead while she liveth'" (*Jo. ev. tr.* 47.8, NPNF1 7.263; cf. *Serm.* 15.6, NPNF1 6.308; *De Trin.* 4.3.5, NPNF1 3.72). Augustine's tendency to take this verse in the broadest possible sense is perhaps most clearly evident in his commentary on Psalm 132. There, the "widows" of 1 Timothy 5 become, in a masterly analogy, the whole church. Just as the Pastor's widow, recognizing that she has no earthly assistance, finds solace in God's divine aid, so "the whole Church," if she recognizes that she is alone, "desolate in this world," and seeks God's help, will find comfort and life (*En. ps.* 132.16, NPNF1 8.620).

Not less than 60 years old (v. 9)

Not only must widows be virtuous, and not hedonistic, but they must also be at least 60 years of age. Tertullian feels that the Pastor's restrictions, including that of age, were needed "in order, forsooth, that their [i.e., widows'] experimental training in all the affections may, on the one hand, have rendered them capable of readily aiding all others with counsel and comfort, and that, on the other, they may none the less have travelled down the whole course of probation whereby a female can be tested" (*Virg.* 9, ANF 4.33). Both Jerome (*C. Jov.* 1.14, NPNF2 6.359) and Thomas Aquinas (2007: 66) assume that 60 was the age beyond which manual labor becomes impossible for a widow, necessitating her public support. Sexual security, implied in the citation from Tertullian above, is the principal reason for the age requirement, according to Erasmus. Because widows will work in close proximity with bishops, priests, and deacons, who might be tempted sexually, it is best to assign women as their coworkers who are beyond the "lubricious time of life" (*Paraphrases*, 1993: 30), and who, moreover, have proven themselves beyond reproach in their morality (29).

There have been, however, if not outright doubts about the Pastor's wisdom on the age issue, then at least various attempts to circumvent it. Jerome writes that even a younger woman who is widowed ought not to take the Pastor's "three-score years" to heart. Certainly she cannot expect assistance from the church. Jerome's correspondent Salvina, a women of great means with standing at the imperial court (she later also became a deaconess and lent support to John Chrysostom), would not require this at any rate. Still, Jerome counsels, with reference to Pastorals generally, and to chapter 5 in particular:

> Do not be disturbed because the apostle allows none to be chosen as a widow under threescore years old, neither suppose that he intends to reject those who are still young. Believe that you are indeed chosen by him who said to his disciple, "Let no man despise thy youth" [1 Tim. 4:12], your want of age that is, not your want of continence. . . . You must take what I am going to say as addressed not to you but to your girlish years. A widow "that liveth in pleasure is dead while she liveth." [5:6] (*Ep.* 79.7, NPNF2 6.166)

She must have washed the saint's feet (v. 10)

Among the other requirements for a widow is that she should have "devoted herself to doing good in every way" in her life, including that of washing "the saint's feet" (v. 10). Foot washing, of course, recalls the gospel accounts of Jesus washing the feet of his disciples (John 13:4) or having his own feet washed by the penitent woman (Luke 7:44). As a general practice, perhaps not restricted to widows, Christian foot washing is socially more difficult for women, according to Tertullian, especially if they have unbelieving husbands. For what non-Christian husband, he barks, would "suffer her to creep into prison [an inversion of 2 Tim. 3:6?] to kiss a martyr's bonds? nay, truly, to meet any one of the brethren to exchange the kiss? to offer water for the saints' feet?" (*Ad ux.* 2.4, ANF 4.46). Calvin, seeming to echo such concerns, but for a fully Christian (and class-conscious) world, comments that foot washing, which can seem "mean and almost servile," is therefore a service "characteristic of women who are diligent without being dainty or fastidious" (*Commentary* 1964: 10.256).

Younger widows (vv. 11–16)

Just as the Pastor stipulates that older women may be enrolled in the order of widows, and what their obligations are, so he also explains why younger widows are to be excluded: there will come a day when they "wax wanton against

Christ" and remarry, only to incur "damnation" (KJV). The danger is not just their own, however. Some young widows, whose gossipy socializing worries him, have "already turned away to follow Satan," potentially endangering the community. Because the Pastor advocates marriage generally (see 1 Tim. 4:3; Titus 2:4–5), it may initially seem unusual that the remarriage of widows under the age of 60 troubles him so. The reason may be that members of the order of widows take a pledge of celibacy, so that when one of them remarries she is said to "violat[e her] first pledge," or "cast off her first faith" (KJV).

One cannot be sure that there was an official order of widows within the Pastor's communities. However, Jerome seems to conclude that the "first faith" was a pledge for virgins too, and that breaking that pledge was rather more akin to incest than adultery (*C. Jov.* 1.14, NPNF2 6.356). Basil agrees. In earlier times, he writes, "fallen virgins" could be forgiven to some extent; but as the church started to grow into an international force to be reckoned with, its institutions needed to be more carefully policed. Thus, virgins who pledged themselves to the order of virgins must be severely punished if they fall (*Ep.* 199.18, NPNF2 8.237). The institutionalization of celibacy, especially for younger people, eventually became a problem which these verses from 1 Timothy helped to address. Indeed, Basil worries, in the text just cited, about "girls [who] are brought forward [for religious celibacy] by their parents and brothers, and other kinsfolk, before they are of full age, and have no inner impulse towards a celibate life. The object of the friends [i.e., the family members allegedly concerned for the girls/young women] is simply to provide for themselves. Such women as these," he continues, "must not be readily received, before we have made public investigation of their own sentiments" (237–38). Calvin, later, calls such arrangements "tyrannous" and "monstrous" (1964: 258, 257). Augustine agrees with Basil and the Pastor before him, and Calvin after, that it would be an evil to break one's vow of celibacy. But he praises as "the greatest" vow, that vow of celibacy from "the beginning of life" made by men, in this case, who had never experienced that which they have given up for their entire lives (*En. ps.* 76.11, NPNF1 8.358; cf. Chrysostom, *Hom. 1 Tim.*, NPNF1 13.459, who assumes virgins' vows, which "proceeded from a greater elevation of mind" than those of widows, were simply not intended in the Pastor's critical comments).

One encounters quite a different sentiment in a wonderfully energetic poem, almost a *carpe diem*, "To A Young Person That Was About to Vow Celibacy," by Sir James Chamberlaine, a minor seventeenth century poet of religious verse. The poem bears an epigraph from 1 Timothy 5:14, and begins:

> She who her Reason lays aside,
> And Superstition makes her Guide,

> Can never hope by that false Light,
> To do an action that is right.
> In all religious Duties know,
> Most principally, e're we Vow,
> Right Reason should be sought unto.
> Those which endure her rigid Test,
> Them to embrace and leave the rest.

The young woman is urged to embrace that life God willed for humankind "in Paradise." And if she fears that her religious inclinations will find little outlet in the stresses and cares of marriage and family life?

> This [fear] is a great mistake in thee,
> They [i.e., married people] have their times of Vacancy.
> 'Tis true, so long they cannot be
> As Sanctimon'alists on the Knee,
> Because attended with more care,
> And bus'ness than the Cloyster'd are;
> Yet this their care their duty is,
> Time so imploy'd doth lead to Bliss,
> And is no bar to Happiness.
>
> Religion's active, hates a Drone,
> Who buzzing spends each day alone
> In Pray'r and Contemplation.
> Both fitting duties to be done,
> Great Pillars of Religion [1 Tim. 3:15],
> But she who wholly rests on these,
> Though she may fancy what she please,
> Spends but her days in idleness.
>
> So lives the lazy Nun, the Wife
> Who truly virtuous is, a Life
> Devouter leads than any she
> Who vows Recluse Virginity.

Many readers seem at least tangentially aware that Paul, who urges celibacy but does not require it, is rather different from the Pastor, who acknowledges a space for celibacy but much more assiduously insists upon marriage. On these issues some, like Augustine for instance, accept the Pastor, creatively misreading him, in terms of Paul (of course, they believe the Pastor to be Paul): marriage is good, but it is a good designed to protect human frailty from sin and Satan; celibacy is certainly better (cf. Augustine, *De bono vid.* 11, NPNF1

3.445, which reads 1 Cor. 7:8–9 and 1 Tim. 5:11–15 as essentially equivalent texts). We have just the opposite in the Chamberlaine poem, however – a rejection of Paul in favor of the Pastor. From Chamberlaine's perspective, which is not unlike that of Luther and Calvin, the life of religious celibacy is a life of "superstitious Zeal" which "blind[s the] reason, so much to despise / That state, which Heaven dignifies" (Chamberlaine 1680: 183–86).

Gossips and busybodies (v. 13)

In addition to concerns about the unpredictable sexual appetites of younger widows, the Pastor also expresses his fear that these women will become "busybodies" and gossips. The Pastor thus, once again, contributes to a long tradition which takes women to be unreliable and dangerous. Chrysostom vaguely generalizes the gender dynamics of this passage, but women are still cause of special concern because, in his commentary, "when the care for the husband is withdrawn," that is, when they no longer have a man watching over them, women "naturally become idlers, tattlers, and busybodies. For he who does not attend to his own concerns will be meddling with those of others, even as he who minds his own business will take no account of and have no care about the affairs of another. And nothing is so unbecoming to a woman, as to busy herself in the concerns of others, and it is no less unbecoming to a man" (*Hom. 1 Tim.*, NPNF1 13.459). Calvin, although he sympathizes with the widow who might feel, as in Chamberlaine's poem, that she has been unfairly excluded from a higher calling by virtue of the encouragement to remarry, asserts that what is truly necessary is that men take women in hand to provide them with the kind of Christian life "so as to give the adversary no occasion to revile us." The problem, in his view, is that it is unfortunately all too rare to "find a man who willingly bears the burden of governing a wife! The reason is that it is attended by innumerable vexations," not the least of which, of course, is getting the woman to "submit to the yoke" (*Commentary* 1964: 260).

While most readers would simply take the Pastor's focus on young women as their own, nineteenth century Danish existentialist philosopher Søren Kierkegaard quite radically shifts registers from gender and sexuality to politics in what amounts to an urbane theological conceit. In a homiletic discourse of 1844, entitled "The Expectancy of Eternal Salvation," he imaginatively posits that one seeking information about the "far country" of our salvation is like a "state official" seeking advice on how best to govern. The official would not consult people totally unconnected with, and thus not invested in, his state; nor would he look for help from an enemy. Similarly he would not "call together loafers and irresponsible tramps, 'who learn to run idly from house to house, but not only idly but with gossip and useless traffic' . . . because the recommendations of such people," he goes on, with another citation from the Pastorals, "'give rise to questions' [1 Tim. 1:4] instead of providing the answers" (*Writings* 5.255). The language of the passage continues political – with references to "partisans" and "good citizens" – in a manner that echoes what Dibelius and Conzelmann have most famously emphasized as the "bourgeois" tenor of these letters, whose goal is to promote a certain mode of "good citizenship" for a Christianity that is losing its eschatological edge (D-C 1972: 8). Gone, however, is any reference whatsoever to the weakness of women. The problem, here, is that what the Pastor describes as, and what Chrysostom assumes is, a problem natural to a specific set of women has become a characteristic of a whole class of people whose idleness and lack of interest poses the most extreme danger to their immortal souls.

The Church: Elders (5:17–22; Titus 1:5)

As at 5:3, the reference in this passage to honor ("let elders who rule well be considered worthy of double honor," v. 17) seems likely to refer to payment, an ecclesiastical salary of sorts, although Collins argues that "double" should be read as payment plus special honors, rather than a salary which is twice as much as another's (2002: 144). If the verse means that such elders will be paid twice what someone else is paid, it is unclear whom the Pastor may have in mind. Since the verses immediately preceding this have to do with widows, it is possible that the Pastor means "double the stipend of widows" (Chrysostom, *Hom. 1 Tim.*, NPNF1 13.460; Calvin 1964: 262; Davies 1996: 43; Bassler 1996: 99), although he could just as easily have in mind the payment received for some other office, or indeed for a small subset of presbyters, i.e., those who do an especially good job "labor[ing] in preaching and teaching."

The Pastor tells Timothy not to credit "any accusation against an elder except on the evidence of two or three witnesses" (v. 19). All commentators note the similarity with Deuteronomy 17:7 and 19:15, but why the Pastor insists upon this point now, of course, is uncertain. It is possible that some of the heterodox opponents were attacking duly ordained church officials; but it is also likely that the Pastor simply wants to establish legal procedures for dealing with problem leaders (Towner 2006: 367). The following verse, "as for those who persist in sin," if it refers back to the elders (Bassler 1996: 101; Towner 2006: 370), would seem to imply that the latter reading of the rationale behind v. 19 is correct. Readers in the tradition, however, have often understood this verse to concern discipline in the congregation at large (Collins 2002: 146–48).

Worthy of a double honor (v. 17)

The idea that talented or especially effective church leaders receive a double salary has made some readers slightly uncomfortable. Tertullian scorns those (particularly, church leaders not given to fasting) who thought the "Apostle" was here indicating a double pay; rather, he claimed, the verse refers to the double honor of "being both brethren and officers" (*De jejun.* 17, ANF 4.113–14; cf. Theodoret, *Comm. 1 Tim.*, 2001: 2.225). Thomas Aquinas had no doubts that the verse in question speaks of material, or "corporal," gain (SS Q[103] A[1]); but his appreciation of materiality was broad indeed. If, by honor/ payment one means an out-and-out exchange of cash for "the spiritual grace of the sacraments" then, according to Thomas, one is describing "the sin of simony." On the other hand, priests who receive payment "not as a price of goods, but as a payment for their need," are not simonists at all. The nuances of this difference are, of course, difficult to parse – for example, how might one distinguish between paying for absolution and giving of one's resources as a penance leading to absolution (SS Q[100] A[2])? But Thomas' use of this verse to determine degrees of "honor" could be quite metaphysically esoteric as well, including a disquisition on halos, and whether or not the double honor due to "doctors" of the "church militant" is a halo bigger than that of either virgins or martyrs. It is not likely: the martyr should probably take the crown, in this race [cf. 2 Tim. 2:5; 4:8], even if Thomas refuses to decide definitively on the matter (XP [Sup. TP] Q[96] A[12]).

Calvin is concerned about the payment of ministers because, in the world's "ingratitude," Satan finds a "means of depriving the church of teaching, by frightening many by a dread of poverty and want, so that they are unwilling to bear this burden" (*Commentary* 1964: 262). The ability to attract and maintain worthy ministers has surely been an important concern. Jonathan Edwards' parishioners were cantankerous in their salary negotiations with him (*Works of Jonathan Edwards* 15.148–51, 163), and he sounds a bitter note about this when, in an ordination sermon, he remarks that those who are in "the business of seeking and promoting the eternal welfare and happiness of you and your children" should not at the same time be "disheartened by the difficulties and indigencies of straightened circumstances." 1 Timothy 5:17 is but one of many verses he cites after this to support his cause (25.76–77).

But one can take the idea of double honor too far as well. A recent editorial in the *Salt Lake Tribune* (Salt Lake City, Utah) opines, rather astonishingly, that two pastors accused of embezzling \$8.6 million from their church over the course of their careers may have been more ethical in the discharge of their duties had the precept of 1 Timothy 5:17 been observed (Hodges 2007), i.e., had they been better paid.

John Wesley's comment on this verse strikes a balance between pastoral impoverishment and corruption, or so it would seem, by reading the double honor in terms of gifts bequeathed to the safekeeping of ministers for the benefit of the poor. According to his historical reconstruction, the "churchmen became very rich in after ages" by means of this provision, but "the design of the donors" was originally that men of "pious intent" would "employ" their goods and money "to the glory of God" (*Explanatory Notes* 1850: 545). In the process, presumably, they would set aside just enough for their own upkeep as well.

That is, of course, an idealist's view of the matter. Other readers, going much further than even the most cautious interpretations mentioned above, consider payment of salaries for church offices as nothing but a sign of the church's decline. According to Virginia Woolf:

> The prophet or prophetess whose message was voluntary and untaught became extinct; and their places were taken by the three orders of bishops, priests, and deacons, who are invariably men, and invariably . . . paid men, for when the church became a profession its professors were paid. Thus the profession of religion seems to have been originally much what the profession of literature is now. It was originally open to anyone who had received the gift of prophecy. (*Three Guineas*, 2006: 146)

Woolf's real concern in context is with the dismal salary received by deaconesses in the Church of England when compared to the pay scale of the Church's leadership as a whole. Her comparison of prophecy and literature serves to highlight the unfairness of the situation. A talented and creative woman like Emily Brontë, she argues, "is the spiritual descendant of some ancient prophetess, who prophesied when prophecy was a voluntary and unpaid for occupation." She, or her more religiously minded sisters, should therefore be accorded the honors currently reserved for a cadre of men (147).

Never accept any accusations against an elder (vv. 19–22)

The Pastor goes on to discuss ways in which to protect elders from slanderous "accusation[s]," and then considers the best way to deal with sin in the community more generally. Readers have cited this passage in the context of historically specific crises. Theodoret, for example, reports how an Arian party obtained the exile of the bishop of Antioch by promulgating, and then refusing to substantiate, the calumny that he had sired an illegitimate child (*Ecc. hist.* 1.20, NPNF2 3.57). But they have also taken it as a key defense for ministers. Calvin knows that the principal here articulated, with its origins in Deuteronomy 17:6, should really apply to all people alike, not to ministers in particular. Nevertheless, he considers the protective measure especially useful since "none are more exposed to slanders and insults than godly teachers," and this in part because of a "trick of Satan," who would like nothing better than to "estrange men from their ministers" (*Commentary* 1964: 10.263).

Others, however, can be rebuked publicly without, apparently, following the same procedures, or at least this is how one might read v. 20 ("as for those who persist in sin, rebuke them in the presence of all"), especially if one assumes that the verse does not refer back to elders. Augustine reflects with touching poignancy upon this text, wondering about the efficacy of punishment in light of the weaknesses, and partial ignorance, of those required to "rebuke" sinners:

> What shall I say as to the infliction or remission of punishment, in cases in which we have no other desire than to forward the spiritual welfare of those in regard to whom we judge that they ought or ought not to be punished? Also, if we consider not only the nature and magnitude of faults, but also what each may be able or unable to bear according to his strength of mind, how deep and dark a question it is to adjust the amount of punishment so as to prevent the person who receives it not only from getting no good, but also from suffering loss thereby! Besides, I know not whether a greater number have been improved or made worse when alarmed under threats of such punishment at the hands of men as is an object of fear. What, then, is the path of duty, seeing that it often happens that if you inflict punishment on one he goes to destruction; whereas, if you leave him unpunished, another is destroyed? I confess that I make mistakes daily in regard to this, and that I know not when and how to observe the rule of Scripture: "Them that sin rebuke before all, that others may fear. (*Ep.* 95.3, NPNF1 1.402)

Timothy (5:23–25)

The imperative that Timothy "no longer drink only water" adds a bit of personal flavor to the letter even as it contributes to the polemic against the Pastor's ascetic opponents. As Jennifer Glancy suggests, Timothy can begin drinking wine because he is no longer an immature youth who would be especially at risk, in the medical conventions of the day, to the adverse heat in wine (cf. Clement, *Paed.* 2.2, ANF 2.243, who warns "boys and girls" to "keep as much as possible away from this medicine"); by encouraging the drinking of wine now, the Pastor may be trying to convince "those readers who have followed an ascetic lifestyle to recast their rejection of drink (and food? and marriage?) not as a permanent choice, but as youthful training towards godliness" (Glancy 2003: 244–45).

No longer drink only water (v. 23)

John Chrysostom also recognizes a pedagogical element to this exhortation: we should all learn to accept good advice, even if it comes in the form of censure. He imagines, however, that readers might be puzzled enough by Timothy's ill health to ask why Paul, who could work miracles, didn't cure him. Chrysostom responds that it was: "[n]ot because he could not – for he whose garment had raised the dead was clearly able to do this too, – but because he had a design of importance in withholding such aid. What then was his purpose? That even now, if we see great and virtuous men afflicted with infirmities, we may not be offended, for this was a profitable visitation," one tending to produce humility in leaders, and an awareness among others that even important men were still human beings, subject to "often infirmities" (*Hom. 1 Tim.*, NPNF1 13.464–65). Chrysostom adds, however, that Timothy is still to be moderate in his consumption. This effort to balance the Pastor's promotion of drink with a pronounced concern about the deleterious effects of alcohol is common down the centuries. Luther is an exception. Caring little for anything that smacks of asceticism, Luther almost ridicules Timothy, who had to be forced to take a drop, as "a lean, miserable person" who "ruined himself" and who, because of his stomach ailments, probably "did not keep his head in order" either (*Lectures on 1 Timothy*, *Works* 28.358).

In an anonymously published nineteenth century temperance society dialogue, "The Ills of Dram Drinking," Tom, the alcoholic character, seems rather like Luther's Timothy. Asked, by the teetotaler John, how he is feeling, he replies: "I feel very weak and languid, as well as thirsty and miserable" (*Collection of Temperance Dialogues*, 1869: 35). Temperance leaders sometimes advocated not just moderation but total abstention from alcohol. They could draw only unsuccessfully upon the Bible in support of their efforts, however (Merrill 1988; see also *The Temperance Bible Commentary*, Lees and Burns 1870: 371–75), and clearly your average drinker could cite biblical precedent just as easily, although perhaps with less gravitas, than they could:

TOM: Did not Solomon say a pint of beer was a good thing for a working-man?

JOHN: No.

TOM: Then didn't somebody tell Timothy to take a drop of gin for his stomach's sake?

JOHN: Not exactly that either; but is there anything the matter with your stomach?

TOM: It's rather empty, that's all.

JOHN: Then what do you think is the best thing to fill it with?

TOM: Why, some beer, to be sure. (*Collection of Temperance Dialogues* 36)

Some men's sins precede them (vv. 24–25)

The chapter concludes with a pithy, proverbial reflection upon sin (in the wonderful language of the Wycliffe translation: "sum mennus synnes ben opyn, bifor goynge to dom; but of summen thei comen aftir"). Most readers down the centuries have read these verses, regarding sins both evident and hidden, in the way that Augustine argues one should, as a limiting factor in judgment: "[l]et us judge, therefore, with respect to those [i.e., sins] which are manifest; but respecting those which are concealed, let us leave the judgment to God: for they also cannot be hid, whether they be good or evil, when the time shall come for them to be manifested" (*Serm. Dom. mon.* 2.18.60, NPNF1 6.54).

In this last chapter of the letter, the Pastor covers a lot of ground. He begins by discussing the obligations of Christian slaves, those who belong to Christian masters as well as those owned by pagans. Godliness returns, briefly, as a theme, as do the opponents. One of the Pastor's principal concerns here, though, is with the possession and distribution of wealth. Some members of the church are quite well off, and the Pastor instructs them that they should cultivate generosity rather than greed. He also charges Timothy, in a soaring theological oath, to keep his gospel and his mission pure, and to avoid the ways of the heretics.

The Pastoral Epistles Through the Centuries, First Edition. Jay Twomey.
© 2009 by Jay Twomey. Published 2020 by John Wiley & Sons Ltd.

The Church: Slaves (6:1–2; Titus 2:9)

The New Testament generally has little or nothing to say against slavery – even if the many references to slavery in early Christian texts (e.g., 1 Cor. 7:21–23; Philem; Gal. 4:1; but see Gal 3:28) show that it "was a difficult problem for the church" (Towner 2006: 379) – so one should not expect the Pastor to be an exception. These letters are sometimes thought to have helped slaves by providing them with "new and incomparably higher motives" (Easton 1948: 93; cf. Wesley, *Explanatory Notes*, 1850: 558; Kelly 1981: 243) even if, as most commentators note, the Pastor has no similar admonitions that slave-owners should treat their slaves well (contrast Eph. 6:9). Such affirmative readings are surprising on ethical grounds (motives aside, these slaves are still enslaved human beings), but also from a historical point of view: as Albert Harrill notes, in the American context the Pastor's comments on slavery "proved to proslavery adherents that abolitionism was incompatible with Christian orthodoxy" (Harrill 2000: 171; cf. Davies 1996: 47). Other modern readers are more skeptical, of course. A common criticism of the Pastorals as a whole is that they seem designed to consolidate power in the Christian community in the hands of the wealthier male householders, to endorse the norms of Hellenistic culture, at the expense of nearly everyone else (Verner 1983: 175; Davies 1996: 100–01; Bassler 1996: 203). Contrary to what one might expect of the authentic Paul, "the author [of Titus] is quite willing to sacrifice the fuller life the women and slaves have found in Christ for respectability among pagans" (Dewey 1998: 452).

The yoke of slavery (v. 1)

Major figures in the history of this passage's interpretation have predictably, if unfortunately, embraced as eternally valid the Pastor's historically conditioned acceptance of slavery, albeit for a variety of different reasons in many different social-political contexts. Most interpreters take seriously the idea in v. 1 that the proper behavior of slaves or servants will keep "the name of God and the teaching" from being "blasphemed." A greater degree of complexity arises with respect to the nature and quality of the relationship between slaves and masters, especially if the masters are Christians themselves. In John Chrysostom's view, slaves ought to behave because they are the beneficiaries of their masters' "toil and trouble for [their] repose" (*Hom. 1 Tim.*, NPNF1 13.465). Yet in deploying a traditional analogy between the slave's service for his or her master, and the believer's for God, Chrysostom establishes quite clearly his sense that the

Pastor's message is for the master's, not the slave's, benefit. His exhortation, "let us only serve our Master as our servants [our 'household slaves': *oiketai*] serve us" (466; PG 62.589), can only intensify distinctions between masters and slaves, as human masters and God are analogous in Chrysostom's parallelism. Nonetheless, human masters can learn something of religious psychology and the proper religious attitude from the slaves' example as well: "They receive many insults from fear of us, and endure them in silence with the patience of philosophers. . . . If we threaten them, they are at once awed. Is not this philosophy? For say not they are under necessity, when thou too art under a necessity in the fear of hell. And yet dost thou not learn wisdom, nor render to God as much honor, as thou receivest from thy servants." Chrysostom does acknowledge, however, that slavery "is not from nature," that "it is the result of some particular cause, or circumstances" (466; cf. *Hom. Tit.*, NPNF1 13.533–35).

For Thomas Aquinas, "the yoke of slavery" means that like domestic animals, slaves are not in control of their own lives (2007: 76). Neither are they equal to their masters, as some mistakenly assume, just because both are Christian. Equality in one thing, in this case religion, does not indicate equality across the board (ibid.). Thomas does feel in general that honor is due only to the virtuous, not simply to those who happen to have authority, but he makes an exception for the cruel and "wicked" who, "on account of their having a share of the dignity of God Who is the Father and Lord of all," should be honored no matter what (ST SS Q[63] A[3]). Slave-owners, it would seem, fall fairly easily into this category.

Calvin, in his commentary on 1 Timothy, puts the matter more positively: "it is no small honor, that God has made us [i.e., both slaves and non-slaves] equal to the lords of this earth" in matters religious. Still, this only means that slaves of Christian masters should bear the yoke of slavery all the more willingly (*Commentary* 1964: 271), and they certainly "should not ask whether they deserve that lot or a better one; it should be enough that they are bound to that condition" (270). Calvin is also acutely aware that ancient Christian slaves were not hired hands and could be used, as he puts it in his sermons on 1 Timothy, "as sharply and rigorously" as their owners chose, and that slavery such as he finds mentioned in the New Testament "was very cruel." Yet in a sense the contrast between harsh slavery and more tolerable forms of servitude merely provides him with an opportunity for arguing a fortiori that contemporary servants have no excuse whatsoever for disobedience. He also echoes Chrysostom, as well as Ephesians 6:7 and Colossians 3:23, in saying that slaves, in serving their masters, are ultimately serving God (1983: 549; cf. 1964: 270).

Luther's view, although characteristically more colorfully expressed, is rather similar. His discussion of this verse in his *Treatise on Good Works* grounds the slave's or servant's activity in a more general obligation to obey authority implied by the Decalogue's commandment that we honor our parents (Exod. 20:12). Because of this commandment, Luther argues, or more precisely because of the sequence of commandments capped by this one, disobedience becomes "a sin worse than murder, unchastity, theft, dishonesty, and all that goes with them" (*Treatise on Good Works, Works* 44.81). Hence, obedience should be a basic element of all believers' lives.

> And yet . . . in the case of servants [obedience] is the one work by which they may be saved. They cannot make many pilgrimages, or do this and that. They have enough to do if their hearts are simply set on gladly doing or leaving undone what they know pleases their masters and mistresses, and to do all this in the simplest faith. . . . This kind of faith makes all works good. Yes, faith must cause the works; faith is the man in charge. (97–98)

Although the Pastor says nothing about how slave-owners should treat their slaves, beyond indicating the need for strict control (cf. 1 Tim. 3:4), Luther, like many other responsible readers of Ephesians 6:9 and Colossians 4:1, insists that masters and mistresses should treat servants well. Just "as masters do not want God to deal most severely with them, but want many things overlooked through grace, they too should be all the more gentle toward their servants and overlook some things" (98). Erasmus, in his *Paraphrases on 1 Timothy*, seems to put most of the emphasis on precisely this sort of mutuality for those households in which both master and slave are Christians: "this is no longer slavery in the usual sense," he says, "but a reciprocation of duties" (1993: 34).

Clearly, in many instances, the idea of slavery deriving from this verse serves Christian interpreters' general theological and homiletic purposes, even when the actual social effects of slavery are barely taken into account. In fact, as we have seen happen elsewhere (e.g., at 5:6), readers democratize this text in ways that extend its significance to non-slaves as well. Luther, again, recognizes that the Pastor is speaking of slaves, people "who were the property of their masters, as sheep are in our regions, who had been captured in war or who had been purchased" (*Lectures on Titus, Works* 29:60). He is more interested in this passage's significance as a theological explanation of the calling of 1 Corinthians 7:17 ("let each of you lead the life that the Lord has assigned, to which God *called* you"), though, which leads him also to generalize its meaning for all readers. Anyone who is "completely sure that he serves God and does what God wishes," despite the inevitable attacks of Satan, is adorning the doctrine: "A servant girl can say . . . 'I have washed the pots, lit the fire in the oven, and made the beds.' She confidently expects the appearing of Christ because she has done these works in Christ," and they please him. The same goes for anyone working confidently at his or her lot in life. Luther jokes that "it is a great thing that He is willing to grant eternal life for the washing of pots"; but then clarifies in all seriousness that in fact Christ does grant eternal life "to those who have lived in this way" (66).

In recent Christian self-help and inspirational literature, books with titles along the lines of *The 12 Essentials of Godly Success* (in which the Pastor's slaves become "workers," Nelson 2005: 143) also promote the many ways in which believers can "adorn the doctrine of God" (KJV) with their lives. There is an important difference between this kind of interpretation and that of Luther, however. Luther, even as he places slavery in a distant historical past, still casts the lives of contemporary believers in servile terms. We are "only dregs ourselves" he says (*Lectures on Titus, Works* 29.61). It is not quite true to say that slavery drops out of the picture entirely in these recent Christian self-help manuals. In Nelson's book, for instance, v. 9 is cited fully, so that attentive readers can see the original verse had slaves in view. Nevertheless, in the application, that ancient (and not-so-ancient) horizon does essentially vanish, and readers are left only with the vaguest feeling that one person's mildly satisfying inspiration may be another person's living hell.

However, many readers have focused more precisely on the role verses such as ours play in justifying the institution of slavery. James Shannon, for example, a president of the University of Missouri in the 1850s, sought biblical warrant for his pro-slavery agenda, and found it in 1 Timothy 6:1–5, which text led him to assume "that they had some abolition *ignoramuses* even in Paul's day; and that inspired Apostle pronounced them '*men of corrupt minds,* and *destitute of the truth,*' and commanded Christians to withdraw from their society" (Shannon 1855: 14). Similarly, Presbyterian minister Fred Ross, in his 1853 oration "Slavery Ordained of God," argued from these verses that "God has really sanctioned the relation of master and slave as those of husband and wife, and parent and child" (Ross 1857: 64).

Slaves themselves were taught, in sermons and catechisms relying in part upon the Pastoral Epistles, that the Bible supported slavery and that service to slave-owners was equally service to God (Bay 2000: 125–26; Wiethoff 2002: 137). One catechism, which also urged masters to treat slaves well, cites 1 Timothy and Titus, along with Colossians:

Q: What command has God given to Servants, concerning obedience to their Masters?
A: Servants obey in all things your Masters according to the flesh, not in eye-service as men-pleasers, but in singleness of heart, fearing God [Col 3:22].

Q: What are Servants to count their Master worthy of?
A: All honor.
Q: How are they to do service for their Master?
A: *With good will*, doing service unto the Lord and not unto men.
Q: How are they to try to please their Masters?
A: Please them well in all things, not answering them again.
Q: Is it right in a Servant when commanded to be sullen and slow, and answer his Master again?
A: No. (in Clarke 2005: 134)

Needless to say, such religious instruction was the essence of the Christianity Frederick Douglass eviscerates at the end of his famous *Narrative* in his "Parody" of a homiletic psalm: "Come, saints and sinners, hear me tell / How pious priests whip Jack and Nell, / And women buy and children sell, / And preach all sinners down to hell, / And sing of heavenly union" (Douglass 2005: 126).

While it is not impossible to find even today defenses of slavery based upon the Pastorals – on the Web and in the work of obscure pamphleteers – Black theologians and Civil Rights preachers have effectively reappropriated the Bible, and its emancipatory potential, for congregations throughout the USA, generally by excluding biblical endorsements of slavery as too closely linked to white theology (see Hopkins 1999: 20). Still, the Pastor's use of that traditional image for slavery, the "yoke" (cf. Lev. 26:13; 1 Kings 12:4; Isa. 10:27; Gal. 5:1), has been adapted polemically in twentieth century African-American literature in the work of poets Imamu Amiri Baraka and Wanda Coleman. Baraka calls "Afrikan People all over the world / Under the yoke, the gun, the hammer, the lash" to revolution (Baraka 1973: 1). Coleman's poem "Manuela Come Out the Kitchen," envisions a revolution as well, this time of minority women, who, in seizing control of the means of production (understood quite generally as cultural and political self-representation), will create a better world:

> my father dies under the yoke/lash/noose/bullet/unemployment
> and misery in general. leaves me a bitter legacy of
> rage hope dignity
> . . .
> so what to do? you ask
> join me. i'm dynamite in an apron
> we'll kill the cook, take the recipe book
> and make cake
>
> enough for all.

(Coleman 1983: 51)

The Church: Wealthy Christians (6:6–10, 17–19)

It has struck some commentators (e.g., Bassler 1996: 111) as strange that the Pastor both lambastes the asceticism of his opponents in these letters (1 Tim. 4:3), yet encourages a certain ascetic ethos himself, urging contentment with mere "food and clothing" (v. 8). Likely he is simply incorporating, as he does elsewhere (i.e., in the references to athletics at 1 Tim. 4:8; 2 Tim. 2:3–7; 4:7) elements of Hellenistic thought, in this case a certain Stoicism (D-C 1972: 85; Collins 2002: 156–57), without necessarily developing these elements in any systematic way. The Pastor is actually much more consistent in advocating the maintenance of the social status quo. Indeed, his own frequent use of financial terms such as "deposit" and "foundation" (cf. Collins 2002: 173; D-C 1972: 91–92; see also Towner 2006: 430, 489, who refers to the content of the deposit as a "commodity") makes his comfortable treatment of wealth seem not out of place at all. Moreover, as noted earlier (at 1 Tim. 3:1–13), Kidd argues effectively that one of the Pastor's tasks in these letters is to convince his community, not to divest themselves, but rather to reprioritize their relationship with money as a device: it is not for the accumulation of honor and power, but rather for the good of the community (1990).

The notion in verse 10, that "the love of money is a root of all kinds of evil," even if it is an ancient commonplace not original to the Pastor (D-C 1972: 85–86), has had an enormous significance. Easton (1948: 165), however, says that "by inserting a gratuitous definite article before 'root' the King James Version converted the proverb into a root of all kinds of errors," implying thereby that this translation encourages a genealogy of evil unintended by the Pastor.

Food and clothing, we will be content with these (v. 8)

Christians are given mixed signals by the Pastor in these verses concerning the importance of money in the life of the community. On the one hand, they are exhorted to be content with the bare essentials of clothing and food (6:8), and not to seek wealth, for the "love of money is a root of all kinds of evil" (6:10). On the other, they are given every reason to believe that wealthy Christians, who in their wealth have recourse to the essentials in some abundance, can contribute not only to the community, but also to their own salvation (6:17–19).

Figures in the history of monasticism, for instance, emphasize the poverty and even asceticism in v. 8. John Cassian, in a remark in the *Institutes* which is both normative and philological, is firm that here Paul means "'covering' . . . not 'raiment,' as is wrongly found in some Latin copies: that is, what may merely cover the body, not what may please the fancy by the splendour of the attire," (1.2, NPNF2 11.202). St. Francis reads this passage back, as it were, into the gospel. "All the brothers," he writes, "should strive to follow the humility and the poverty of our Lord Jesus Christ and remember that we should have nothing in the world except, as the Apostle says, 'having something to wear, we be content with these'" (*Earlier Rule* 9.1, 1982: 117). The life imagined is one of utter simplicity, utterly in accord with Job 1:21 and Ecclesiastes 5:15.

This ascetic standard, however, is not the only measure for interpreting this verse. In John Wesley's hands the Pastor's comment on self-sufficiency is expanded to encompass various contexts of eighteenth century economic life. Certainly the verse enjoins one to seek but the rudiments of life. According to Wesley, however, in the Pastor's general scheme "it is allowed, (1.) That we are to provide necessaries and conveniences for those of our own household: (2.) That men in business are to lay up as much as is necessary for the carrying on of that business: (3.) That we are to leave our children what will supply them with necessaries and conveniences after we have left the world: and (4.) That we are to provide things honest in the sight of all men, so as to 'owe no man anything.' But to lay up more, when this is done, is what our Lord has flatly forbidden" ("The Danger of Riches," *Works* 7.3). It is uncertain how, given the leeway Wesley grants for business interests and inheritances, one ought to understand what this "more" means. Still, the sense among scholars since Dibelius that the spirit of the Pastorals, when compared to Paul or the gospels, is profoundly *bürgerlich*, "bourgeois," seems pertinent for Wesley's reading as well. One wonders what Wesley, or the Pastor, would think about the perennial debates in the American Congress over the repeal of the estate tax.

The love of money is a root of all kinds of evil – exegetical treatments (v. 10)

We have noted, above, that the NRSV provides a forceful, but complicated, rendering of the idea in v. 10. However, as the history of interpretation bears out, many besides the King James translators have had recourse in this verse to a totalizing heuristic for the comprehension of evil in human life. The problem has been not the singularity of avarice, but rather how to square the influential ethical bankruptcy of the love of money in this letter with a cartel of other vices similarly colluding in the history of human malfeasance.

Augustine, for instance, because he would rather that pride take the blame for evil, finds ways of linking pride and "the love of money." A specific motivation for this arises from conflicting biblical passages. How, he asks, can the Pastor be correct if Sirach 10:15 says that pride is the beginning of sin? Wouldn't this make pride the root of all evil? His answer is that pride and avarice are more or less equivalent in that they both indicate a going "beyond that which sufficeth" (*Jo. ev. tr.* 8.6, NPNF1 7.508). With a slightly different emphasis on pride not simply as the equivalent, but as a consequence of greed, Thomas nonetheless concurs with Augustine since what we want in seeking riches is to "stand out" or to excel above others, "and this is pride" (Thomas Aquinas 2007: 83). The same goes for all vices, Thomas says. Even if other motivations intervene, even if other resources than avarice are drawn upon, in any particular sin, still, if one were to trace the genealogy of this or that immoral deed back to its ultimate source, one would be forced to recognize that "there is no evil that does not at some time arise from covetousness" (*Summa Theologica* SS Q[119] A[2]).

For others, such as Tertullian and John Cassian, pride is less significant an ill. The love of money can only be the significant source of evil it is for the Pastor if it is equated with the biblical horror of idolatry. Both Tertullian (*De idol.* 11, ANF 3.67) and Cassian (*Inst.* 7.7, NPNF2 11.172) thus find it convenient to link this verse with Colossians 3:5, in which covetousness is called idolatry, in order to justify avarice's pride of place, so to speak, in the hierarchy of corrupting ills. Tertullian also makes the connection between the love of money and idolatry the better to differentiate among the trades, those contributing to evil in the world and those with ethical merit (ibid.). A similar perspective finds voice in the liberation theology of Gustavo Gutierrez, in all other respects an unlikely conversation partner for Tertullian. Gutierrez goes further than Tertullian (or Cassian) in providing a psychological basis for seeing avarice as idolatry: "the primary distinguishing mark of idolatry in the Bible is that one trusts in an idol and not in God"; consequently, as form of such misplaced trust, "greed divinizes money and turns it into an absolute" (*The God of Life*, 1991: 61).

Painter Brian Kirhagis literalizes the verse by imagining a warped, almost industrial tree, against a blighted urban landscape, with dollar bills sprouting from its branches and its roots reaching into the subterranean flames of hell. The apples littering the ground beneath the tree suggest a one-to-one relationship between the root of all evil and the transgression in the garden.

Of course, money is not in itself the problem. Jesus may have wanted his followers to sell everything and follow him, as Jerome notes, but Christian wealth is for all that neither illicit nor without its spiritual benefits, even for those who know they should, but for one reason or another cannot, "literally

Figure 3 Brian Kirhagis. "The Root of All Evil" 2007. Oil, acrylic, paper & metal on canvas. 24″ × 54″. *Source*: www.brikart.net

fulfill [the] directions" of Matthew 19:21 (*Ep.* 79.3, NPNF2 6.165). One could hardly argue otherwise given the Pastor's kindly regard for "them that are rich in this world" in 6:17–19. John Wesley not only agrees with Jerome in this, but goes further in articulating the moral possibilities of a Christian economy: Certainly if we inhabited a truly Christian state of innocence everything would be held in common and we'd not need money. "But, in the present state of mankind, [money] is an excellent gift of God, answering the noblest ends. In the hands of his children, it is food for the hungry, drink for the thirsty, raiment for the naked: It gives to the traveler and the stranger where to lay his head. By it we may supply the place of an husband to the widow, and of a father to the fatherless. We maybe a defense for the oppressed, a means of health to the sick, of ease to them that are in pain; it may be as eyes to the blind, as feet to the lame; yea, a lifter up from the gates of death!" ("The Use of Money," *Works* 6.126).

Martin Luther King would concur. King, in a provocative sermon entitled "Paul's Letter to American Christians," remarks, with a certain approbation, "you have become the richest nation in the world, and you have built up the greatest system of production that history has ever known. All of this is marvelous." He continues, however: "but Americans, there is the danger that you will misuse your Capitalism. I still contend that money can be the root of all evil. It can cause one to live a life of gross materialism. I am afraid that many among you are more concerned about making a living than making a life. You are prone to judge the success of your profession by the index of your salary and the size of the wheel base on your automobile, rather than the quality of your service to humanity." King also goes on to argue that Communism, "based on an ethical relativism and a metaphysical materialism," is not a viable alternative, morally, to American capitalism (*Papers* 4.416).

Sixty-five years prior to King's sermon, Pope Leo XIII had similarly read the Pastor's injunction against "love of money" in terms of the rival economic models of capitalism and Marxism/Communism. But his encyclical *Rerum Novarum* asserts, rather from the perspective of the haves, that "Christian morality, when adequately and completely practiced, leads of itself to temporal prosperity, for it merits the blessing of that God who is the source of all blessings; it powerfully restrains the greed of possession and the thirst for pleasure – twin plagues, which too often make a man who is void of self-restraint miserable in the midst of abundance, it makes men supply for the lack of means through economy, teaching them to be content with frugal living, and further, keeping them out of the reach of those vices which devour not small incomes merely, but large fortunes, and dissipate many a goodly inheritance" (in Carlen 1981: 2.248). Martin Luther King's sermon, needless to say, is rather more strongly supportive of the have-nots; and King accordingly makes the case for a more equitable distribution of resources by recognizing that avarice is productive of evil not only, or even principally, at the personal level, as Leo XIII would have it, but at the level of large-scale systems of economic power.

The love of money is a root of all kinds of evil – literary treatments (v. 10)

Literary versions of the root of all evil, as diverse as they are, constitute an effort to grapple with both the comprehensiveness and the consequences of the Pastor's warning. In this, many produce readings similar to the interpretive work discussed above. Sir Guyon, rejecting the temptations of Mammon in Spenser's *The Faerie Queene*, for instance, endorses the Pastor's view while broadening "evil" into "disquietness" (II.vi.12.2, 1981: 283). Mammon's vast treasures lie behind "a litle dore . . . / That to the gate of Hell, which gaped wide, / Was next adioyning":

> Before the dore sat selfe-consuming Care,
> Day and night keeping wary watch and ward,
> For feare lest Force or Fraud should unaware
> Breake in, and spoile the treasure there in gard . . .
> (II.vii.24.5–25.4, 1981: 286)

Herman Melville's *Typee* portrays a world in which not the love of money, but money itself, "that root of all evils," plays no role: "There were none of those thousand sources of irritation that the ingenuity of civilized man has created to mar his own felicity. There were no foreclosures of mortgages, no pressed notes . . . no unreasonable tailors and shoemakers, perversely bent on being paid . . . no proud and hard-hearted nabobs in Typee" (1846: 1.160). In Melville, this utopian vision is the antithesis of the Care-wracked realm of Mammon; it is also, perhaps, the paradise of a poor young writer who can't seem to raise the cash for his simplest needs. Elwin Ransom, the hero of C. S. Lewis' *Perelandra*, presents a more complicated, if less urgent, analysis of avarice as "this itch to have things over again, as if life were a film that could be unrolled twice or even made to work backwards . . . was it possibly the root of all evil? No: of course the love of money was called that. But money itself – perhaps one valued it chiefly as a defence against chance, a security for being able to have things over again, a means of arresting the unrolling of the film" (1961: 48).

Other writers have extended the Pastor's meaning well beyond the language of the text itself through critical irony, such as we find in Chaucer's *Pardoner's Tale*. The Pardoner, who preaches solely for gain, explains to his fellow pilgrims:

"Lordings (quoth he), in churchë when I preach, / I painë me to have an hautein speech, / And ring it out, as round as doth a bell, / For I know all by rotë that I tell. / My theme is always one, and ever was; / *Radix malorum est cupiditas*" (6 [C] 329–34, 1987: 194). The Pardoner's ironic appropriation of this verse is sharply "subversive," and is at one with his other borrowings from 1 Timothy; indeed *The Pardoner's Tale* has been read as "a deviant corollary of the epistle" more generally (Montelaro 1991: 9). The irony here, of course, ultimately reflects back upon the corruption this character represents, just as it does in Dickens' *Little Dorrit* when Bar, a caricature of the law, flatters the morally sullied Mr. Merdle by calling him "one of the greatest converters of the root of all evil into the root of all good" (1857: 183).

Some literary readings so decontextualize the "root of all evils" that it loses its economic character, thus permitting the targeting of a broader set of social standards and institutions. William Blake, in a move not entirely uncharacteristic of the Pastor elsewhere, superimposes the Fall upon this verse, rendering reason itself, in its capacity for self-subversion, a source of unhappiness, especially for human sexuality: "Two Horn'd Reasoning Cloven Fiction / In Doubt which is Self contradiction / A dark Hermaphrodite We stood / Rational Truth Root of Evil & Good" (*Gates of Paradise*, 1965: 265). Both Kierkegaard and D. H. Lawrence adopt a Blakean tone in defining "the root of all evils" as, respectively, "boredom" (*Either/Or*, 1971: 1.281) and the "fear of society," the product of a "mutilated social consciousness" (Lawrence, "Fear of Society is the Root of All Evil," 1993: 512), while in Graham Greene's droll sensibility it is nothing other than gossip (Greene, "The Root of All Evil," 1973).

Chinese-American poet Wang Ping adapts the "root of all evil" for a complex layering of cultural and ethical considerations in her poem "Flash of Selfish Consciousness." The poem begins by acknowledging that "evil has many faces and we must dig / into the bottom of the soul to catch / flashes of selfish consciousness" (Wang 1998: 96). Selfishness is not an easy stand-in for the Pastor's "love of money," though; indeed, while the idea of digging into the soul to unearth the root of all evils would be striking, the image actually derives, according to the poem, from the "*Red Treasure Book*," a collection of Mao Zedong's sayings, required reading for the Chinese, especially during the Cultural Revolution. Rather, "the root of all evil" is defined by the speaker's mother in the poem as sex:

> 'This is the last time, daughter:
> sex is the root of all sickness and evil deeds.
> Look at me. Since your father's death, I got
> my health back and my eternal happiness.'
> (98)

However, as sex, here, functions as a mode of selfish consumption, in this case of women and their independence by men, the mother's words undermine the Maoist politics of self-criticism (not to mention the Pastor's misogyny) by considering evil anything that hinders personal, private, fulfillment. Although it is not clear that the daughter accepts the mother's definition (indeed, she seems to reject the mother altogether), the poem as a whole ultimately muses upon conventionally adjudicated conceptions of evil, not in order to avoid them, but instead to find liberation, and sometimes even love, in their embrace (102).

Pierced themselves with many pains (v. 10b)

The Pastor does not limit himself to a theory of the origins of evil, however. He also suggests something, in the most general terms, as is his wont, about the very human consequences of a life lived in the "senseless and harmful desires" of avarice. Some intriguing voices in the tradition have taken a special interest in this part of the discussion. Chrysostom offers a window into the corruption to which avarice was prone in fourth century Antioch when he asks his congregants whether it is "not a foolish desire when men like to keep idiots and dwarfs, not from benevolent motives but for their pleasure . . ." (*Hom. 1 Tim.*, NPNF1 13.468). Chrysostom also recognizes that a less inhumane avariciousness, the desire to possess beautiful things, is both far from uncommon and far less hurtful. His task, however, is to convert this materialism into a desire for true beauty, for qualities which, like godliness and righteousness, are truly beautiful "in themselves" (ibid.: 470).

Catherine of Siena similarly rues the choices individuals make in their greed, but for ontological, rather than ethical reasons. Speaking as Truth, in her *Dialogue*, Catherine explains that avarice is the root of all evil not only because it produces all other vices, but, even more importantly, because "it makes people cruel to themselves. It takes away the worth of the infinite and makes it finite . . . [people] are never satisfied because they love something that is less than themselves. All created things were made to serve people, not for people to become their servants" (1980: 316–17).

Those in the present age who are rich (v. 17)

There are, the Pastor acknowledges in vv. 17–19, believers who are rich as well. Readers have, contrary to the tendency in Cassian and St. Francis noted above, both taken for granted, and carefully exploited, this plain fact of Christian wealth. Origen's concern with these verses is largely rhetorical, an effort to counter Celsus' arguments against Christianity – in this case, that the law (unlike Christianity) promotes this-worldly wealth as a sign of God's grace. Origen retorts that wealth is not the reward Celsus imagines it to be on his reading of scripture; what matters is not actual money or an abundance of material goods, but a spiritual wealth. "Consider if it is not according to God's promise," Origen asks, "that he who is rich in all utterance, in all knowledge, in all wisdom, in all good works [1 Cor. 1:5], may not out of these treasures of utterance, of wisdom, and of knowledge, lend to many nations" (*C. Cels.* 7.21, ANF 4.619). His emphasis thus falls on, and yet far exceeds, the good deeds to which the Pastor obliges the Christian economic elite, for those wealthy in spirit, like Paul himself, do the whole world good by communicating the gospel. Augustine also deflects attention away from the language of wealth, focusing instead upon the moral qualities of the Pastor's rich; what matters for the rich as for anyone else is that they be not "highminded," that they achieve a poverty which will be spiritually efficacious since "to the poor and needy . . . [God] inclines his ear" (*En. ps.* 86.3, NPNF1 8.410).

A rather more materialist interpretation – although one no less dependent upon the text – is voiced by Salvian the Presbyter, a fifth century Gallic priest and critic of Roman corruption, who produces from these verses something along the lines of a Christian exchange, a trickle-down theory of salvation. In Salvian's view, Paul here indicates how God wisely gives riches "to the wealthy . . . in order that they may grow rich by good works." The extra riches which accrue to the benevolently wealthy are, undoubtedly, spiritual, but Salvian still uses the language of exchange to explain that whatever the rich give to the poor will be "returned by God with interest" (*Ad ecclesiasm* 3.1, 1947: 320).

A more frankly economic reading is performed by John Locke in a discussion of the natural law of property. If property is that upon which one expends labor in order to remove it, as it were, from nature as everyone's common possession, then can't the most productive and most powerful simply gobble up everything for themselves? No, he replies, because "the same law of nature, that does by this means give us property, does also bound that property too. 'God has given us all things richly' . . . is the voice of reason confirmed by inspiration. But how far has he given it us? To enjoy. As much as any one can make use of to advantage of life before it spoils" is property. "Nothing was made by God for man to spoil or destroy" (*Second Treatise on Government*, 1966: 17). To the extent that Locke's appropriation of v. 17 for a liberal sense of property, in view of the common good, genuinely touches upon the Pastor's general intention, its recovery for New Testament criticism may help revive an interest in the Pastorals as documents fraught not merely with prescription, but certain creative, if ultimately ambiguous, possibilities as well. While Locke and others may strive to find an affirmative economics in these verses, Calvin worries about their potential theological misreading. One isn't to suppose, as the "Papists" do, that one can earn one's salvation by good works, despite what the Pastor says, even if "it is true that everything spent on the poor is acceptable to God" (*Commentary* 1964: 283). For, Calvin continues, "even the most perfect of us scarcely fulfill the hundredth of their full duty." Thus, "there is not one of us who would not be bankrupt" if God were suddenly to call us to account for our lives (1856: 172).

Theological Speculation: God's Dwelling and Being (6:12–16; 1 Tim. 1:17)

This passage begins with what is probably a creedal reference to Christ's crucifixion (explicitly mentioned nowhere in the Pastoral Epistles), with the addition of a link between Jesus' confession and Timothy's of the previous verse, perhaps on the basis of the willingness of both to testify before unbelievers (Towner 2006: 412–14; Davies 1996: 52–53), and then concludes with a beautiful "hymn to the sovereignty of God as all-powerful, immortal and invisible" (New Oxford Annotated Bible, 3rd edn (NRSV) 15–16n.). As in the earlier doxology (1:17), which opens the letter, this closing passage emphasizes God's radical difference from all earthly rulers, and especially from the emperor cult (Bassler 1996: 116). The terms here are not quite expressed in the same way as in chapter 1, however. For one thing, God is not only immortal, but "he alone has immortality" and he "dwells in unapproachable light" (v. 16). Hanson notes that the first idea reflects "a very Jewish concept. . . . [t]he soul is not naturally immortal, as Plato taught, but life beyond death is the gift of God." He also suggests that the vision of an "unapproachable light" is derived from such biblical sources as the Sinai experience and the opening verses of the Gospel of John (1982: 113; cf. Collins 2002: 168; Towner 2006: 420). One of the curious consequences of portraying God in so transcendent a manner, however, is that he seems utterly removed not only from humanity, but from the very earthly Christ of this epistle (Collins 2002: 166). Additionally, Hanson (1982: 62) and Collins (2002: 46) note that the Bible almost always conjoins a negative descriptor ("invisible") for God with some positive feature, for instance the ways in which God nevertheless makes himself visible in creation or in Christ. That the Pastor does not do so on this occasion, and certainly not at 1:17, may suggest that his doxology, in its original context – most scholars believe it is a "liturgical fragment" (Bassler 1996: 45) – had been designed to challenge the claims to divine status of (historical, visible) Hellenistic rulers (Towner 2006: 152).

The good confession (v. 13)

In reading this verse of uncertain provenance, and reference, Chrysostom plays it safe, as do modern commentators, by assuming merely that if the Pastor had in mind an actual statement of Jesus' it must have been something from the Passion narratives in the gospels (*Hom. 1 Tim.*, NPNF1 13.471). In his commentary, Theodoret seems to imagine that Jesus may actually have preached to Pilate, since in his reading, "by good confession of the Lord" the letter refers "to the salvation of the world" (*Comm. 1 Tim.*, 2001: 2.229). It is possible that Theodoret, like Matthew Henry in his commentary (1721–25: 312), has John 18:37–38 in mind, which would put his exegesis of this verse in service also of an understanding of the "truth" Jesus professes before Pilate in that gospel.

Many readers find a normative element in this verse, insisting that, like Timothy, all Christians must confess their faith, especially when pressed to do so. Seventeenth century English Presbyterian John Flavel is intriguing in this regard, since he tries to indicate more precisely, and thus to limit, the circumstances under which Christians must make their "good confession":

> Herein Christ has ruled out the way of our duty, and by his own example, as well as precept, obliged us to a sincere confession of him, and his truth, when we are required lawfully so to do, i.e. when we are before a lawful magistrate, and the questions are not curious or captious; when we cannot hold our peace, but our silence will be interpretatively a denying of the truth; finally, when the glory of God, honour of his truth, and edification of others, are more attainable by our open confession, than they can be by our silence; then must we with Christ, give direct, plain, sincere answers. (*The Fountain of Life* 24, 1701: 1.118)

Calvin voices what amounts to the consensus view among modern commentators, that "confession" essentially duplicates "testimony," and thus that both terms evoke martyrdom. For Calvin, however, the idea that Jesus' "voluntary submission to death" was a "good confession" is still important since it doesn't just bear witness to, but actually proves, in a way that other famous martyrdoms (such as Socrates') cannot, the truth of his "doctrine" (*Commentary* 1964: 278).

Unapproachable light (vv. 15–16)

As in 1 Timothy 1:17, the Pastor here calls attention to God's eternity; but he does so with the curious statement that God "alone . . . has immortality." This claim poses something of a problem for the understanding of believers' own immortal souls. For Origen, the soul is eternal, and receives its immortality from God who grants eternal life (*Cant.* Prol., 1979: 226; cf. Calvin, *Commentary* 1964: 280). Augustine, on the other hand, for whom the soul is immortal only "in a certain manner," in that the soul has no eternal preexistence, points out that "true immortality is unchangeableness; which no creature can possess, since it belongs to the creator alone" (*De Trin.* 1.1.2, NPNF1 3.18).

One of the most interesting readings is that of Francisco de Osuna, which is less concerned with the implications for human immortality, but takes God's special immortality as the basis for an epistemologically articulated ontology:

> [T]here can be no forgetfulness in God because as Saint Paul says, 'he alone is immortal,' and thus the infinite knowledge engendered by his understanding remains forever in his eternal memory where all things live and are never forgotten. The idea for every single thing and the seminal reason for every possibility exist in his memory better than on a plan, so that even if something were to die in itself, it would not perish in God's memory where all things are recorded and comprehended in such a way that the angels can read as if from a perfect book what God wishes them to know. In that book alone the essence of individual people is found, and there they are immortal, participating in the immortality possessed only by God, to whom and through whom and in whom all things live. (*Third Spiritual Alphabet*, 1981: 295)

Just as it is not clear in what sense God is alone immortal, so the Pastor's poetic turn of phrase regarding the one who dwells in inaccessible light has also puzzled readers, in part because of the distinctions the doxology in vv. 15–16 appears to establish between God and Christ. Clement of Alexandria seems to have imagined that this verse refers to Christ (*Exc. Theod.* 10.5, 12.3, 1970: 79, 83). In Faustus of Milevis' Manichean cosmology, by contrast, it is God the "Father [who] properly dwells in the highest or principal light, which Paul calls 'light inaccessible,'" while the Son inhabits the lesser "second or visible light," namely the sun and moon, and the Spirit makes a capacious home "in the whole circle of the atmosphere" (*C. Faust.* 20.2, NPNF1 4.253). Taking up yet a different interpretive perspective, Methodius of Olympus suggests that God, akin both to the Platonic cosmos and demiurge at once, "abides in Himself and is Light itself in secret and unapproachable places, embracing all things in the orbit of His power; creating and arranging them – He it was who made the soul in the image of His likeness," i.e., of the Son (*Banquet of the Ten Virgins* 6.1, 1958: 91).

Although each of these figures wrote prior to the great Arian crises of the fourth century, their collective indecision in reading this verse is indicative of later usage as well. Augustine insists that all "orthodox believers" see in this unapproachable light nothing other than the "one divine being, in an inseparable triune existence" (*C. Faust.* 20.7, NPNF1 4.255) – and Dante, a millennium later, will follow Augustine in his Trinitarian vision of the "Highest Light . . . raised so far above / the minds of mortals," the "Eternal Light," that "Love that moves the sun and the other stars" (*Paradiso* 33.67–68, 124, 145, 1984: 299–303).

But even supporters of the Council of Nicea's Trinitarian formulation, who were concerned to undermine the Arian contentions that the Father alone is truly divine from eternity and that the Son was his first creature, might find the Pastor's image rich and yet uncertain. Gregory of Nyssa, for example, attempting to refute the view that the divine light only pertains to God the Father, seems merely to invert the terms of a heretical equation by claiming that "the Son is light unapproachable in which the Father dwells, or in whom the Father is" (*C. Eun.* 12.2, NPNF2 5.243). Gregory similarly finds that the reference to immortality in this verse pertains to Christ as well, because Christ is life, and "life is immortality" (ibid.: 105). So who, exactly, inhabits the supreme incandescence? The Son, the Father, the Holy Spirit? The Trinity, or some subset or re-characterization thereof, as in Henry Suso's sense that the text concerns "Eternal Wisdom" (*Wisdom's Watch upon The Hours,* 1994: 121)?

Writers in a speculative mode are often less interested in answering such questions precisely, less invested in establishing who dwells in the light, than in the light itself, or more properly, what knowing this light implies for the believer. Thus, for figures such as Pseudo-Dionysius, drawing upon and developing "self-subverting" metaphors of light and darkness characteristic of certain mystics and negative theologians (Turner 1995: 21), "the divine darkness is that 'unapproachable light' where God is said to live. And if it is invisible because of a superabundant clarity, if it cannot be approached because of the outpouring of its transcendent gift of light, yet it is here that is found everyone worthy to know God and to look upon him" (*Epistle* 5, 1987: 265). Similarly, Nicolas of Cusa claims that the one whom the religious person "worships as inaccessible light is not light as is corporeal light, whose opposite is darkness, but is most simple and infinite light, in which darkness is infinite light; and that this infinite light always shines in the darkness of our ignorance," which cannot comprehend it (*De doct. ign.* 1.26.86, 1997: 125–26). Nicolas feels that the unapproachability of God's light should be taken quite literally, such that one cannot even pray to God effectively since he is in fact "unapproachable by every means" short of Grace (ibid.: 246). In Thomas Aquinas' view, not even Christ, at least in terms of his "created intellect," could transcend this infinite gulf and know God (Thomas Aquinas 2007: 88). One of the implications of this line of thought is that the very description of God as light is, from the outset, problematic. If God is so entirely unknowable to the intellect, and in terms of the world of the senses, then what does it mean to call God light at all?

Indeed, it troubles some, such as Theodoret of Cyrus, that the writer of 1 Timothy would "circumscribe" the divine with reference to a visible and specific dwelling space – as abstract as it might be (*Comm. 1 Tim.*, 2001: 2.229–30). As Cassiodorus reminds his readers, "such splendor, brightness, brilliance, and majesty as is conceivable to the human mind is inferior to God . . . We must not with false presumption . . . form some mental picture of him . . . God has no shape, no outline" (*Ex. ps.* 141, 1991: 405). Still, the Pastor, in Chrysostom's terms (which are echoed by Theodoret), has done the best he could, given that "when the tongue would utter something great, it fails in power" (*Hom. 1 Tim.*, NPNF1 13.471). And as we must rely upon the senses and language in any case, perhaps we should simply embrace the inherent limitations of theological expression. This, it seems, is the tenor of Guigo de Ponte's homely, almost Hardyesque, adaptation of a common analogy to suggest that God's light is not so ultimately unknowable after all: "one can indeed see the sun clearly without being blinded by its brilliance – if one is in open country early in the morning. That is how God is seen in heaven" (*On Contemplation* 2.8, 1997: 207; cf. Novatian *On the Trinity* 18, ANF 5.627–28). Jonathan Edwards seems to have had just this sort of experience, musing upon 1 Timothy 1:17 as he came to appreciate, with a "*delightful* conviction," the notion of God's absolute sovereignty. He finds that this idea, like our verse, fills him with "a new sort of affection," and he keeps "saying, as it were singing over these words of Scripture" to himself:

> [soon] after this my sense of divine things gradually increased, and became more and more lively, and had more of that inward sweetness. The appearance of everything was altered . . . God's excellency, his wisdom, his purity and love, seemed to appear in every thing; in the sun, moon, and stars; in the clouds and blue sky; in the grass, flowers, trees; in the water, and all nature; which used greatly to fix my mind. ("Personal Narrative," *Works of Jonathan Edwards* 16.792)

Translations of this verse into English have maintained the key emphasis on divine light at a distance. Wycliffe's translation reads: God "aloone hath vndeedlynesse, and dwellith in liyt, to which no man may come." In Tyndale's translation, the divinity of this verse is specifically Christ who, since he "dwelleth in light that no man can attain" has rather a moral or epistemological, as well as metaphysical, otherness. The King James Version echoes Wycliffe's and Tyndale's language in portraying a God "who alone hath immortality, dwelling in the light which no man can approach unto." Most later translations follow the King James Version, more or less, although often without the definite article before "light." One interesting variant, however, is the "inspired version" of Joseph Smith, which inverts and in the process interiorizes the text in its preference for a God "whom no man hath seen, nor can see, unto whom no man can approach, only he who hath the light and the hope of immortality dwelling in him" (Joseph Smith Translation). Smith's prophetic reading undermines precisely that which the verse seems to establish: God's unreachability. As such, it participates in a strand of the tradition that would, like mystical theologians, seek to overcome the divine–human gulf. Meister Eckhart, in fact, believes that the verse provides direct access to God in his claim that people modeling their spiritual quest on "our Lord [who] went to heaven, high above all light and above all understanding and all comprehension . . . are thus carried above all light dwell in unity. For this reason Saint Paul says: 'God dwells in an inaccessible light' . . . which is a pure unity in itself" (Sermon 25, 1980: 358). Even far less mystical thinkers could come to similar conclusions about the accessibility of the inaccessible. Erasmus, fusing 1 Timothy 6:16 with James 4:8 – "draw nigh to God and he will draw nigh to you" – concludes, hopefully, that "if you try with all your might to rise out of the darkness and confusion of your sensory experience, He will graciously come to meet you from His inaccessible Light and inscrutable Stillness, where" all doubt and diversion are "put to rest" (*Enchiridion*, 1963: 130).

The power of this image of God's light is taken up in different registers in nineteenth and twentieth century creative works. The following excerpt from David Harsent's poem "The Blessed Punchinello, Mart." appropriates a certain divinity for the mock heroic martyrdom of Mr. Punch, of the Punch and Judy tradition:

> He would live in unapproachable light
> and the numbing silence of denial,
> weathered in desert air
> to leather and bone, a shriveled sun dial
>
> welded by bone to the pillar: and record
> rumours of the world
> as a feather on a stripped nerve.
>   (Harsent 1984: 49)

The same verse, however, is liable to an almost scientific mysticism, as in T. H. Chivers' nineteenth century poem "God Dwells in Light: Sacred Song":

> God dwells in light!
> And holds within the hollow of His hand
> The universe of worlds which gem the night,
> Which, through Heaven's sea, at his divine command,
> Freighted with His own smiles, now sail at even,
> Fearless of storms, around the sun in Heaven.
>
> (Chivers 1845: 27)

Chivers' physicalism is echoed in the twentieth century in composer Stephen Taylor's piece "Unapproachable Light," or rather in his explanation that the work "was inspired by images of stars being born in the farthest reaches of the cosmos, unimaginably distant," and that 1 Timothy 1:16 "captured the power and remoteness of the Universe" (Taylor 1999: 6).

The Opponents: Dissent (6:2b–5, 20, 2 Timothy: 12, 14)

Timothy is warned here, as elsewhere in the letter, about false teachers. These verses teach us little that is new about the Pastor's opponents, beyond that fact that they are tempted toward dissension and contradiction (vv. 4, 20). We do learn something, however, about how the Pastor understands his gospel. It is a "deposit" [*paratheke*, "what has been entrusted," (NRSV)] to be "guarded" and handed on only to trustworthy successors (cf. 2 Tim. 2:2). By deposit, the Pastor means his version of "the Pauline articulation of the faith . . . that is being endangered by heretical distortions, additions, deletions" (Towner 2006: 431). Collins characterizes it as "a cameo description of the gospel message, the essence of the creed, a norm of catechesis" (2002: 213). When the "deposit" reappears in 2 Timothy 1:12, 14, "Paul" claims, additionally, that God is its ultimate guarantor. Yet the language in that passage is unclear. "Paul," knowing whom he trusts, can tell Timothy that he, i.e., God or Christ, "is able to guard until that day what I have entrusted to him." However, one can also translate the final clause: "what has been entrusted to me" (RSV). Most modern commentators opt for the second of these renderings, while earlier readers tend to prefer the first.

Guard what has been entrusted to you (v. 20)

Readers have not been uniform in their understanding of the nature or content of the deposit. For some it is a reference to God's grace (cf. Theodoret, *Comm.*

1 Tim., 2001: 2.230; Calvin 1964: 283). To others the word evokes esoteric instructions for the initiate (cf. Tertullian *Praescr.* 25, ANF 3.255; Pseudo-Dionysius *On the Divine Names.* 1.8, 1987: 58). Figures in the Catholic tradition have frequently thought of this deposit as their own special theological and spiritual inheritance. In fact, the document which opens the new Catholic Catechism is called "Fidei Depositum." Written by John Paul II, this introductory text begins with the claim that "guarding the deposit of faith is the mission which the Lord entrusted to His church, and which she fulfills in every age" (US Catholic Church 1995: 1; cf. Abbott 1966: 117–18).

As noted above, the deposit at 2 Timothy 1:12, 14, is not entrusted to Timothy but, at least potentially, to God. Augustine takes "Paul" to be entrusting God with his faith (*De gest. Pel.* 35, NPNF1 5.199). Toward the opening of *On the Trinity*, Augustine himself also prays to God, like the Pastor's "Paul," and commits "my trust and desire to him, who is sufficiently able to keep those things which he has given me, and to render those which he has promised" (3, NPNF1 3.20). In this case he trusts and desires both that his readers will engage with him charitably, and that God or other men will inspire or admonish him, as needs be, toward an ever more accurate theology. Chrysostom assumes, similarly, that it is God whom "Paul" has entrusted with something, either the faith itself or "the faithful," individuals like Timothy. Taking up the latter reading, Chrysostom says that "Paul" "is insensible to sufferings, from the hope that he entertains of his disciples" (*Hom. 1 Tim.*, NPNF1 13.481), a sure hope, given God's fiduciary role in this reading. In Calvin's view, "Paul" commits unto God his salvation, for "if our salvation depended upon ourselves, it would be continually exposed to very many dangers; but being committed to such a guardian it is out of all danger" (1964: 300). This very sentiment is expressed in a hymn by Isaac Watts. The individual soul, whose own name is "worthless," can place his trust in God, for:

> Firm as His throne His promise stands,
> And he can well secure
> What I've committed to his hands
> Till the decisive hour.
> (Hymn 103, 1856: 345)

Controversy, disputes and contradictions (vv. 4, 20)

Clearly, since the Pastor feels he must constantly be on guard against his opponents, his community must have been rather complex, a zone of competing theological perspectives. One might creatively extrapolate from the data of the

Pastorals and conclude that ascetics, mythographers, genealogists, and others were actively at work within the Ephesian community, and all of them were at odds, apparently, with the Pastor. Early readers of the Pastorals, as I mentioned briefly in the introduction to the commentary, often assumed that the opponents addressed here were Gnostics. Irenaeus borrows from v. 20 for the title of his "Refutation and Subversion of Knowledge Falsely So-Called," more commonly known as *Against Heresies*. And in that work he also castigates the Gnostics who, "'doting about questions' [v. 4], do imagine that what the apostles have declared about God should be allegorized" (3.12.11, ANF 1.434; see also Eusebius, *Eccl. Hist.* 4.7; NPNF2 1.178). Tertullian considered that the doctrine Timothy was charged to keep, in combating false knowledge, was strictly opposed to the "madness" of certain Gnostics, who insisted that the early church had propagated a secret teaching along side the publicly proclaimed word (*Praescr.* 25; ANF 3.255). Chrysostom also suggested that "perhaps [the Pastor] says this (e.g., v. 20), because some then assumed the name of Gnostics, as knowing more than others"; however true this may be, Chrysostom added, the warning in this verse can be generalized for the benefit of all believers too: knowledge can only come by faith, and thus "when anything springs from our reasonings, it is not knowledge" (*Hom. 1 Tim.*, NPNF1 13.472).

As oppositional as many readings of v. 20 could be, it has nevertheless been recognized, at least occasionally, that the development of multiple, even multiply conflictual, strands of tradition might be good for Christianity, despite a strong desire for uniformity and consistency. Celsus had claimed that Christians of his day, in the cynical pursuit of power, shattered an earlier consensus – implying that all Christians had originally been harmoniously "of one mind" (cf. 2 Cor. 13:11; Phil. 2:2). Origen responds, in his *Contra Celsum*, by using these lines from 1 Timothy to prove that dissent and the promotion of what today we would call alternative Christianities had been part of the tradition from the very beginning (3.11, ANF 4.488–89). Most readers including Origen assume that dissent is unproductive, and some appropriate the Pastor's remarks about his opponents for their own polemical purposes. Luther's homiletic adaptation of the epistolary conclusion of 1 Timothy is particularly striking, both in its critical purpose and in its wildly anachronistic reconstruction of Paul's meaning: "Here in explicit terms and in a way that cannot be challenged, the apostle truly condemns what the universities teach. . . . The apostle well commands us that we should guard the doctrine that has been entrusted to our care. He calls the natural philosophy of Aristotle unChristian, idle words without substance; in fact, it is opposed to Christ; he says, it is 'falsely called knowledge.'" ("Gospel for the Festival of Epiphany," *Works* 52.166–67). Erasmus similarly mocks scholastic theology, in his *In Praise of*

Folly, but recalls nostalgically via these verses that "all the quarrels and disputes of [Paul's] time were coarse and crude by comparison with" what are derided as "the supersubtleties of the doctors of theology" (2003: 93). Even Matthew Arnold can cite v. 4 in order to slander contemporary "preachers of predestination and justification," of whom he was rather weary, as "just the people [Paul] would have called 'diseased about questions and word-battlings'" (*Dogma and Dissent*, 1968: 69).

The second letter to Timothy opens with the longest, if not the only (but see 1 Tim. 1:12–14), thanksgiving section of the Pastoral corpus. "Paul" reminds Timothy of his pious upbringing and then turns to the subject at hand: he is suffering in prison and expects that he will not be released, indeed that he will not survive. One of his goals, however, is to encourage Timothy to suffer bravely. The chapter concludes with "Paul" reporting upon his isolation: all his coworkers have abandoned him, with the exception of Onesiphorus, who is accorded special praise.

The Pastoral Epistles Through the Centuries, First Edition. Jay Twomey.
© 2009 by Jay Twomey. Published 2020 by John Wiley & Sons Ltd.

The Thanksgiving (1:3–7)

Like the thanksgiving in an authentic Pauline epistle, this text sets out some of the main elements of 2 Timothy as a whole, including the theme of maintaining faith in the face of suffering (Timothy's tears, Paul's imprisonment) and the emphasis, evident throughout the Pastorals, upon the tradition behind that faith, its "stability and antiquity" (Bassler 1996: 129) and therefore its trustworthiness (cf. the frequent use of the formula "this saying is sure," literally "trustworthy [*pistos*, faithful] is the saying," 1 Tim. 1:15; 3:1; 4:9; 2 Tim. 2:11; Titus 3:8). These initial verses, in conjunction with 4:9, 12, also frame the letter in terms of Paul's desire to have Timothy by his side at this, his most trying hour.

Eunice and Lois (v. 5)

Readers through the centuries have taken a special interest in the relationships this letter commemorates. The Pastor seems to invoke the memory of Timothy's grandmother Lois and mother Eunice as a way of uniting "Paul" and Timothy as men working in continuity with their ancestors, the better to insist upon the continuity of the Christian message itself, from its earliest articulation to every moment in its future propagation (2:2; 1:12; 1 Tim. 6:20). That the "Paul" of 2 Timothy 1:3 seems at odds with the "Paul" of 1 Timothy 1:13–16, the one a man of "clear conscience" in accord with his ancestors, the other a "blasphemer," is easily explained, Chrysostom felt, by the fact that "Paul" never failed in pursuing his own intentions with all integrity. Even as a persecutor, Chrysostom has his Paul say, "I never gave up any good that I purposed, for any human cause." "I was never a hypocrite, thinking one thing and doing another" (*Hom. 2 Tim.*, NPNF1 13.476; Theodoret 2001: 2.236). Calvin takes issue with Chrysostom's reading, which unfortunately made too great an allowance for private will, and too little for ethical or religious correctness. In his view one cannot claim to have a pure conscience if one is not rightly reverential. "Paul's" remark, then, needs to be understood in a historically specific sense: he tells Timothy that "he worships the same God as his ancestors, but now he does it with a pure and heart-felt affection, since he has been enlightened by the gospel" (*Commentary* 1964: 291). Calvin's "Paul" does not merely have an affectionate relationship with Timothy, whose hoped-for visit will, the Pastor writes, fill him with "joy," but he also worships with affection.

Many readers have simply taken the information supplied with regard to Timothy's upbringing as an ideal of religious education. As Theodoret puts it, "nothing brings such benefit as an example from home" (2001: 2.237), an opinion seconded in nearly identical terms by a variety of others in the tradition (cf. Calvin, *Commentary* 1964: 292). Some of these have also explicated Timothy's relationship with his mother and grandmother by way of endorsing the role of strong family commitments in the production of Christian sensibilities. Thomas Fuller, the seventeenth century English churchman and wit, believing that Timothy's mother and grandmother were dead at the time of the letter's composition, feels that "Paul's" recollection is especially powerful because "[i]t is good to feed our soules on the memories of pious persons" ("How Far Grace Can be Entailed," 1640: 151). Interestingly, however, Fuller appeals in this sermon less to the young Christian than to his or her parents, who are told that they can outlive death in raising their offspring properly.

> Saint Paul beholding Timothies Goodnesse, is minded thereby to remember his Mother, and Grand-mother Eunice and Lois; they can never bee dead, whiles hee is alive. . . . Dost thou desire to have thy memory continued? Art thou ambitious to be revenged of death, and to out-last her spight? . . . give thy children godly education, and the fight of their goodnesse will furbish up thy memory, in the mouthes and minds of others, that it never rusts in oblivion. (152)

Fuller's sermon does more than play upon the self-interests of parents, though; it pays special attention to the status of these two women, especially as the teachers of Timothy (see 3:16). Aware of the Pastoral's prohibition against women having "authority over a man" (1 Tim. 2:12), Fuller nevertheless speculates that Timothy's father is probably absent from our passage because "he was not so eminent, and appearing in Piety" as Eunice or Lois. Theirs was not a special case, however, for all women should similarly strive "to excell their husbands in Goodnesse; it is no trespasse of their modesty, nor breach of the obedience they vowed to their husbands in marriage, to strive to bee Superiours, and above them in Piety" (153). Horace Bushnell, in his *Christian Nurture*, concludes that Timothy's father was probably an idolater, a wholly negative influence on his son's life. Happily, that influence was far too weak to supersede the teachings of Eunice and Lois. This does not necessarily mean that women ought to strive to outpace their husbands in religious worth, however. In Bushnell's view, one parent is usually better suited to Christian child-rearing than the other. That this parent is usually the mother only helps to reinforce a sentimentalist, rather than a feminist, position (1876: 268). Timothy – and the emphasis here is on the son rather than his maternal forbears – is reminded by "Paul" of a truth which is powerfully rooted in such sentimentalism: "Timothy was supposed to have had a complete set of recollections from his mother woven into his very feeling of the truth itself. It was

2 Timothy 1   117

more true because it had been taught him by her. There was even a sense of her loving personally in it, by which it had always been, and was always to be, endeared" (370).

Timothy: Ordination (1:6–8; 1 Tim. 1:18, 4:14–15)

Hilary of Poitiers, commenting perhaps upon the oddness of the fact that "Paul" would have to remind Timothy of something he had known all his life, remarks that "the infirmity of man needs time to review before the true and perfect tribunal of the mind, that which is poured indiscriminately into the ears. Comprehension follows the spoken words more slowly than hearing, for it is the ear which hears, but the reason which understands, though it is God Who reveals the inner meaning to those who seek it" (*De trin.* 11.23, NPNF2 9.210). But if all mankind suffers from such an infirmity, Timothy can seem in particularly bad shape. As Bassler puts it, Timothy's "spirit is weak" and his "fortitude is flagging" (1996: 129), and the Pastor must urge him to "rekindle" (v. 6) his gift, not to be frightened or cowardly (v. 7), and not to be ashamed (vv. 8, 12, 16; 2:15). Bassler also points out that the historical Timothy is of little importance here since the letters can also be read as giving general advice to church leaders (ibid.).

The language of cowardice and shame, then, especially in conjunction with the reference to ordination (v. 6), might rather have in view the association with Joshua (cf. Josh. 1:9) already developed in 1 Timothy 4:14. Indeed, Marjorie Warkentin claims that "Paul" is envisioned in these passages not as an elder ordaining Timothy for a specifically pastoral function, but rather as a leader electing Timothy as his own replacement in the manner of Moses' selection of Joshua (Warkentin 1982: 136–42; cf. Collins 2002: 196–97). Like Moses, "Paul" conveys authority through the laying on of his hands (Num. 27:18–23). Nevertheless, these passages, along with other New Testament parallels (Acts 6:6; 8:17; 13:3; 19:6), are frequently cited in studies of the origins of rites of ordination. A curious problem in the Pastorals is just why "Paul" seems to have two different memories of his ordination of Timothy. In the one (1 Tim. 4:14), Timothy is ordained by a "council of elders"; in the other (2 Tim. 1:6), by "Paul" alone. Scholars have assumed that, short of contradicting himself, the Pastor is simply focusing on the same event differently (Bassler 1996: 130; Collins 2002: 197), although some believe that two separate events are here being recalled (Towner 2006: 325).

The gift received at ordination is never named, although it is difficult to disagree with Bultmann and others, who picture the Pastor's Christianity as essentially post-charismatic (1955: 2.108; D-C 1972: 71; Bassler 1996: 89), that the Pastor has limited the vivid Pauline concept and experience of spiritual gifts to the fulfilling of a ministerial function.

Rekindle the gift of God (v. 6)

Timothy is encouraged to embrace his own not insubstantial, and indeed God-given, capacities. At his ordination (see 1 Tim. 4:14) he was granted a gift of God, and he is asked to rekindle, to "stir up" (KJV) or "fan into flame" (NIV), that gift now. For Chrysostom this seems to imply that grace is dependent to some extent upon the believer's ardor. "Paul" urges Timothy "to rekindle" his gift because "it requires much zeal to stir up the gift of God. As fire requires fuel, so grace requires our alacrity, that it may be ever fervent" (*Hom. 2 Tim.*, NPNF1 13.477). Theodoret makes the same point, albeit in more striking terms: "just as the lamp's oil makes the flame stronger, so the soul's excellent enthusiasm attracts the grace of the all-holy Spirit" (2001: 2.237). This language of "fanning into flame," incidentally, has been taken up by many recent ministries and Christian media outlets online, whose websites frequently feature images not merely of rekindled embers but positive infernos.

But what is the gift itself? The collocation of vv. 6 and 9 provides Chrysostom and Theodoret with something of an answer: the gift is grace. One could also consider, with Matthew Henry, that the "spirit of power and of love and of self-discipline" of v. 7 is Timothy's, and thus every minister's, gift (1721–25: 315). John Henry Newman, perhaps conjoining 1:6 and 2:2, believes the gift to be the apostolic succession, "an honourable badge, far higher than that secular respectability, or cultivation, or polish, or learning, or rank, which gives you a hearing with the many" (*Tracts* 1 1969: 3).

At his ordination Timothy was also the object of prophecies (1 Tim. 1:18). Perhaps these are the gift? Calvin, ever the astute detector of scriptural tensions and apparent contradictions, imagines that "some will now object" to "Paul's" exhortation that Timothy obey the prophetic word. After all, if Timothy's role has been confirmed in the Spirit, then how could he possibly falsify "prophecies uttered by God?" Calvin answers this imaginary cavil by assuring his readers that "the outcome could only be what God had promised" (*Commentary* 1964: 201), because of God's sovereignty, of course, but also because if Timothy embraces "faith and a good conscience" then "the rest will follow" (202).

The question can be posed more critically as well. Assuming, with any variety of readers, that it is the gift of carrying out the duties of the office – or as Thomas Aquinas puts it with reference to v. 6, "a certain excellence of power over the Divine mysteries" (ST TP Q[84] A[4]) – what has happened to that gift over the course of ages? Ancient and modern commentators frequently lament that the idea of the gift has deteriorated from what one finds in the New Testament. James Owen complains that "the Church degenerated from the first Purity," and that this led to a consolidation of the powers of ordination into the hands of bishops alone, who become despotic ecclesiastical authorities, rather than representatives of the true king (*A Plea for Scripture Ordination*, 1694: 49). Thomas Jefferson, after citing the Pastor on ordination, offers a theopolitical reading of the text and subsequent church history. Bishops, because they resemble monarchs, become "tools of the crown," whereas "government by a presbytery which resembles republican government . . . is known to be . . . congenial with friendly liberty" ("Notes on Religion," 1893: 97–98). The Protestantism at work here is quite evidently polemical, even as Owen and Jefferson have different ends in view – the first longs for a spirit-driven ministry under the sovereignty of a single divine king, the second for a democratic order of men. Jefferson's position may be closer, in fact, to Calvin's, for Calvin argues that "to be honored by the praises of prophets was not at that time an ordinary occurrence" (*Commentary* 1964: 201); "Paul" sought prophetic warrant for the youthful Timothy simply in order to forestall charges of "innovating rashness" (ibid.). The office of the presbyter is, Calvin says in the *Institutes*, "a faithful symbol of spiritual grace" (4.19.28, 1960: 2.1476).

Owen's position, by contrast, resembles that of early figures in the tradition, who could similarly feel the loss of religious immediacy from "Paul's" time to their own. Chrysostom, for example, waxes critically nostalgic for a time when priests were selected with the direct aid of the divine: "But then, when nothing human was done, the appointment of Priests too was by prophecy" from the Holy Spirit (*Hom. 1 Tim.*, NPNF1 13.423).

One can also understand these infusions of the spirit as gifts not to ministers alone, but to all Christians. Augustine reads this verse as evidence that God grants to humanity the very ability to act religiously in this life (*Cont. epist. Pelag.* 4.10, NPNF1 5.421). An American minister of the revolutionary era, Ebenezer Devotion, agrees with the Augustinian view, but feels that in fact, "[t]hro' the Prevalence of this Spirit of Fear which God has not given, Men have tamely bowed their Necks to Slavery, quitted their natural Rights, and given up their Liberties as Men, and in Exchange therefor have suffer'd the Yoak, the galling Yoak of Tyranny and Oppression to be put upon them . . . this Spirit shows itself in all despotick Governments, civil and ecclesiastical" (in Noll 1976: 299). The spirit of power can thus also be the spirit of revolution. Or, if not revolution, then existentially aristocratic resolution? Kierkegaard, like Devotion, laments the prevalence of cowardice in the world, and similarly suggests that people find "the spirit of fear" more appealing. Indeed, "cowardliness is precisely the most flexible, the most adroit, the most pleasant, so to speak, of all the passions" ("Against Cowardliness," *Writings* 5:353). By contrast, the spirit of power which Kierkegaard redefines as resolution, "joins a person with the eternal, brings the eternal into time for him, jars him out of the drowsiness of uniformity and habit, cuts off the tedious bickering of troublesome thoughts, and pronounces a benediction upon even the weakest beginning, when it is indeed a beginning" (347). He goes on to say that this kind of talk, essential though it is, also can lead to idealism, dreams of heroism. Instead, what is most necessary is that we come to realize what we are: beings in the grip of sin, failing our own souls. Only insofar as one recognizes one's weaknesses can one receive the "knighthood" which God "confer[s] . . . with his powerful hand" (353).

Not a spirit of cowardice, but rather of power (v. 7)

Modern commentators, searching for a theology in the Pastorals, make much of this chapter and especially its epiphany concept ("the *appearing* of our Savior" in v. 10; see Collins 2002: 202–09); but in the process they tend to separate theology from exhortation, Christology from fear and suffering. Traditional readers, on the other hand, have sometimes been rather more attentive to the way this theology functions in context. Chrysostom, for example, occasionally places a much greater emphasis on the personalia and the implicit warnings to Timothy. He understands "Paul" to be walking a fine line between hope and despair in this text. "Paul" himself is imprisoned and knows that preaching the gospel entails suffering. But he offers a hopeful theology of God's power and immortality, principally as a means of "encouraging" and "consoling" his protégé (*Hom. 2 Tim.*, NPNF1 13.480). Tertullian had similarly cited 2 Timothy 1:7–8 in order to buck up those likely to face martyrdom, providing a certain comfort in claiming that "we suffer with bravery from love of God and with a sound mind, when we suffer on account of innocence" (*Scorpiace* 13, 2004: 133). Calvin understands a minister's fear to be part of the Pastor's focus in this passage. The goal is to engage in a constant struggle with, and consistently overcome, by the grace of God, the weaknesses to which ministers are prone (Calvin 1964: 294).

Theological Speculation: God's Plan (1:9–10; 4:1, 8; 1 Tim. 6:14; Titus 1:2; 3:4–5)

These important verses have contributed to discussions of Christ's divine preexistence, the meaning of his appearance in time, and, perhaps most significantly, predestination – none of which concepts are entirely extricable

Figure 4   A "spirit of power"? Detail from a twelfth century French Bible, Monastery of Saint-André-au-Bois. Opening of 2 Timothy. *Source*: Bibliothèque Municipale de Boulogne-sur-Mer

from the others. God, who "called us with a holy calling" (v. 9), is here, as in 1 Timothy 1:1, described as a savior, as is Christ Jesus (v. 10). And Jesus, in his epiphany, his "appearing," which in the Pastorals can refer both to the second coming and to the earthly ministry (D-C 1972: 105; Young 1994: 63–64), has made manifest that grace which was his (and at least potentially ours) "before the ages began" (v. 10). This short "theological hymn" (Collins 2002: 199) concludes with the remark that Jesus "abolished death and brought immortality to light through the gospel" (v. 10). Towner suggests, in a brief paraphrase, that "through the gospel" means "[t]hrough Christ" (2006: 472), not through the text we are reading. Knight, while maintaining a distinction between the event and its proclamation, claims that the Pastor has effectively "fused" these "two horizons" (1992: 376). Perhaps it is useful to note in this regard that epiphany theologies have, historically, been derived from events in history and from the reporting of those events in texts (D-C 1972: 104).

Saved, not according to our works (v. 9a–b)

The Pastor, in speaking of the priority of God's "purpose and grace" over "our works" (v. 9), provides key support for the Augustinian/Calvinist doctrines of predestination, unmerited grace, and so on. Quite early on, in fact, the idea that God had chosen for salvation a certain elect group was given voice by Origen, who reads Christ's appearing as a manifestation "to each one of those who are perfect," an epiphany "which enlightens the reason in the true knowledge of things." These perfect ones, however, can reach out in an ameliorative gesture and offer healing to others considered wicked, binding their "wounds by His word, and . . . apply[ing] to the soul, festering amid evils, the drugs obtained from the word . . . which are analogous to the wine and oil, and plasters, and other healing appliances which belong to the art of medicine" (*C. Cels.* 3.61, ANF 4.488; cf. 2 Tim. 2:25). Many readers down the centuries have heard just such a promising tone in this text. Erasmus, paraphrasing the Pastor, feels that a "way" to immortality is "opened . . . through the preaching of the gospel which promises the same reward [i.e., immortality] to those who imitate the cross of Christ" (1993: 42). That is, despite the apparent exclusivity of our verse, one can choose one's own salvation, at least to some extent. And within Protestantism, interpreters such as John Wesley will insist that the "holy calling" of this verse "claims us *all* for God" (*Explanatory Notes* 1850: 550, italics added).

It is the Augustinian/Calvinist perspective, however, that really claims this material as its own. For Augustine, Paul himself is the perfect example of God's unmerited grace. After all, he was a persecutor of Christians, a blasphemer (1 Tim. 1:13), even a slave "to various passions and pleasures, passing [his] days in malice and envy" (cf. Titus 3:3). "Nothing, to be sure, but punishment was due to such a course of evil desert," Augustine exclaims. Yet, God, who "returns good for evil by his grace," saved "Paul" despite his merits (*Gr. et lib. arb.* 12, NPNF1 5.449). And when one is saved, "called according to the purpose," then one can never be lost, for God cannot be mistaken in his purposes, cannot be "overcome by human sin" (*Corrept.* 14, NPNF1 5.477). Indeed, God will always be correct in his judgment of human agents, Augustine writes in a reading of Titus 3:5, because "works proceed from faith, and not faith from works. Therefore it is from Him that we have works of righteousness, from whom comes also faith itself" (*De gr. et lib. arb.* 17, NPNF1 5.451).

Calvin cites this passage much more frequently, but interprets it in essentially the same way. Calvin himself calls the doctrine of predestination a *decretum horribile*. It relies upon scriptural evidence for both the moral decrepitude of humankind (after the Fall) and the necessity of grace for salvation. One can see the basic logic at work in this passage from the *Institutes of the Christian Religion*:

> It is truly wonderful that man, condemned to such disgrace, dares still assume that he has anything left [in himself, for the good]. Let us therefore admit . . . that the Lord "called us with a holy calling, not according to our works, but according to his own purpose and . . . grace," and that "the generosity and love of God our Savior was manifested toward us, for he saved us, not because of deeds done by us in righteousness, but on account of his own mercy he saved us." . . . By this confession we deprive man of all righteousness, even to the slightest particle. (3.14.5, 1960: 1.772)

Recent scholarship on Calvin, however, tends to stress what Calvin saw as positive in his theology of predestination, which he never quite claims to understand in any event (see, for example, Hesselink 2004: 83–84). The vision of grace without works does not become quite as optimistic as it does in Erasmus or Wesley; still we can find Calvin reading 2 Timothy 1:9 in moods of mildly joyous affirmation: "if we have faith in the Scriptures – which expressly proclaim that in Christ the grace and gentleness of the Lord have fully appeared . . . – let us not doubt that the Heavenly Father's clemency flows forth . . . rather than that it is cut off or curtailed" (4.1.26, 1960: 2.1038–39). Isaac Watts, in a hymn that ends, in fact, with the word "joy," similarly incorporates our text into a hopeful vision of election:

> Not for our duties, or deserts,
> But of his own abounding grace,
> He works salvation in our hearts,
> And forms a people for his praise.
>
> 'Twas his own purpose that begun
> To rescue rebels doomed to die;
> He gave us grace in Christ his Son,
> Before he spread the starry sky.
> (Hymn 137, 1856: 361)

It may be difficult to imagine how one could sustain an alternative reading of these verses (2 Tim. 1:9; Titus 3:5), or to square them with 1 Timothy 2:4 and 4:10, both of which state plainly that God saves, or wants to save, all people.

However, nineteenth century Liverpudlian minister David Thom makes an effort to appropriate for Universalist theology the Calvinist import of our text. If God is both perfectly just and perfectly merciful, he argues, then logically all humans must suffer the punishment they deserve, and yet all must be saved – or, all must be granted the perfect mercy they do not deserve. In his reading of v. 5, which is curiously at home with the doctrine of imputed justification, Thom takes the contrastive "but" to mark a very real dichotomy between justice and mercy. The idea of "works of righteousness," is a matter of justice, and thus does not involve salvation; instead, it is "according to his mercy, that God saves us" (*The Assurance of Faith* 1833: 2.65). Hence there is no place in this passage for a theory of predestination according to which only some are saved, for God's perfect mercy requires the granting, universally, of eternal life.

Grace, given before, now revealed (v. 9c)

There is another dimension to this text's role in soteriological debates. The idea that "grace was given to us in Christ Jesus before the ages began, but . . . has [only] now been revealed through the appearing of our Savior" has been a problem for many, as it seems to suggest both that grace has always been available, and that it is activated, as it were, only after Christ appears in the world. Irenaeus seems to have 2 Timothy 1:9–10 in mind when he comments upon the apparent inefficacy of God's plan for human salvation prior to the incarnation: "as long as incorruptability was invisible and unrevealed, it did not help us, but He became visible so that we might fully participate in incorruption" (*Preaching of the Apostles* 30, 1987: 47). Others in the tradition have also worried about those who died prior to Christ's appearing. Or, as Calvin puts it, was "all this . . . hidden from the fathers who lived under the Law" (1964: 297)? Augustine, reflecting upon Ezekiel 36:23–29, answers this concern by arguing that a "spiritual Israel," the church, the salvation of the elect, is and has always been a part of God's divine plan. Thus "what the fathers believed would be given in its own time was to them, on account of the unchangeableness of the promise and purpose, the same as if it were already given; just as the apostle, writing to Timothy, speaks of the grace which is given to the saints" (*De doc. Chr.* 3.34, NPNF1 2.571; cf. Calvin 1964: 297). But Thomas Hobbes supposes, since immortality comes "to light through the gospel" (v. 10), that "before the Gospel of Christ, nothing was immortal but God" (1994: 4.351).

Just as the promise of salvation precedes the incarnation, according to our text, so too does Christ himself seem to preexist creation. Indeed, Athanasius assumes that the Pastor is, in this verse, actually interpreting the preexistence language of Proverbs 8 (*Orat. cont. Ar.* 2.22, NPNF2 4.389), according to which Wisdom was "set up at the first, before the beginning of the earth" (v. 23, NRSV). Christ the savior can grant salvation to all, throughout history, because, as Matthew Henry comments, he "had lain in the bosom of the Father from eternity, and was perfectly apprised of all his gracious purposes" (1721–25: 316).

"Paul" (1:13–18; 4:11, 19)

The sound teaching, a technical term for the pattern, or even "rough sketch" (Hanson 1982: 125), of the gospel message transmitted by the Pastor to his communities, is frequently alluded to in these letters (see the discussion of "deposit" at 1 Tim. 6:20; cf. 1 Tim. 1:10; 4:6; 6:3; Titus 1:9; 2:1), but is never – aside from what can be gleaned from the content of the letters themselves – fully explained. The word translated here as "sound" literally means healthy, hygienic, which leads Towner to the following polemical contrast: the Pastor's message is "positively health-producing," whereas "the opponents' . . . doctrines are infectious, diseased, and capable of destroying the spiritual health of those who come under their influence" (2006: 131), a contrast restated, gruesomely as we shall see, in 2 Timothy 2:17. The Pastor doesn't often mention the Holy Spirit (see Titus 3:5). Here the Spirit may be invoked as part of the continuing recollection of Timothy's ordination, and of the gifts mentioned in vv. 6–7 (Towner 2006: 479). At the end of this section, as at the end of 1 Timothy 1, we read of former coworkers who have "turned away from" "Paul." The sole exception is Onesiphorus, who "often refreshed" "Paul," seeking him out in Rome, unashamed of his "chain" (v. 16). Onesiphorus plays a larger role in the apocryphal *Acts of Paul*, where he is also an exemplary helper of the apostles. Donelson, suspicious of what he calls the unusually "excessive praises lavished upon Onesiphorus," thinks it possible that if the Pastor is writing about his contemporary moment, rather than the Pauline past, he may be "flattering and vindicating to his readers some of their contemporaries, perhaps even himself" (1986: 60). Beyond his specific role as a character in the Paul story, Onesiphorus has played a minor role in doctrinal controversies. Both because of the Pastor's reference to "that day" (v. 18) and because, at 4:19, "Paul" sends his greetings to "the household of Onesiphorus," but not to the man himself, readers have frequently assumed that Onesiphorus was dead when this letter was written (Bassler 1996: 137). If this is the case, Collins claims, then "the prayer of verse 18 [is] one of the earliest examples of Christian prayer for the dead" (2002: 217).

Standard of sound teaching (v. 13)

Timothy is to hold to this standard or pattern, and Theodoret understands this to mean that Timothy is to imitate "Paul" as he would "imitate the painters . . . and as they take note of originals, painting copies of them with precision, so too keep as a kind of original the teaching given by me about faith and love" (*Comm. in 1 Tim.*, 2001: 2.239). For Chrysostom, on the other hand, "Paul" is the artist, and he explains to Timothy that "I have impressed on thee the image of virtue, fixing in thy soul a sort of rule, and model, and outline of all things pleasing to God" (*Hom. 1 Tim.*, NPNF1 13.484).

The Holy Spirit and the Lord (vv. 14, 18)

For Chrysostom, however, "Paul" goes on to refer to the Holy Spirit because no one can hold to the pattern, can "guard the good treasure," by virtue of their intentions or strength of character alone. This is "[b]ecause there are many robbers, and thick darkness, and the devil still at hand to plot against us; and we know not what is the hour, what the occasion for him to set upon us. How then, he means, shall we be sufficient for the keeping of them? 'By the Holy Ghost'; that is if we have the Spirit with us, if we do not expel grace, He will stand by us" (*Hom. 1 Tim.*, NPNF1 13.484).

For some early readers in the tradition, this reference to the Spirit, especially when it is linked to v. 18's unusual allusion to two Lords ("may the Lord grant that he will find mercy from the Lord"), helps to affirm the economy of the Trinitarian Godhead. This is not to say that one of the Lords in v. 18 is necessarily understood to be the Spirit. Interpreters like Chrysostom have tended to think, instead, that the Pastor has Christ and God in view here (*Hom. 1 Tim.*, NPNF1 13.485; Hanson 1982: 127). Chrysostom, nevertheless, is concerned to undermine Marcionite readings, which apparently saw this verse as endorsing a ditheism even Marcion would have considered unchristian (Marcion himself either excluded, or used a collection of Paul's letters which never incorporated, the Pastoral Epistles; see Gamble 2006: 208–10). On the contrary, Chrysostom proposes, the two references to Lord in this verse mean that the Father and the Son are united in one substance. The same logic is at work in Ambrose as well, who reads our text alongside a passage from Genesis:

> Moses called Him One, and yet also relates that the Lord rained down fire from the Lord [Gen. 19:24]. The Apostle, too, says: "The Lord grant unto him to find mercy of the Lord." The Lord rains down from the Lord; the Lord grants mercy

from the Lord. The Lord is neither divided when He rains from the Lord, nor is there a separation when He grants mercy from the Lord, but in each case the oneness of the Lordship is expressed. . . . So, as we do not say that there are two Lords, when we so style both the Father and the Son, so, too, we do not say that there are three Lords, when we confess the Spirit to be Lord. (*De spir. sanct.* 3.15, NPNF2 10.150)

Basil, also in the context of a discussion of the Spirit's Trinitarian status, reads 1:14 specifically in terms of what he sees as the privilege of certain individuals in their relationship to the third member of the Trinity. For ordinary believers, he says, it is not exactly appropriate to claim to be invested by the Spirit when worshiping, because the Spirit in fact produces in us that capacity for praise in the first place. However, "to a Paul it is becoming to say 'I think also that I have the Spirit of God' [1 Cor. 7:40], and again, 'that good thing which was committed to thee keep by the Holy Ghost which dwelleth in us'" (*De spir. sanct.* 26, NPNF2 8.39). Such men as Paul, and Daniel, are virtuous enough to claim this for themselves without seeming presumptuous in the least.

Onesiphorus (v. 16)

The Pastor's praise of Onesiphorus may seem lavish to Donelson (see above), but among some readers, the praise was not lavish enough. Theodore L. Cuyler, a prominent nineteenth century Presbyterian minister of Brooklyn, complains about the lack of moral courage in American Christianity. He looks to Onesiphorus as his model, writing, in the inspirational rhetoric of the day, "of that noble piece of manhood" who ought to be considered "immortal" despite his all-too-brief presence in the Pastorals. As "a faithful friend in all weathers . . . Onesiphorus is a lesson to us in these days," Cuyler writes. If only we had more men like him now, the world would be a different place. "If Onesiphorus were a member of an American church," he would side with those who, like Paul, spoke the unpopular but "plain pungent truth." Paraphrasing the Pastor, albeit by eliminating the eschatological hint at v. 18, Cuyler concludes his essay with a prayer of his own: "May the Lord multiply in these days 'the house of Onesiphorus'" ("Brave Onesiphorus – A Talk for The Times," 1898: 4).

Assuming that Onesiphorus has died, Protestant readers, generally opposed to the Catholic belief in Purgatory and the practice of praying for the dead there, have often drawn upon this text in support of their perspectives. Many, though, like Luther (*Works* 52.180), believing that the doctrine of Purgatory has no biblical warrant, nevertheless are willing to allow that prayers for the dead are still harmless, essentially a sign of the generosity of one's spirit. At most, one can say, with David Blondel, that one's prayers for the dead may contribute somehow to the perfection of their ultimate blessedness, even though souls can only be saved by God's "Mercy, which Onesiphorus, and all the rest of the Elect shall finde, when that day [i.e., the day of final judgment] comes" (Blondel 1661: 264).

"Paul" now reminds Timothy of what he has learned. He continues to warn him of the difficulties he is likely to face, but also indicates that there will be a reward for those who "endure." As he does elsewhere in these letters, the Pastor castigates his opponents and their teachings. However, he strikes a conciliatory note in the last third of the chapter, seeming to suggest that the church is a big enough tent for all comers.

The Church: Pauline Succession (2:1–2)

The deposit Timothy is to guard is also to be passed on by him "to faithful people who will be able to teach others as well." Dibelius and Conzelmann

The Pastoral Epistles Through the Centuries, First Edition. Jay Twomey.
© 2009 by Jay Twomey. Published 2020 by John Wiley & Sons Ltd.

(1972: 108), Hanson (1982: 128), and most other commentators do not believe that this verse envisions a line of apostolic succession. The doctrine of succession develops in response to authoritative claims made upon the tradition by "heretics"; for "if it was the case that a doctrine could be validated by the claim that it derived, by succession, from a secret or esoteric tradition handed down by Jesus to his disciples, then any doctrine at all could be validated in this way" (Minns 2006: 269). In Davies' view, the evidence against a Pastoral doctrine of succession is that one would expect the Pastor to insist upon uniformity in transmission, so that an endless chain of delegates might be in constant possession of exactly the same message, across the ages. What one finds instead is an invitation, she argues, to put "the teaching into practice" in ways that are bound to be idiosyncratic (1996: 68). If this is so then perhaps 2 Timothy deserves to be considered the most doctrinally and theologically flexible of these letters (Bassler 1996: 156–57).

Entrust to faithful people (v. 2)

Readers in the tradition, however, have much more frequently assumed that 2 Timothy 2:2 is something of a charge to Timothy to think carefully about his duties because he is indeed a key link in what is to be a much greater chain. Irenaeus traces the line of succession through 2 Timothy when he explains that "[t]he blessed apostles, then, having founded and built up the Church, committed into the hands of Linus the office of the episcopate. Of this Linus, Paul makes mention in the Epistles to Timothy [2 Tim. 4:21]. To him succeeded Anacletus; and after him, in the third place from the apostles, Clement was allotted the bishopric" (AH 3.3.3, ANF 1.416). This same Clement is said to have written a letter which endorses, although without citing the Pastorals, a belief in succession as well (*1 Clement* 42, 44).

In order to protect what the orthodox considered the truth of the gospel, they had first of all to establish a lineage traceable back to Jesus himself. And secondly they had to show that the teachings propagated by that lineage are public and verifiable, that is, not esoteric or limited to a privileged few. Tertullian cites this verse (as well as 1 Tim. 6:20, 2 Tim. 1:14) in his *Prescription Against Heretics* to insist upon the publicity of the gospel:

> [T]here is no mysterious hint darkly suggested in this expression about (some) far-fetched doctrine, but that a warning is rather given against receiving any other (doctrine) than that which Timothy had heard from himself, as I take it publicly: "Before many witnesses" is his phrase. Now, if they refuse to allow that the church is meant by these "many witnesses," it matters nothing, since

nothing could have been secret which was produced "before many witnesses."
(25, ANF 3.255)

Tertullian feels confident of his demonstration that "this doctrine of ours . . . has
its origin in the tradition of the apostles," which is guaranteed by God, and that,
therefore, "all other doctrines . . . *ipso facto* proceed from falsehood" (252).
Aquinas too combats arguments that a secret tradition developed within
the church alongside publicly known Christian teachings, and understands
"through many witnesses" to mean both "though the law and the prophets"
and "through the apostles" (Thomas Aquinas 2007: 110). Calvin, less invested
in the Catholic idea of succession, nevertheless ascribes to "Paul" a desire to
secure, permanently, the specific content of his ministry for future generations.
This apparently had not been done effectively in the church as a whole, Calvin
notes: "we see what Satan accomplished a little after the death of the apostles,
for, as though there had been no preaching for many centuries, he raised up
innumerable madnesses which in their monstrous absurdity outdid the super-
stitions of all the Gentiles" (1964: 306). "Paul," however (and would one expect
anything less from a figure so important to the Reformers?), could see such
disasters looming on the horizon, and this is why he here takes his precautions
(ibid.). The Catholic bloggers who have taken it upon themselves to debunk
Dan Brown's 2003 bestseller *The Da Vinci Code* will also allude to 2 Timothy
2:2 in proving that the church has no secret, or politically (or Satanically)
twisted, tradition (see The Da Vinci Code Fraud website, for example).

This is not to say, however, that even proponents of the publicly and apos-
tolically attested gospel haven't also wanted to limit the availability of its
content to some degree. The Pastor wants Timothy to seek out "faithful people,"
and more specifically those who "will be able to teach others." This might mean,
as Hippolytus conjectured, that "the blessed (apostle) delivered these things
with a pious caution, which," even though they "could be easily known by all,"
required the proper faith to be understood, a faith sorely lacking in many. We
risk great "danger," he argues, "if, rashly and without thought, we commit the
revelations of God to profane and unworthy men" (*Treatise on Christ and
Antichrist* 1, ANF 5.204). Origen feels that among the things entrusted to a few,
select men, like Timothy, would most certainly have been the "ineffable mysteries" of Paul's extra-worldly journey from 2 Corinthians 12:1–5 (*Homilies on
Joshua* 23.4, FC 105.202–03). One Hierotheus, whom Pseudo-Dionysius claims
as his teacher, is said (by his student) to have achieved insights into the divine
not unlike the Paul of 2 Corinthians. And even though Pseudo-Dionysius
knows that he falls "very short of that understanding which the divine men
possessed concerning heavenly truths," still he passes along the teachings of his
master at least in part because "Paul" in 2 Timothy 2:2 commands us to learn

what we can, "and to share these treasures generously with others" (*De div. nom.* 3.3, 1987: 71). In the *Summa Theologica*, Thomas Aquinas allows an even greater leeway for secrecy of a special kind. Jesus himself sometimes taught in enigmatic parables when he felt the crowds were insufficiently capable of grasping his message. "Nevertheless," Aquinas explains, "our Lord expounded the open and unveiled truth of these parables to His disciples, so that they might hand it down to others worthy of it" (TP Q[42] A[3]).

The Church: Christian Soldiers (2:3–7)

The imaginative world of, or rather behind, the Pastoral Epistles has entered the consciousness and language of Anglo-American culture, via the King James Version, in expressions such as "fight the good fight" (1 Tim. 6:12; see commentary at 2 Tim. 4:7) and "the root of all evil" (1 Tim. 6:10). The analogies in 2:3–6, comparing the Christian to a soldier, athlete, and farmer, while less broadly known, at least in the language specific to the Pastorals, have been productive of a great deal of creative reflection through the centuries. Modern commentators tend to stress that the Pastor's emphasis on suffering (e.g., 1:8; 4:6) continues here, that "Paul" is developing the motifs of suffering, and also the reward for patient endurance, that characterize the rest of this testamentary letter. While these issues certainly pertain to the interpretation of these verses through the centuries, they also reflect the effort to understand the letter's overall coherence and integrity. In his study of the historical significance of the motif of the Christian soldier, *Militia Christi*, Harnack explains how these verses (as well as other New Testament parallels, such as Eph. 6:11, 13), independent of their literary context in the letter, have been received. The idea of 2 Timothy 2:3, as the tradition has understood it, is that:

> Above the Catholic priesthood and above the Catholic orders of monks in all the centuries stand the words 'No soldier entangles himself in civilian pursuits.' They have often become a declaration of war. Above all else, however, they have caused the 'civilian' life and the 'civilian' calling to appear to be of inferior value . . . Here we have two military axioms which were accepted in earliest Christianity: the Christian missionary and teacher gets his living from others and does not involve himself in 'civilian' pursuits. They are polar in their effect and therefore imply a whole class structure. (1981: 38–39)

Harnack's program was to show that earliest Christianity was essentially pacifist, but that its militaristic metaphors for spirituality helped, especially after its development into a state religion under Constantine, to transform it into militarized social order. Scholars have debated the merits of this view, with some arguing that there is, in fact, precious little evidence for an actual pacifism early on, even in the writings of figures like Tertullian and Origen who forbade Christians military service (see Helgeland 1974).

Like a good soldier (v. 3)

For our purposes, of course, deciding the historical question is less urgent than surveying the interpretive rhetoric. There are two relatively interconnected, but still distinguishable trajectories that readings of this verse take through the centuries. The first, generally emphasizing v. 3, endorses a literal, or an aggressively figurative, or at least an uncomplicatedly accepting understanding of the Pastor's soldier imagery.

Cyprian can speak of those undergoing martyrdom in the most enthusiastic, and militaristic, of ways:

> The scourge, often repeated with all its rage, could not conquer invincible faith, even although the membrane which enclosed the entrails were broken, and it was no longer the limbs but the wounds of the servants of God that were tortured. Blood was flowing which might quench the blaze of persecution, which might subdue the flames of Gehenna with its glorious gore. Oh, what a spectacle was that to the Lord, – how sublime, how great, how acceptable to the eyes of God in the allegiance and devotion of His soldiers! (*Epistle* 8, ANF 5.288)

These soldiers, needless to say, are not taking up arms against worldly enemies but are rather, as the Pastor has advised Timothy to do, "shar[ing] in the suffering" of Christ. Chrysostom, who foregrounds the figurative nature of the Pastor's language, interprets "soldier of Christ" as one who can be bound (2 Tim. 2:9) and yet still be effective, since the battles in which he engages are those of the word (*Hom. 1 Tim.*, NPNF1 13.488–89). As usual, Chrysostom assumes that "Paul" is partly interested in solacing Timothy despite the dangers facing him; and so he begins his commentary on these verses by extrapolating on the Pastor's analogy: "the Captain, who sees his General wounded and recovered again, is much encouraged. And thus it produces some consolation to the faithful . . . [f]or when Timothy heard, that he who possessed so great powers, who had conquered the whole world, is a prisoner, and afflicted, yet is not impatient . . . would not consider that it proceeded from human weakness, nor from the circumstance of his being a disciple, and inferior to Paul, since his teacher too suffered the like, but that all this happened from the natural course of things" (488). Although Augustine uses military analogies sporadically elsewhere (see *De nat. et grat.* 68, NPNF1 5.145; *Ep.* 99. NPNF1 1.411), he develops them at length in his *On the Work of Monks*. To the monastic life come those who, like soldiers, must battle against sin and temptation, striving to please Christ while remaining unencumbered by the affairs of the world. Similarly John Cassian, writing of the difficult trials monks face, not just in general, but even at certain hours of the day (the acedia one often suffers at noon, for instance), makes the most of the Pastor's martial imagery.

> [T]he wretched soul, embarrassed by such contrivances of the enemy, is disturbed, until, worn out by the spirit of accidie, as by some strong battering ram, it either learns to sink into slumber, or, driven out from the confinement of its cell, accustoms itself to seek for consolation under these attacks in visiting some brother, only to be afterwards weakened the more by this remedy which it seeks for the present. . . . and so the soldier of Christ becomes a runaway from His service, and a deserter, and "entangles himself in secular business," without at all pleasing Him to whom he engaged himself. (*Inst.* 10.3, NPNF2 11.267)

Despite the language used, however, Cassian's figurative appropriation of this text, like that of Chrysostom and Augustine, is far removed from any actual aggression. The focus is entirely upon how the soldier/monk fails in his duty by entangling himself in the world, that is, by seeking out the society of another religious, and even by going about to look for some refreshment, "for the mind of an idler cannot think of anything but food and the belly" (*Inst.* 10.6, NPNF2 11.268).

Stephen Coven, in his *The Militant Christian; or, The Good Soldier of Jesus Christ*, explores every possible tactical dimension of the Pastor's analogy; but his figurative reading is infused with a passion for combat. The prayers of the Christian soldier, for example, are likened to engines of war:

> Oh, What a Terrible Engine is this! able to affright, to astonish, and confound the Enemies of Christ! . . . . Christs Soldiers Engine is the most Terrible and Dreadful that is in all the World. This Engine will not only shoot Arrows, and great Stones; but Snares, Fire and Brimstone; Blood and Wrath, Plagues and Death, to all Irreconcilable Enemies of the Militant Church. (1669: 172)

Elsewhere in this meditation on 2 Timothy 2:3, Coven even issues orders like a drill sergeant, calling out "march" (31) and "as you were" (54). Coven, a Restoration nonconformist, naturally sees the Christian's enemies within the soul, in terms of Satanic influences, but also out in the larger political/religious arena, where one's failure to support a state-sanctioned polity led to serious social and political consequences.

Perhaps the most famously militaristic use of the idea of the soldier of Christ is the hymn "Onward Christian Soldiers," by Sabine Baring-Gould. Although the hymn does not cite from the Pastorals directly, the influence of 2 Timothy 2:3 is felt unmistakably in the first several verses:

> Onward, Christian soldiers,
> Marching as to war,
> With the cross of Jesus
> Going on before.
> Christ, the royal Master,
> Leads against the foe;
> Forward into battle,
> See, His banners go!
>
> (in *Hymns Ancient
> and Modern* 1904: 545)

In 1986 the United Methodist Church decided, temporarily, to drop "Onward, Christian Soldiers" from its hymnal as too militaristic – until the backlash from rank and file Methodists forced the Church to surrender, and keep the hymn after all ("Methodist Hymnal Committee Blasted" 1986).

The spirit of the Christian warrior is more complicated, although not actually rejected, in Gerard Manley Hopkins' poem "The Soldier." The soldier of the title is Christ himself, in fact, and not soldiers fighting in his name. Hopkins, who served as a military chaplain, wonders: "Why do we all, seeing of a soldier, bless him? bless / our redcoats, our tars? Both these being, the greater part, / but frail clay, nay but foul clay" (Hopkins 1986: 168). The reason, he suggests, is vanity, the desire to link oneself to the manliness of soldiers via a kind of patriotic projection. But Hopkins imagines Christ looking down on humanity, and surveying the acts of men. "Christ our King, He knows war, served this soldiering through." Christ doesn't seize upon acts of military valor, however, but instead, "seeing somewhere some man do[ing] all that man can do" exclaims: "O Christ-done deed! So God-made-flesh does too." Other writers associated both with the military and the ministry, such as Rick Bereit, have absolutely no qualms about endorsing the most literal reading of 2:3–4 possible. Bereit's 2002 book, *In His Service: A Guide to Christian Living in the Military*, reads "the soldier's aim is to please the enlisting officer" quite literally and unproblematically as advice for advancing up the military ranks (68).

Hopkins' contemporary, Christina Rossetti, draws upon the language of the King James Version in her poem "Endure Hardness" ("endure hardness as a good soldier of Jesus Christ," KJV), and yet removes the militaristic element from the Pastor's imagery altogether. In the poem it is not the Christian soldier who must "endure hardness," but the blackthorn:

> A cold wind stirs the blackthorn
> To burgeon and to blow,
> Besprinkling half-green hedges
> With flakes and sprays of snow.
>
> Thro' coldness and thro' keenness,
> Dear hearts, take comfort so:
> Somewhere or other doubtless
> These make the blackthorn blow.
>   (1979–90: 2.297)

Or rather, it is the reader, the "dear heart" of the second stanza who, knowing that the blackthorn is in blossom, can take hope in the cold harshness of late winter, and thus can endure until spring. Interestingly, the logic of the poem is not at all unlike the encouraging message of so many readings of 2 Timothy 2:3–4. If Paul can endure, if Christ can endure such suffering, such hardness, then so can we.

Entangled in everyday affairs (v. 4)

Of the two verses, and the two trajectories, we are considering in this section, v. 4 has produced the more non-militaristic readings. Many of these reflect a certain ambiguity with regard to the Pastor's military imagery, while others either neglect the analogy, or go so far as to reject the real-world implications of his soldiering altogether.

Augustine, for example, who like Chrysostom assumes that "Paul" is writing to Timothy in part to lend him moral support, imagines that if the latter is a "soldier of Christ," he is a weak-bodied one. Because of his infirmities (cf. 1 Tim. 5:23), Timothy is unable to engage in any effective manual labor; as a result, he is likely to "seek some business in which the stress of his mind would become entangled." Physical labor, according to Augustine, is not necessarily proscribed in our verse because a worker can, at least ideally, keep "the mind free." Other sorts of occupations, however, busy "the mind itself with cares of collecting money without the body's labor, as do either dealers, or bailiffs, or undertakers, for these with care of the mind conduct their business, not with their hands do work, and in that regard occupy their mind itself with solicitude of getting" (*De op. mon.* 16, NPNF1 3.511–12). "Paul" is simply making it clear to Timothy that he needs to avoid all such labor.

Aquinas agrees with Augustine that there are distinctions to be drawn among the variety of "everyday affairs" one can get entangled in. Generally, occupations in any sort of business are forbidden to "bishops and clerics" because "they unsettle the mind too much" (ST SS Q[40] A[2]). Or they do if one is primarily motivated by greed. It may be necessary, however, to engage even in commerce in order to assist others in need, and to that charitable end Thomas allows that "monks or clerics . . . with their superior's permission . . . may occupy themselves with due moderation in the administration and direction of secular business" (ST SS Q[187] A[2]; *pace* Cassian, who can treat even charitable work as a tempting distraction, cf. *Inst.* 10.2, NPNF2 11.267). Aquinas, intriguingly, so fully understands the Pastor's soldier analogy to be figurative that he actually cites it, without irony, as evidence that bishops and priests are not to fight in wars: "Now warlike pursuits are altogether incompatible with the duties of a bishop and a cleric . . . because . . . [they] are full of unrest, so that they hinder the mind very much from the contemplation of Divine things. . . . Wherefore just as commercial enterprises [motivated by private gain] are forbidden to clerics, because they unsettle the mind too much, so too are warlike pursuits, according to 2 Tim. 2:4." In this reading, "warlike pursuits" are the Pastor's "everyday affairs," and the solider is, in a very direct and uncomplicated way, nothing but a cleric (a precise inversion of Bereit's militaristic literalism). Thomas Aquinas, unlike many in the tradition, also argues that clerics should rather "shed their own blood for Christ" than take the life of another (ST SS Q[187] A[2]). Calvin, too, despite his sometime reputation as an advocate of theopolitical violence, takes the opportunity in his commentary to repudiate those for whom Christian warfare would mean "struggl[ing] fiercely with their adversaries." The task "Paul" sets Timothy here is patient endurance rather than "inflicting evil on others" (*Commentary* 1964: 306; cf. Pellerin 2003). Calvin seems to have in mind something along the lines of a Christian jihad, insofar as jihad is taken to mean, simply, a struggle, and more specifically a struggle with the forces within. Both ministers and ordinary Christians alike, he argues, are advised by "Paul," in these instructions to Timothy, to find and eliminate from within them "what keeps them from Christ, that our heavenly commander may have as much authority over us as any mortal man claims over the soldiers of the world who have pledged themselves to his service" (307). For Calvin, incidentally, "everyday affairs" were not necessarily financial in nature, but everything and anything that might conflict with service. Other readers also use the Pastor's counsel in contexts entirely removed from anything remotely martial. William Prynne, the seventeenth century Puritan, loosely adopting the form of a tragedy for his work attacking the theater (the 1,000-page screed entitled *Histrio-Mastix: The Players Scourge*) cites canon 14 of the ninth century Council of Mainz, which ordered that ministers and monks could not engage in such worldly affairs as dicing and hawking including, Prynne adds, "all Stage-playes, dancing, and scurrilous songs and musicke" (1633: 591). But whereas the conciliar document Prynne cites limits its restrictions to the clergy and religious, Prynne himself, not unlike Calvin of course, argues that what goes for Timothy, goes for everyone (570).

Some critical responses to v. 4 suggest that while certainly there are limits, still religious individuals, the clergy included, can tangle in the world to a significant extent. John Henry Newman, rebutting an argument about the apolitical nature of the clergy, comments that, while a clergyman really shouldn't be fully engaged in active political life, "it is absurd to say that the affairs of this world should not at all engage his attention. If so, this world is not a preparation for another" (*Tracts* 2 1969: 1). Newman goes on to list the possible political work of the clergy: the recognition of national sins, support for the poor and chastisement of the wealthy and powerful, and, most importantly for him in this context, the protection of the church from state interference. William L. Banks, an African-American minister, writing of the Civil Rights period, complains that "Some Negro ministers have become so involved in the civil rights struggle that perhaps they could be better called politicians, sociologists, religious humanists, or religious philosophers rather than preachers of the Gospel. They seem totally unaware that 'No man that warreth entangleth himself with the affairs of this life; that he may please him who hath chosen him to be a soldier [KJV]'" (in Cone 1993: 2.80). James Cone offers a short critique of this position, noting that "throughout the period of slavery and even after emancipation, Black clergy had fewer scruples than their White counterparts about entangling themselves with the 'affairs of this life.'" He adds the African American ministers have often been "pragmatic, hard-headed leaders," "not saintly hermits who withdrew from the world" (80).

"Paul": The Gospel (2:8–10)

The Pastor, writing as "Paul," frames his gospel with the themes of this letter, suffering and memory: "Remember Jesus Christ, raised from the dead, a descendant of David – that is my gospel, for which I suffer hardship" (vv. 8–9). There are similarities with credal statements found elsewhere in the New Testament, 1 Corinthians 15:1–4 for example, and especially Romans 1:3–4, which also links the resurrection to Jesus' Davidic heritage. 2 Timothy 2:8, however, does not mention Jesus' divine sonship, and it inverts the authentic Pauline text by referring to the resurrection before the descent from David. Modern commentators, often at a loss to explain both the formula and its idiosyncrasy in this context, usually assume that the Pastor is simply drawing upon traditional materials without really engaging with their theopolitical content. Because the Pastor seems relatively uninterested in Jesus' Davidic or messianic status elsewhere (but see v. 12, "reign with him"), it is also supposed that the formula "a descendant of David," literally "of the seed of David" (cf. Rom. 1:3; John 7:42), may function, indirectly but perhaps in tandem with 1 Timothy 2:5 and 3:16, to emphasize Jesus' humanity (Bassler 1996: 142; Collins 2002: 223). On the other hand, the Pastor need not mention David if this is his only goal, so perhaps some flavor, at least, of a messianic affirmation does remain (Towner 1989: 102).

Raised from the dead, a descendent of David (v. 8)

The majority of readers in the tradition have in fact been quite comfortable with what appears to modern readers as an ambiguity requiring decision. Most, like Augustine, simply take for granted that v. 8 means both that Jesus was fully human (C. *Faust.* 2.2, NPNF1 4.157) and that he was the Davidic messiah (*En. ps.* 78.36, NPNF1 8.379), choosing one or the other reading depending upon their polemical or contextual needs. The fact that the Pastor consistently condemns the use of genealogies, and yet in essence cites one here, has not gone without comment. Wesley's note on this verse, "this one genealogy attend to," is a gem of unintended irony (*Explanatory Notes* 1850: 551).

The word of God is not chained (v. 9)

Such, then, is "Paul's" gospel, for which he has been imprisoned. "But the word of God," he comments, "is not chained." For many readers this is evidence not only of "Paul's" indomitable spirit, but also the power of the word of God itself. Chrysostom, in a lively if mixed metaphor, compares the word both to a sunbeam and a bird in its essential freedom: "[f]or just as it is not possible to bind a sunbeam, or to shut it up within the house, so neither [is] the preaching of the word; and what was much more, the teacher was bound, and yet the word flew abroad; he inhabited the prison, and yet his doctrine rapidly winged its way every where throughout the world!" (*Hom. stat.* 16.12, NPNF1 9.450).

Theological Speculation: Divine Consistency (2:11–13; Titus 1:2)

Most of the traditional commentary on, and use of, this passage has arisen in response to vv. 11–13, the hymnic list of parallel clauses ending with "if we are

faithless, he remains faithful – for he cannot deny himself." The language of
v. 11, "if we be dead with him, we shall also live with him" (KJV), "expresses
the ultimate meaning of baptism" (Collins 2002: 227; cf. Origen *C. Cels.* 2.69,
ANF 4.459; Chrysostom, *Hom. 2 Tim.*, NPNF1 13.492). Catholic writings
cite this verse in support of other sacraments as well, such as the Eucharist
(Rahner, *On the Theology of Death*, 1973: 77) and the anointing of the sick (US
Catholic Church 1995: 417). Unlike the three clauses which precede it, the final
element in the hymn, v. 13b, includes an explanatory addendum. It also differs
from the previous clauses, and 12b especially (which it most closely resembles),
by providing for a somewhat inadequate, or confusing, divine response. Collins
calls it "ironic" (2002: 228), meaning in this context simply that 13b is the
opposite of what one might have expected. Dibelius and Conzelmann, broadening the focus, say quite bluntly that "the idea of v. 13 does not belong in the
context of 2 Tim. 2" (1972: 109). Bassler considers v. 13 to be, potentially, "in
complete contradiction to the message of the preceding line" (1996: 146). The
structural strangeness of the hymn, however, is less significant than the theological ambiguity of the last verse. Modern commentators agree that there are
at least two basic ways of understanding this faithfulness, be it Christ's or,
especially in light of Romans 3:3, God's (ibid.). In Hanson's pithy formulation,
that Christ remains faithful is either "a threat or a promise." If he is faithful to
justice, which requires punishment, then it is a threat. If, by contrast, he is
faithful to his church even when that church is suffering a plague of faithless
heretics, then it is a promise. Hanson concludes that "in view of the author's
[i.e., the Pastor's] admirable emphasis on the universal scope of God's love in
Christ, we should surely regard it as a promise" (1982: 132; cf. Bassler 1996:
147; Towner 2006: 514).

If we die, if we endure (vv. 11–12)

Those who suffer, whether from sickness or from other causes, have often
turned to this verse seeking solace. As Calvin remarks with vv. 11 and 12 in
mind: "who could fail to be stirred by this exhortation . . . since we shall have
such a happy deliverance from . . . our afflictions" (*Commentary* 1964: 310).
The language of endurance in v. 12 was adopted by Pope Leo XIII in a way
similar to Calvin's appreciative question, but with a rather focused political
project in mind. The 1891 anti-Socialist encyclical, *Rerum Novarum*, aims to
encourage the working masses to place their hopes for ease and freedom from
affliction in the future, when they will "reign" with Christ: "As for riches and
the other things which men call good and desirable, whether we have them in
abundance, or are lacking in them – so far as eternal happiness is concerned

– it makes no difference." The encyclical goes on to emphasize Christ's suffering, and declares that " '[i]f we suffer with Him, we shall also reign with Him.' Christ's labors and sufferings, accepted of His own free will, have marvelously sweetened all suffering and all labor" (in Carlen 1981: 2.246). Leo admits that the worker's life is a difficult one (242), it is true, but the solution he proposes, in the end, is that workers should embrace their difficulties, dutifully, and hope for the best.

He remains faithful (v. 13a)

Readers through the centuries have explored what Hanson (see above) calls the promise and threat of v. 13. Most pre-modern readers, however, like our modern commentators, share in the consensus that this text is a promise: despite the inexorable claims of justice, God will extend his mercy to the faithful. Aquinas understands that v. 13 can be construed as a menacing threat, but he counters that "God acts mercifully, not indeed by going against His justice, but by doing something more than justice; thus a man who pays another two hundred pieces of money, though owing him only one hundred, does nothing against justice, but acts liberally or mercifully. The case is the same with one who pardons an offence committed against him, for in remitting it he may be said to bestow a gift" (ST FP Q[21] A[3]). This is a rather generous view; and one might ask how such generosity is to be accounted for given Christ's "denial" of those who deny him, in the preceding verse. Kierkegaard notices the problem, but argues that there is a difference between denying and being unfaithful. You can be unfaithful without also denying Christ. "The one is the stern word, the other is the gentle word; so here we have the Law and the Gospel; but both words are the truth." But since he is speaking to Christian believers, he knows that outright denial is but a minimal possibility. Thus "surely it is the latter word which is pre-eminently appropriate for us to dwell upon today. We allow the dreadful aspect to pass unnoticed, not as though it were irrelevant to us; oh no, so long as he lives no man is saved in such a way that it would not be possible for him to be lost" ("He Abideth Faithful," 1961: 289).

He cannot deny himself (v. 13b)

While this claim serves to clarify Christ's fidelity, it has often been taken alone for its theological, indeed philosophical, importance. And because the theologeme is expressed negatively, readers have been especially interested in understanding how a negative attribute can be positively expressed for a theology of divine omnipotence. Augustine believes that the problem is merely apparent, that in fact omnipotence is easily and frequently delimited by negatives:

> God is Almighty, and yet, though Almighty, He cannot die, cannot be deceived, cannot lie; and, as the Apostle says, "cannot deny Himself." How many things that He cannot do, and yet is Almighty! yea therefore is Almighty, because He cannot do these things. (*De symb. cat.* 2, NPNF1 3.369)

Theodoret covers similar ground in his third *Dialogue*, "The Impassible," except he seems more comfortable than Augustine with certain incapacities of the divine. He argues, for instance, that God's inability to sin, his inability to cease to exist "is proof not of weakness, but of infinite power," whereas "to be able [to do these things] would certainly be proof not of power but of impotence." Therefore one is to understand the "cannot" of this verse as "indicative of infinite power, for even though all men deny Him He says God is Himself, and cannot exist otherwise than in His own nature, for His being is indestructible. . . . [T]he impossibility of change for the worse proves infinity of power (NPNF2 3.219–20; cf. Titus 1:2, echoed in *1 Clement* 27, ANF 1.12). In full agreement, Pseudo-Dionysius mocks anyone who would even consider deriving God's weakness from 2 Timothy 2:13. Such a person is like "one of those incompetent athletes who is under the illusion that his competitor is weak. He judges him by his own standards, and so he misses him each time as he sends a mighty blow at his shadow" (1987: 112).

The tenet that God "cannot deny himself" has also been useful within Calvinism. Calvin, almost echoing Pseudo-Dionysius, writes that this verse denies "ungodly apostates" the hope that otherwise would "soothe" them, namely that Christ is as "double-faced and variable" as they are (1964: 311). In the view of nineteenth century American Calvinists, the heirs of Jonathan Edwards, God's utter unchangeability in matters of election does not lead to the "fatalism" that an Arminian would fear (Jackson 1998: 236). Morality simply does not depend upon the will. Nevertheless, in the words of one of Edwards' nineteenth century readers, moral people are still moral:

> The most perfect moral agents in being are destitute of this property in question [i.e., free will] which is asserted to be requisite to moral agency. Such is God. . . . He cannot deny Himself. . . . The elect angels can never become the subjects of sinful choices. Regenerate men, who are kept by the power of God through faith unto salvation, cannot prevailingly sin, or utterly fall away. Are they not moral agents? Are they the less excellent and praiseworthy, for being so inflexible holy,

that they cannot become the prey of sin and Satan? ("The Power of Contrary Choice," 1840: 544)

For the Neo-Edwardseans (as for Calvin), the stark clarity of a binary opposition between promise and threat is highlighted when the inability of the divine to deny itself, to change its mind, becomes the incapacity of believers and nonbelievers alike either to risk or to salvage their fates. His God is still sovereign, of course, but "destitute" of a certain freedom he is also vaguely machinic. The sense of the mechanical arising from the contemplation of God's un(self-)deniability comes to the fore in a sermon by R. Winter Hamilton, a nineteenth century Congregationalist from Leeds. He preaches, in this sermon on the atonement, that God's self-sacrifice wasn't a change in the divine plan, a response to a fallen world. Rather the cross was his decision from all eternity, an essential component of "[t]he unfailing resolve, the calm majesty" of his will. This resolve, which facilitates the salvation or damnation of individuals, is described almost as one would describe natural processes, or laws: "The splendor of his glory never trembles with a varying light, nor shoots forth a wavering effulgence. . . . His moral perfections, with the respect due to them as the standards of all happiness in the universe – his moral rules, with the necessity of enforcing all their original exactitude to make them not only 'just' but 'good' – these are the grounds of his conduct. He cannot deny himself. His will is but the activity of his nature, and that activity can only move in the line of eternal right" ("Atonement," 1864: 227–28).

Up to now we have considered v. 13b with regard to issues of particular theological import. The final two examples, while still theologically relevant, are given to show the complex, real-world effects reflection upon this verse can have. In 1521, Martin Luther wrote his "On Monastic Vows," which argues against celibacy and was instrumental in the decision to release monks and nuns from their vows. Luther deploys our text as a wedge to separate the religious from the institutions to which they had pledged themselves. He argues, on the basis of the single and eternal constancy of the divine, that God's commandments always trump any human instruments and decisions. Monks and nuns, for instance, have taken a vow which removes them from their families, and isolates them from the world at large. But, Luther asserts:

[Y]ou cannot take vows which deny obedience to parents and service to neighbor; for God has commanded obedience to parents and service to neighbor. Therefore with absolute confidence you should so interpret your vow that when your parent or neighbor has need of you, you may be absolutely certain on divine authority that you need keep your vow no longer. . . . The monastic vow ought to be efficacious for the commandments of God. . . . Have no doubt about it,

God himself cannot demand a vow of you or recognize a deed that is contrary
to a single iota of his commandment. He is faithful and true; he cannot deny
himself. (*Works* 44.331)

Luther's plain message is that the monastic life is a denial of God. Interestingly,
this was the argument Luther's father had used to try to prevent his son from
entering the monastery in the first place years before (Marius 1999: 311).

The second example comes from the early twentieth century poet George
Barlow, whose appropriation of the Pastor's theology for erotic purposes is
gentle and yet charged with near-scandalous humor. The poem is entitled
A Poet's Gethsemane. In the first section, we read of a young man whose love
has abandoned him and written him, cruelly, that she had decided to marry
another. The young man has had a vision, though, or rather a series of them,
in which his love appears in his bedroom each night for six nights in a row,
and sleeps with him. This experience is a promising one, and it fires the young
man's hopes:

> That was the Vision. – I believed
> The living God had sent it me:
> With joyous full heart I received
> Its message of great ecstasy.
> She was my wife. So God had said,
> Who sent her angel to my bed.
>
> And, now that God had done this thing,
> Could any hold that God would lie?
> That he would steal my wife, and fling
> Deep into hell irrevocably
> The soul who had believed his word?
> Could God deny himself? Absurd!
>   (1902–14: 6.80–81)

When, on the basis of this reasoning, he goes to the woman's house and is
rebuffed, he finds it theologically shattering "that this should be / The end of
all God's pageantry!" Most ironically, however, the young man's vision of divine
consistency is not just negated, but entirely inverted, as the woman herself, in
a note she writes her former lover, now becomes the threatening divine, dashing
the promise entirely:

> "Leave me," she said, "and be a man:
> Yes, leave me and all thought of me.
> I do not change: I never can."
>   (83)

The Opponents (2:14–18)

The Pastor asks Timothy to "remind them," the congregation, or perhaps leaders of the congregation, in Ephesus, of the gospel message and the hymn just discussed. He then advises him to present himself as a "worker," like Paul and his associates, who is both "unashamed" and capable of "rightly dividing the word of truth" (v. 15, KJV). The metaphor, translating a word that literally means "to cut straight," has been interpreted as a reference to plowing, to the sharing of food at a meal, to masonry (Towner 2006: 521–22 n. 32). The image may depend upon similar language in the wisdom literature, and here it works in consonance with the warnings against false teachers to mean something like "hold to the standard of sound teaching" (1:13).

Rightly explaining the word of truth (v. 15)

"Rightly dividing," for readers through the centuries, has simply meant "rightly explaining" (NRSV), as when Augustine remembers the perspicacity of Ambrose's preaching in his *Confessions* (6.4, NPNF1 1.91). Some, however, have taken up the metaphor itself with a certain vigor. In Chrysostom's interpretation, Timothy is urged to "cut away what is spurious, with much vehemence assail it, and extirpate it. With the sword of the Spirit cut off from your preaching . . . whatever is superfluous and foreign to it" (*Hom. 2 Tim.*, NPNF1 13.493; cf. Erasmus *Paraphrases* 1993: 46). The King James translation of this verse (see also Tyndale's version), emphasizing as it does the idea of division, has produced its own conceptual possibilities. For Cyrus Scofield, editor of the *Scofield Reference Bible*, an essential resource for Dispensationalist thought, the idea that there are divisions in the truth seems evident even from the way "Paul" addresses Timothy:

> In 2 Timothy 2 the believer is presented in seven characters. He is called a son (verse 1), a soldier (verse 3), an athlete (verse 5), a husbandman (verse 6), a workman (verse 15), a vessel (verse 21), and a servant (verse 24).
>
> With each of these characters there is a well-suited exhortation. As a son, Timothy is exhorted to be strong in grace. Grace goes with sonship, just as law goes with servitude – as we learn from Galatians. Then, as a soldier, Timothy is exhorted to endure hardness and to avoid worldly entanglements; these are right elements of good soldiership. As a vessel, he is to be cleansed, separated; as a servant, gentle, patient, meek; and so of each of these seven aspects of his life as a Christian.

Scofield concludes, in this preface to a summary overview of the Bible, appropriately entitled *Rightly Dividing the Word of Truth*, that "the Word of truth, then, has right divisions, and it must be evident that, as one cannot be 'a workman that needeth not to be ashamed' without observing them, so any study of that Word which ignores those divisions must be in large measure profitless and confusing" (1957: 4). More commonly, "dividing the word of truth" is idiomatic for distinguishing *between* truth and falsehood (for example), and can be deployed with enormous flexibility. The speaker in Thomas Jordan's poem "Peccavi," written "to a vertuous Lady, who was vitiously solicited by a Gentleman whilst she was in her mourning," seems to have absorbed language similar to the Pastor's when he casually observes:

> It is a truth divided from all doubt,
> That ne'er a Nun'ry can keep Cupid out.
> (Jordan 1680: n.p.)

Their talk will spread like gangrene (v. 17)

It is essential that the truth be rightly divided because the word of false teachers like Hymenaeus and Philetus (1 Tim. 1:19–20), if unchecked, "will spread like gangrene," or "will eat as doth a canker" (KJV). Calvin provides a mini dissertation at this point in his commentary on the medical history of "gangrene" (1964: 314), but concludes, with modern commentators, that the specific term is less important than the idea of a disease which spreads, dangerously, into the otherwise healthy body of the community. How does this disease spread? Cyprian imagines the gangrene "creep[ing into] to the ears of the hearers" like a worm (*Ep.* 72.15, ANF 5.383), and Thomas Aquinas pictures the heretics "vomiting" their "deadly" matter into a discourse which initially seemed "true and profitable" (2007: 119). Just as the gangrene can spread throughout the Pastor's church, so too can it infect the tradition at any point in the future. This is the implicit premise of *Gangraena*, a work of heresiology by the Presbyterian Thomas Edwards, written in horror at the growth of religious toleration and independency in the period before the English Civil War. The first part of the book is subtitled: "a catalogue and discovery of many of the errors, heresies, blasphemies and pernicious practices of the sectaries of this time, vented and acted in England," during the 1640s. Edwards thinks of himself in the company of the religious greats, and even sounds something like an elderly Timothy when, in his preface, he pleads with mock humility that although he is certainly a lesser figure than "those learned Fathers, Augustine, Athanasius, and those first Reformers, Luther, Zuinglius, Calvin," still " '[t]is honour enough for me to be somewhat like to them in sufferings" (1646: xxi). Ann Hughes notes that the scholarship on *Gangraena* to date has been mostly sympathetic to those whom Edwards attacks, including especially John Milton, while the author himself has usually been "dismiss[ed] . . . as an intolerant, paranoid hysteric" (Hughes 2004: 3).

The Church: A Large House (2:19–26)

The complexity of the church is the subject of the remainder of this chapter. The Pastor uses unusually inclusive and conciliatory language here, envisioning the household of god (1 Tim. 3:15) as a "great house" (KJV) in which there are diverse "vessels" (KJV) or "utensils not only of gold and silver, but also of wood and clay" (v. 20, NRSV). All the vessels or utensils seem to serve a purpose, although, in the NRSV translation, some are more "special" than others. The Pastor, in encouraging everyone to "turn away from wickedness" (v. 19) and promising that "all who cleanse themselves of the things I have mentioned will become special utensils" (v. 21), seems to hark back to the notion of universal salvation (1 Tim. 2:4). Even the opponents here are given a second chance; perhaps, the Pastor writes, "they will repent and come to know the truth." Their opposition is not really their fault after all, since they have "been held captive" in "the snare of the devil," forced "to do his will" (vv. 25–26). The advice to steer clear of "senseless controversies" (v. 23) here has less to do with the Pastor's anti-intellectual rejection of his opponents, than with a strategy for productive pastoral care: "the Lord's servant must not be quarrelsome but kindly . . . correcting . . . with gentleness" (vv. 24–25). Bassler finds the Pastor's perspective here a breath of fresh air, quite unlike what one encounters all too often in 1 Timothy and Titus (1996: 156–57). Perhaps the Pastor is trying to craft what would seem to be the appropriate mood for a testament of "Paul's," especially given "Paul's" own closeness to his heavenly reward (see at 4:6–8)? One must guard against an undue rosiness, of course. All commentators note that v. 19, "the Lord knows those who are his," is almost a direct quote from Numbers 16:5, where God is about to crush Korah's rebellious company (Num. 16:26–27). Also, the NRSV translation is perhaps not quite as accurate as the KJV at v. 20b, which refers to the "vessels" of the great house in terms of "honor" and "dishonor," instead of "special use" and "ordinary" use. Here the Pastor seems to be drawing directly upon Romans 9:19, where Paul, in a moment of "arduous, dark, and far-reaching theology" (Hanson 1982: 139), provides Christian readers with a key argument for predestination. Pulling these two citations together, one could insist that the Pastor is, in fact, drawing a line in the sand, telling the faithful of his community to "cleanse themselves" by separating from the opponents, whom God will surely destroy. This is a reasonable position to take. But it does seem more likely that readings such as those proposed by Bassler or Towner are correct. Clearly the citations and the language are intended to produce "a strong warning to be heeded by all. . . . but thoughts of judgment, still implicit but muted, open out to an invitation to all to seek cleansing and conversion" (Towner 2006: 542–43).

Utensils of gold and silver (vv. 20–1)

This optimistic reading is a venerable one. In the mid-third century Cyprian writes to counter the argument that those who apostatize in times of persecution are forever to be excluded from the Christian community. The vessels of 2 Timothy 2:20 do indeed represent the saved and the damned, he says, but no one in this life can determine who's who, for "the vessels of wood are not burnt up except in the day of the Lord by the flame of the divine burning, and the vessels of clay are only broken by Him to whom is given the rod of iron" (*Ep.* 51.25, ANF 5.334). It is not only that we cannot make this determination, but also that sinners, in Cyprian's view, are not always sinners, that is, they can repent and thus they can become "special utensils" again. In Chrysostom's view, the "large house" of this verse is not the church, but the world as a whole. It would not be said of the church, he claims, since in the church there are only vessels of "gold and silver." Humanity in general, though, is a mixed pantry, with both types of vessels passively or actively supporting God's plan. Like Cyprian, he feels also that there is nothing static in these types either; one can change for the better or worse, as the examples of Paul and Judas show: "Paul was an earthen vessel, and became a golden one. Judas was a golden vessel, and became an earthen one" (*Hom. 2 Tim.*, NPNF1 13.496). A reading that has much in common with these, but actually departs from them quite radically, is that of Origen. The vessels in the great house of the world are all individuals, useful in their own way (*C. Cels.* 4.70, ANF 4.528), and facing judgment (*De prin.* 2.10.8, ANF 4.293). The judgment is not to damnation or salvation, however, but rather to dishonorable or honorable service in the next reincarnation. When the Pastor advises that believers "cleanse themselves," Origen says, he means "that he who shall purge himself when he is in this life, will be prepared for every good work in that which is to come; while he who does not purge himself will be, according to the amount of his impurity, a vessel unto dishonour" (ibid.). In the nineteenth century, Universalists return to v. 20 with the Origenist intention of teaching the eventual salvation of all. Elhanan Winchester, in his book *The Universal Restoration*, explains that while there are differences of quality among souls, it ought to be observed "that honor and dishonor are comparative terms," and that while dishonorable vessels are incapable of perfection now, and will "suffer with Christ here" in this life, they will be purged of sin for the life to come (1819: 200–01; but see Babcock, 1983, who claims that Universalists are mistaken to consider Origen an early precursor since his theology was indistinguishable from anti-Gnostic polemic, as if real theology cannot emerge in polemical or apologetic writings). The hope such readings provide for Christian vessels of the dishonorable sort is evident. Tapping into this strain of readings, Chaucer's Wife of Bath tells her fellow pilgrims that she too has a legitimate role to play in a Christian world. Perhaps it is not as noble as Paul's, she admits in the Prologue to her tale, but then:

> Of myn estaat I nyl nat make no boost,
> For wel ye knowe, a lord in his houshold,
> He hath nat every vessel al of gold;
> Somme been of tree, and doon hir lord servyse.
> God clepeth folk to hym in sondry wyse,
> And everich hath of God a propre yifte –
> Som this, som that, as hym liketh shifte.
>   Virginitee is greet perfeccion,
> And continence eek with devocion.
> But Crist, that of perfeccion is welle,
> Bad nat every wight he sholde go selle
> Al that he hadde, and gyve it to the poore,
> And in swich wise folwe hym and his foore.
> He spak to hem that wolde lyve parfitly,
> And lordynges, by youre leve, that am nat I.
>   (III[D] 98–112; 1987: 106)

Doris Shoukri, in a study of the ways in which the Wife of Bath "paraphrases St. Paul," claims that moments such as this are "misapplications" of "his words . . . to argue the case for those who would be less than perfect" (1999: 106). However, Chaucer's vivacious widow, despite her biting sarcasm, seems quite representative of a key strand of interpretation in her handling of this text.

Utensils of wood and clay (vv. 20–21)

What we have been calling the optimistic reading of this passage is countered not by a pessimistic one, or not necessarily, but rather by interpretations that highlight issues of predestination and final judgment. Origen, like many through the centuries, turns to 2 Timothy 2:19 as a "favorite" text "on God's foreknowledge" (Grant 1948: 244), endorsing the intriguing position that God's knowledge is limited to "those who are his." God is not "ignorant" of human affairs, obviously, but he "does not deign to know him who has turned away from him [God] and does not know him." Such a one is "considered . . . unworthy of knowledge of God." Origen prays for himself and his readers that God "may see fit to know us" so that we, in turn, might know the Godhead (*Hom. Gen.* 4.6, FC 71.110). While Origen believes that every soul will ultimately come into that knowledge, Augustine, and the tradition he establishes, holds to a theology of predestination according to which some are saved while others are damned for all eternity. Accordingly, the mixture of vessels in God's great house does not indicate neutrally the complexity of the church's social and ethical constitution, but rather the fact that there are two camps within the Christian world:

> Of this countless multitude [of vessels] are found to be not only the crowd which within the Church afflicts the hearts of the saints, who are so few in comparison with so vast a host, but also the heresies and schisms which exist in those who have burst the meshes of the net, and may now be said to be rather out of the house than in the house, of whom it is said, "They went out from us, but they were not of us" [1 John 2:19]. For they are more thoroughly separated, now that they are also divided from us in the body, than are those who live within the Church in a carnal and worldly fashion, and are separated from us in the spirit. (*De bapt.* 7.52, NPNF1 4.512)

Reading in Augustine's commentary on Ps. 67.7 that God is able "to make men of one mood to dwell in a house," Finbarr Clancy hears an echo of 2 Timothy 20, and on this basis argues that for Augustine "God does not dwell in all members of his house. His home is only among those united in mind and heart" (1993: 245). The vessels of gold and silver alone, then, are worthy. Or rather, only they have received God's grace, only they are predestined for mercy, because they are his.

They will repent and know the truth (vv. 21, 25–26)

However, the suggestion that repentance can bring about one's salvation causes Augustine a problem. If, as the entire text up to this point seems to suggest to him, figures like Hymenaeus and Philetus (v. 17) are likely damned, is it really possible that these vessels of wood and clay might, by "cleansing themselves," be saved? No, he replies, since the verse refers only to those who are already saints. "Paul" is simply telling Timothy to steer clear of sinners, heretics, schismatics, and the like (*De bapt.* 4.14, NPNF1 4.456). But if not, should one pray for them? Unfortunately, he can provide no very good answer to this question. The church, gendered feminine here, prays for her enemies because she is expected to, "she prays for her enemies who yet live in this world; and yet she is not heard in behalf of all. But she is heard in the case of those only who, though they oppose the Church, are yet predestinated to become her sons through her intercession" (*De civ. Dei* 21.24, 2000: 794). However, one never knows when God will look savingly into a sinner's heart, and so prayers such as these, words of rebuke, and sincere acts of penitence ought never to be considered wholly ineffective either, as long as we understand that no one can be sincere in repentance, or respond fruitfully to rebuke, without the grace of God (*Corrept.* 10, NPNF1 5.475; *Ench.* 82, NPNF1 3.264).

Much the same reading is found in Calvin, of course, who comments that the more optimistic interpretations are "quite frivolous" (*Commentary* 1964: 318). Additionally, he reads the last verse of the chapter, in which the Pastor writes that Satan has held the reprobate captive, as proof of just how condign the damnation of sinners is:

> [T]he fact that they are in this kind of captivity does not give the ungodly any excuse for claiming that they do not sin, because they act at Satan's instigation; for although the irresistible impulses to evil that carry them away result from Satan's domination over them, they do nothing under compulsion, but with their whole heart are inclined to go where Satan drives them. The result is that their captivity is voluntary. (ibid.: 321)

For Luther, this verse was all the evidence needed to prove "that the free will is dead and non-existent" (*Works* 4.89).

Escape from the snare of the devil (v. 26)

It would be absurd to say, however, that for the Reformers and their heirs there is no merit in repentance, in trying to "escape from the snare of the devil" (see also 1 Tim. 3:7). Certainly the Puritans in Salem Village, Massachusetts, during the witch hysteria, called ardently upon their congregations to free themselves from the snare, to "[a]wake[n] . . . and remain no longer under the dominion of that Prince of Cruelty and malice, whose Tyrannical Fury, we see thus exerted, against the Bodies and Minds of these afflicted persons" ("Christ's

Fidelity," a sermon by Deodet Lawson, in Trask 1997: 93; cf. Calvin, *Institutes* 1.14.18, 1960: 177). Milton, a near contemporary of the Salem Witch trials, although writing from what seems another planet altogether, opens Book 4 of *Paradise Lost* with an equally fraught echo of the Pastor's prose.

> O for that warning voice, which he who saw
> The Apocalypse heard cry in Heaven aloud,
> Then when the Dragon, put to second rout,
> Came furious down to be revenged on men,
> Wo to the inhabitants on Earth! that now,
> While time was, our first parents had been warned
> The coming of their secret foe, and 'scaped
> Haply so 'scaped his mortal snare.
>
> (1–8; 1961: 115)

His Adam, however, his "afflicted person," is fully responsible for his own choices. As God famously puts it in Book 3:

> . . . Whose fault?
> Whose but his own? Ingrate, he had of me
> All he could have; I made him just and right,
> Sufficient to have stood, though free to fall.
>
> (96–99; 1961: 94–95)

If one were seeking a compromise position between the ameliorist's more optimistic reading, and that of the advocates of strict predestinationist theologies, perhaps Horace Bushnell's would be most suitable. A nineteenth century heir to New England Calvinism, and yet a founding father of theological liberalism, Bushnell straddles the divide in his adaptation of v. 19. In that place, he writes, "Paul represents the Christian soul as a coin having two seals or mottoes" (1864: 203). The motto "the Lord knows those who are his" is evidence of grace, and is appropriate when the soul is experiencing "the felt impulse of God." The other motto, "let everyone who calls upon the name of the Lord turn away from wickedness," is adequate to those periods when one feels a loss of that "divine impulse"; at such times "some sharp revision of the life, some new girding up of the will in sacrifice and self-discipline, is urgently demanded." In other words, this double inscription, and by extension this whole concluding passage from 2 Timothy 2, really means: "Let the soul go by inspiration when the gale of the Spirit is in it, and when it has any way stifled or lost the Spirit, let it put itself down upon duty by the will" (202).

Reprising the eschatological message of 1 Timothy 4:1, the Pastor once again adapts a traditional vice list to characterize his opponents, adding here that these false teachers have a nefarious way with women. Timothy is told to avoid such men, and to remain firm in his godliness, following "Paul's" own model, as well as the teachings of his mother and grandmother. His upbringing in the scriptures will aid him in his pursuit of salvation, the Pastor concludes, because "all scripture is inspired by God."

The Pastoral Epistles Through the Centuries, First Edition. Jay Twomey.
© 2009 by Jay Twomey. Published 2020 by John Wiley & Sons Ltd.

The Opponents: Home Breakers (3:1–9)

As at 1 Timothy 4:1, the Pastor here intensifies warnings about his opponents with an apocalyptic proclamation: "in the last days perilous times shall come" (KJV). The crisis Timothy faces in Ephesus is apparently quite a dangerous challenge. Thus the chapter continues with a vice list, one longer and, if possible, even more frightening than that found in 1 Timothy 1. In v. 5 we read that these "profligates," these "unholy . . . haters of the good," these "abusive . . . inhuman . . . brutes," about whom Timothy is warned, apparently belong to the congregation. They are Christians "holding to the outward form of godliness, but denying its power." We have noted that the vice list is a traditional literary form, designed to cast the broadest possible aspersions rather than accurately to depict sets of specific individuals. The use of this list to depict the Pastor's own community, however, raises eyebrows among some modern commentators. Hanson questions the Pastor's literary skill, here, when he remarks that "it is rather surprising, after this horrific list of evil characters, to find that they are apparently respectable members of the church" (1982: 145). Some of these men even "creep into houses" and make "captives" of the community's "silly women," who are said to be "laden with sins" and incapable of true learning (v. 6 KJV). This view of women is consistent with the Pastor's attitudes elsewhere in these letters (cf. 1 Tim. 2:9–15; 5:13–15; Titus 2:3–5), even if the immediate rhetorical target here may be the community's men, as "Greco-Roman men would have been appalled at the prospect of their women coming under the influence of other men, and at the disruption of their households this would cause" (Davies 1996: 78). Indeed, Harnack argues that this passage, like 2:3–4, is a sign of the influence of military images and language on the Pastorals (cf. Bassler 1996: 160). He paraphrases the verse as follows: these men are "heretics, who like cunning foes sneak into the houses and take away the women as captives" (1981: 39). Thus the Pastor may been have been encouraging the Christian men in Ephesus to help him mount a more successful defense against his opponents by tapping into their patriarchal fears. Finally, the reference to Jannes and Jambres, the two magicians who, according to extra-biblical traditions, opposed Moses, is another instance of the many ways in which the Pastor wants to cast his "Paul" as a Moses-figure (see Martin 1997).

Distressing times will come (v. 1)

American folk artist and Baptist minister Howard Finster incorporates elements of this and the Pastor's other vice lists into his painting *A Feeling*

Figure 5 "A Feeling of Darkness Creeping up on the World" by Howard Finster no 2358-May 1982. Jim, Beth and Matt Arient.

of Darkness, the very title of which invokes the "perilous times" (KJV) of our verse. In the painting, the world is engulfed in darkness and all signs of civilized life are under attack by America folk versions of Hieronymus Bosch's beasts. Finster's trademark clouds, each with a face, and the sky and mountains in the background, all bear mottoes warning against "haters of those who are good," "backstabbers," "kidnappers," "deceivers," and "wife stealers" (v. 6). Contemporary criminal types – such as "gangsters," "lazy deadbeats," writers of "bad checks," and much worse – extend the Pastor's catalogue, just as the painting as a whole powerfully extends the Pastor's apocalyptic moment into an almost overwhelming visionary experience.

The outward form of godliness (v. 5)

The opponents are accused of being all form and no content. Chrysostom and Luther each insist upon the impoverishment of religiosity in its merely "outward form"; however, for the former the real power behind religious appearances can only be felt in works, while for the latter it is precisely works that are formally religious but ultimately impotent (Chrysostom, *Hom. 2 Tim.*, NPNF1 13.505; Luther, "The Freedom of a Christian," *Works* 31.363, 376). Chrysostom, in the same context, also recognizes that "form" can be a positive term, and gives examples from aesthetics. Augustine, going further, suggests that the form of religion can be, in itself, holy and good (*Ep. Jo.* 2.9, NPNF1 7.472). This appreciation of form, even mere form, is endorsed by Symeon the New Theologian, welcoming monks who "have fled from [worldly] life and its cares and have run into the haven of life and have wrapped [themselves] . . . in the outward form of religion" (*Discourses* 9.9, 1980: 159). He praises this effort, even as he warns that it is just the beginning.

Those who make their way into households, captivating silly women (vv. 6–7)

The Pastor makes it clear, however, that in those of whom he is speaking there is no connection whatsoever between form and content. And at any rate, these false teachers are much more dangerous as actors in his social world, stealing into houses and snaring the women. One would expect readers in the tradition to take up the Pastor's patriarchalism with some enthusiasm, and indeed this is the case. Chrysostom, although he mitigates his gender politics somewhat by hinting that the Pastor has only certain women in mind, not all women by nature, feels that the derogatory diminutive (*gynaikaria*, little women) would be apt even when men are being described because "to be deceived is the part of silly women" (*Hom. 2 Tim.*, NPNF1 13.505). Jerome is scornful of teachers who exploit "silly women," but is equally dismissive of the involvement of women in religious "sects" (*Ep.* 133.4, NPNF2 6.275), a further slap at the Pastor's opponents.

Langland, in *Piers Plowman*, links v. 6 with 1 Timothy 2:15 and in doing so translates the Pastor's concerns into a semi-bawdy joke about a friar, a "lymytour, [who] tho my lord was oute . . . salvede so oure wommen til some were with childe" (Text C, pass. 23.346, 1954: 1.599). Erasmus also brings the Pastor's concerns colorfully to life:

> To this class belong those who insinuate themselves into the homes of others, using the opening given them by their feigned religion, their coarse clothes, their sham severity, and the artfully induced paleness of their features. Once inside they hunt for foolish little women so that through them they may impose more easily on the men just as the serpent deceived Adam through Eve. . . . (*Paraphrases* 1993: 49).

This mini-narrativization of v. 6 does allow for a "class" of women who are not so easily duped, but one notices that they are protected more by sticking to their roles as "good wives" than by their own intellectual resources (compare with Astell, below).

One does find, however, counter-perspectives to, and critical rejections of, the patriarchal anxiety of vv. 6–7. Here we will note just two, both of which are interesting for the way they work against the Pastor, but from within his own rhetoric. Mary Astell, agitating in the late seventeenth century for women's education, or in actuality for the opportunity to create a religious/philosophical academy for women, asks in her *Serious Proposal to the Ladies*: if "GOD has given Women as well as Men intelligent Souls, why should they be forbidden to improve them" (2002: 80). She writes that while women are not permitted to "teach in the Church," they should nonetheless be allowed to "understand our *own* duty, and not be forc'd to take it upon trust from others" (81). The chances of misunderstanding, "in these *last* and *perilous* days," are great. In fact, there is simply no point in worrying about home-invading heretics anymore since so many "Deceivers . . . have Authority to proclaim their Errors on the *House top*" (81–82). Presumably Astell's goal, in context, is to manipulate male concerns about the permeability of the domestic sphere. Given the pervasiveness of ideas in our culture, she seems to be saying, your desire to protect women by controlling their access to information is doomed to failure. Heresy is abroad. The best way to defend women against it is to allow them the quite masculine luxury of education.

Postmodern American novelist Donald Barthelme takes another tack. He pushes a very male and conservative use of 2 Timothy 2:6–7 into absurdist obsolescence in his novel *The Dead Father*, by rendering the passage offensive in utterly colloquial, utterly familiar terms. The dead father-God of the title pens "A Manual for Sons," in one section of which an anonymous father, trying crudely and incompetently to relate to his son, begins ranting about religion:

> Flee from the wrath to come, boy, that's what I always say. Seen it on a sign one time, FLEE FROM THE WRATH TO COME. Crazy guy goin' down the street holdin' this sign . . . it tickled me. Went round for days sayin' it out loud to myself. . . . Couldn't get it outa my head. See, they're talkin' 'bout God there, that's what that's all about. God, see boy, God. It's this God shit they try and hand you, see, they got a whole routine, see, let's don't talk about it, gets me all pissed off. It fries my ass. Your mother goes for all that shit, see, and of course your mother is a fine woman and a sensible woman but she's just a little bit ape on this church thing we don't discuss it. . . . I don't blame her it was the way she was raised. Her mother was ape on this subject. That's how the churches make their money, see, they get the women. All these dumb-ass women (2004: 126; see also the section "A Tongue-Lashing," 134–35, which cites from the Pastoral Epistles, and elsewhere in the Bible, directly).

The boy in this section is never named, but it would be surprising if he weren't Timothy, given his religious mother and grandmother, and rather alien father. But the father is not quite unfamiliar, either. He has something in common with the Pastor, toying with apocalyptic language while mocking the religiosity of the "silly women" in his life.

Never arriving at a knowledge of the truth (v. 7)

Readers have sometimes opted out of the gender polemics this text encourages when commenting on v. 7. Some have done so simply by reading this verse in a gender-neutral way (cf. some of the responses to 1 Tim. 5:6). Augustine can even suggest that when the passage speaks about those "who are always being instructed" but "can never arrive at a knowledge of the truth" – clearly a reference to the silly women of the preceding verse – it is actually criticizing "certain men" (An. et or. 3.8, NPNF1 5.347); more often than not, though, Augustine cites this verse without regard to gender at all (Jo. ev. tr. 63, NPNF1 7.314; En. ps. 68.36, NPNF1 8.297; similarly Theodoret Comm. 2 Tim., 2001: 2.244; Calvin, Institutes 3.2.5, 1960: 548; Kierkegaard, Writings 15: 65). Oecumenius of Tricca goes even further, noting that not all women are "silly" and easily led captive: "there are women who are virile by nature, just as there are men who are feminine by nature" (in Johnson 2001: 31). The treatment of intellectual and moral characteristics here may be quite traditional, but the idea nevertheless complicates the Pastor's simplistic gender economy.

"Paul": Suffering (3:10–13)

"Paul" now recalls, in summary form, the many times he has suffered persecution. For many modern commentators, this all-too-brief survey of material found in Acts 13–14 is an indication of the letters' inauthenticity. Dibelius and Conzelmann remark that "in a genuine Pauline epistle it would seem strange that the troublesome experiences which Paul and Timothy had together are missing here" (1972: 119). The detailed, more intensely charged memories of persecutions which Paul describes in 2 Corinthians 6:4–10, 11:22–33 contrast so sharply with this passage that Hanson declares it "impossible to believe" that the same man wrote both. He also assumes that the Pastor had read Acts, but given the absence of material more relevant to Paul and Timothy, an absence Hanson notes as well (1982: 149), Collins is probably right in his suggestion that the Pastor merely had access to some stories about Paul similar to the ones Luke uses in Acts (2002: 258). As Bassler and others have rightly noted, the experience of suffering, indeed the theology of suffering in this letter, is balanced here by the promise of rescue (v. 11; 4:8, 17–18), and is grounded in the hymnic claim that those who "endure" will "reign" with Christ (2:11–13; Bassler 1996: 173).

You have observed my persecutions (v. 10)

Like some modern commentators, Chrysostom also wonders about just why "Paul" cites these few, and not other, examples of his suffering. He concludes that as Timothy already knew what had befallen Paul in his ministry, except perhaps for a few "new events," there is no reason to be more detailed. More importantly, "Paul" "is not enumerating [his experiences] . . . particularly, for he is not actuated by ambition or vainglory, but he recounts them for the consolation of his disciple" (*Hom. 2 Tim.*, NPNF1 13.506).

All who want to live a godly life will be persecuted (v. 12)

The real focus, of course, is not so much "Paul's" own suffering, nor the suffering of church leaders like Timothy, both of which have been stressed already, but that all believers will suffer persecution. Readers have frequently stressed both the pain and the gain, as it were, of following "Paul" on the path of faith. Augustine reports the confused response of auditors who hear of the promises of ease in Christ (as, for instance, in Matt. 11:28–30) and yet witness the sufferings of believers. Knowing that "Paul" says persecution comes to the godly, someone will ask: " '[h]ow is the yoke easy, and the burden light,' when to bear this yoke and burden is nothing else, but to live godly in Christ?" (*Serm.* 20.1, NPNF1 6.317). Paul and Jesus and persecuted believers, Augustine answers, do not feel their burdens as pain because the Holy Spirit refreshes them within while they endure torments without: the promise of their eternal reward far outweighs the agony of persecution. He then returns the query, asking, don't merchants, soldiers, and hunters undergo enormous difficulties and privations for what they consider important? Why should the Christian faithful be any different? (20.2, NPNF1 6.317). Bernard of Clairvaux agrees entirely, but says, nonetheless, that one should sympathize with and pray for those experiencing suffering in the faith because we do not know in advance whether the outcome will be for good or ill. If the believer is "submerged" by the "tempest" of their suffering, then the experience will have been for naught (*Ep.* 11.1–2, 1904: 47; cf. *Ep.* 22.2, 1904: 91).

Both Augustine and Bernard could also consider many kinds of non-persecutory suffering to qualify as "persecution" in the Pastor's sense, and readers throughout the tradition have generally shared this broader view of

v. 12 and its New Testament cognates (cf. Leo the Great, *Ep.* 167.2, NPNF1 12.109; Matthew Henry, 1721–25: 322). At moments of crisis, however, during periods of real persecution, interpreting the difficulties of which the Pastor warns becomes a matter of urgency. For some, the Pastor's text means that persecution is necessarily to be endured. Tertullian argued, in his tract against fleeing from persecution, *De fuga in persecutione*, that although the earliest Christians had to do what they could to survive, in order for the gospel to spread, contemporary Christians were expected to face suffering without trying to escape it, for it was of God. In the eighteenth century, George Whitefield, sounding like a Cyprian or Tertullian in his open advocacy of (an albeit historically unlikely) martyrdom, gives a sermon entitled "Persecution, The Christian's Lot," in which he lauds persecution not just as a device for testing one's faith, but for clarifying it, providing one, as it were, with a kind of special revelation: "how many Paradoxes are there to [confuse] a natural Man unless we are persecuted" (1741: 21).

On the other hand, the passage is a problematic one for someone like Athanasius, who does in fact flee, and multiple times over the course of his career. Athanasius, noting that he is accused of cowardice by the very people from whom he fled, argues, like Tertullian, that escape from persecution was often necessary for the greater good of the faith; but unlike Tertullian, he claims that it is still so in his day. "Paul" may have defined the Christian life as subject to persecution, but he also "prepared them that fled for the trial, saying, 'Let us run with patience the race that is set before us' [Heb 12:1]" (*Apol. de fuga* 21, NPNF2 4.262). One must endure persecution, but not seek immediately to succumb to it. Moreover, since his persecutors have clearly learned their skills from Satan, he argues, when they criticize him for fleeing rather than facing suffering, Athanasius can retort that they are essentially Satanic, and that he would rather obey the dictates of God (ibid. 23, NPNF2 4.263; cf. Augustine, *Ep.* 228.6, NPNF1 1.578, who finds Athanasius' flight acceptable only because he wasn't abandoning his congregation to danger).

The Church: Scripture (2:14–17)

Timothy is urged to "continue in what [he has] learned ... knowing from whom [he] learned it." Earlier in the letter, the Pastor mentions Timothy's mother Eunice and grandmother Lois (1:5) and it seems clear that although the Pastor is likely intending to give credit mostly to "Paul" and others (e.g., 1 Tim. 4:14), he is also once again acknowledging these women for their role in educating Timothy in the scriptures from "his childhood" (D-C 1972: 119; Guthrie 1990: 174; Davies 1996: 81; Collins 2002: 261; Towner 2006: 582). The "sacred writings" is a technical term in Hellenistic Judaism for the Hebrew scriptures (D-C 1972: 119). Thus, even if some Christian literature may just have begun to achieve a relatively informal scriptural status during this period, the scriptures on which Timothy was brought up are Jewish (Bassler 1996: 167). Of course, it is not just Timothy's age that makes this passage exegetically viable for educators of all stripes. The Pastor also tells Timothy that the "sacred writings are able to instruct you for salvation." That the Bible itself can function as the principal text in a Christian curriculum is an ancient notion, but one that was at odds with traditional Hellenistic pedagogy (see Young 2006).

This is a principal text for Christian theories of biblical inspiration, although, as Robert Gnuse comments: "the passage hardly says what inspirationists earnestly desire. The passage says nothing about inerrancy or verbal dictation, nor does it speak of a canon of Scripture, nor does it describe the Scriptures as the foundation of Christian theology, and finally it does not even consider the Scriptures as the unique or ultimate criterion of the faith" (1985: 19). Inspiration as a theory builds upon other New Testament resources as well (e.g., 2 Peter 1:20–21), but 2 Timothy 3:16 contributes a particular interest in divine authorship to the debate about inspiration, which is also a debate about biblical authority. All commentators note that the Greek text can mean either that "all scripture that is inspired by God is useful for teaching, etc.," suggesting that there are some scriptures not so inspired, or that "the whole of scripture/every passage of scripture is inspired by God, and is thus useful for teaching, etc." Needless to say, very few readers take up the first option, and indeed for Calvin and others, the fact that alternative translations are possible "makes no difference to the meaning" (1964: 329). Patristic and medieval writers simply took the divine inspiration of scripture for granted, without trying to understand the claim of 3:16 within a general theory of inspiration. Many readers, ancient and modern alike, seem to have understood "this statement on the divine authority of every text of Scripture . . . [as] really preliminary to the main topic of the verse," namely the usefulness of scripture (Towner 2006: 590; cf. Bassler 1996: 174).

Theories of inspiration begin to take serious shape only after the Reformation, when the heirs to the reformers felt the need to distinguish themselves sharply from the Catholic Church, which claimed that without the teachings of the Church, believers – even if they relied upon the Bible – were lost. The Protestant principle of "Sola Scriptura" thus comes to rely upon one or another theory of inspiration as its doctrinal "safeguard" (Pelikan 1971–89: 4.347).

From childhood (v. 15)

Because v. 15 says that Timothy learned his scriptures *apo brephous*, "from infancy," readers have used it to make claims on childhood for religious education. Basil writes in conjunction with this verse that "every time of life, even the very earliest, [is] suitable for receiving applicants" to the order (in McMillan and Fladenmuller 1997: 26). The Wesleys, in a hymn written for children, imagine a child in prayer, taking Timothy as his or her model:

> O that I, like Timothy,
> Might the Holy Scriptures know,
> From mine earliest infancy,
> Till for God mature I grow,
> Made unto salvation wise,
> Ready for the glorious prize.

In the final stanza, the educative function of the written word, read and studied, gives way to a pietist's plea for inspiration:

> Open now mine eyes of faith,
> Open now the book of God,
> Show me here the secret path,
> Leading to Thy bless'd abode:
> Wisdom from above impart,
> Speak the meaning to my heart.
> ("Before Reading the Scriptures"
> 1868: 6.398–99)

Without insisting necessarily upon religious training for its own sake, Horace Bushnell takes Timothy as a model of education more generally. The best and truest education begins in the home, he explains, "and just so it will ever be true of the ripest and tallest of God's saints, who were trained by His truth in their childhood, that however deep in their intelligence or high in their spiritual attainments they have grown to be, the motherly and fatherly word is working in them still; and is, in fact, the core of all spiritual understanding in their character" (*Christian Nurture*, 1876: 367).

Useful for teaching (v. 16)

The Bible can provide true, essential knowledge of God because "all scripture is inspired by God" (v. 16). Frequently, however, interest in inspiration has been limited to the second half of our verse: "and is useful for teaching, for reproof, for correction, and for training in righteousness." Chrysostom, in fact, can cite the entire verse as though it were solely about the functions to which scripture can be put in the discharge of one's priestly duties – for example, in debating with dissenters (*De sac.* 4.8, NPNF1 9.68). Others respond similarly: Augustine mentions it with regard to the critical function of the prophets (*De civ. Dei* 23.17, 2000: 607); John of Damascus (*Exposition of the Orthodox Faith* 4.17, NPNF2 9.89), Martin Luther (*Bondage of the Will*, Works 33.27), and John Wesley ("The Witness of Our Own Spirit," *Works* 5.136) cite it in terms of scripture as theological and moral instruction. Wesley, for instance, completely subordinates the inspired nature of scripture to its usefulness when he claims that these verses are "a lantern unto a Christians feet, and a light in all his paths" (ibid.).

In many cases, on the other hand, even where the emphasis on "usefulness" remains, one can detect a certain theoretical interest in what inspiration might mean. Basil of Caesarea, for instance, worries about the potentially detrimental effects that some more salacious or less morally edifying passages from the Hebrew Bible could have on believers. Not that the Hebrew Bible should not be read, since "all scripture is God inspired and profitable." But just as "[a]ll bread is nutritious, but . . . may be injurious to the sick," so too the spiritual bread of the scriptures needs to be administered carefully (*Ep.* 42.3, NPNF2 8.145). Gregory of Nyssa is more generally concerned that the text of the Old Testament, if read literally, will not produce the spiritual benefit it is designed for. In many places, "the Divine intention lies hid under the body of the Scripture, as it were under a veil, some legislative enactment or some historical narrative being cast over the truths that are contemplated by the mind" (*C. Eun.* 7.1, NPNF2 5.192). It is not everyone, therefore, who can read the inspired word and be instructed by it. Both Basil and Gregory begin with inspiration as a given, and find that they must square this idea with their ambivalent appreciation of some scriptural texts whose signs of inspiration are not self-evident. Gregory's reading is characteristic of a tradition in Christianity that tries carefully and narrowly to guide the processes of signification by characterizing some biblical material as obscure, and perhaps reserving it only for the initiate. It is precisely this attitude that Martin Luther, in the text cited above, is combating. Erasmus had similarly declared that certain passages of scripture are too darkly mysterious, too dangerous, to attempt interpreting on one's own. Luther calls upon 2 Timothy 3:16 in challenging Erasmus "and all the Sophists" to "produce any single mystery that is still abstruse in the Scriptures" (*The Bondage of The Will*, Works 33.27).

The approach one finds in Basil and Gregory can also be reversed, in a sense; that is, one can argue for the scriptural status of non-canonical texts on the basis of their ability to teach and rebuke. Tertullian's appropriation, and unusual reading, of 3:16 is an excellent example of this strategy. In the process of arguing for the scriptural authority of the Book of Enoch, he renders v. 16: "every Scripture suitable for edification is divinely inspired" (*De cultu. fem.* 1.3, ANF 4.16). Enoch, because it can educate the spiritually inquiring Christian mind, in this case because it "tell[s] of Christ," must for that very reason be inspired. Incidentally, in Tertullian's combative anti-Judaism, this is precisely the reason Enoch was rejected "[b]y the Jews" (ibid.). The idea that one may divine the inspired status of a text by means of its spiritually educative potential, however, does not mean that any text "useful for teaching" would be considered scripture, of course. Almost everyone in the tradition would undoubtedly agree with Thomas Aquinas, for instance, that even if other kinds of texts are useful, philosophical treatises for instance, they cannot lead to salvation (ST Q[1] A[1]).

Inspired by God (v. 16)

As noted above, the Reformers and their followers are among the first in the western tradition to develop theories of biblical inspiration. Calvin's own theory resembles (inspires?) those which follow. He begins his commentary on this verse polemically, by averring that the fact of inspiration makes Christianity different from all other religions, because "we know that God has spoken to us." But he continues:

> [T]he prophets did not speak of themselves, but as organs of the Holy Spirit uttered only that which they had been commissioned from heaven to declare. All those who wish to profit from the Scriptures must first accept this as a settled principle, that the Law and the prophets are not teachings handed on at the pleasure of men or produced by men's minds as their source, but are dictated by the Holy Spirit. . . . [I]t has its only source in Him and has nothing of human origin mixed in with it. (*Commentary* 1964: 330)

That the biblical writers were "organs of the Holy Spirit," to whom God "dictated" the message of scripture without any admixture of innovation or error on the part of those writers, is a strong statement of the theory of inspiration.

It has been taken up vigorously by proponents of strict verbal inspiration almost exactly in the form Calvin provides, but with the difference that more recent articulations of the principle take the writers' situations more fully into account. Louis Gaussen's treatise, *Theopneustia: The Plenary Inspiration of the*

Holy Scriptures, a work of this kind, also builds very consistently on our verse from 2 Timothy. The title is a version of the Greek word translated in the NRSV as "inspired by God." Literally, *theopneustos*, which occurs only here in the New Testament, means "God-breathed," and Gaussen, thinking from the perspective of the biblical writers, acknowledges a paradoxically active/passive element in inspiration, since "it is, in fact, with *Theopneustia*, as with efficacious grace.... God does every thing; and man does every thing" (1841: 33–34). However, that experience of being moved to write by the Holy Spirit is transient, whereas the biblical texts remain, and in this way Gaussen affirms the standard view of "God-breathed" as texts "inspired [in their composition] by God." The doctrine of strict verbal, or plenary, inspiration which he forwards in his work allows, as we've just indicated, some flexibility to the writers. As human beings, they retain their idiosyncratic personalities, their styles, and experience the inspiration "in very different degrees" (24–25, 55–56). Nevertheless, as instruments or organs of the Holy Spirit, they can and did write nothing in error, and they wrote exactly what, and only what, the Holy Spirit meant for them to write (37–38, 57). Every single passage, every word, in the Bible is therefore perfect and inerrant.

Far less strident versions of the theory of inspiration are possible, however, and one can balance the view of Gaussen, a Swiss Protestant, with that of someone like John Henry Newman, a convert to Catholicism from the Anglican Church. Newman's essay, "On the Inspiration of Scripture," endorses what he understand to be the dogma of Vatican I, namely that "the whole of Scripture in all its parts is inspired," but with an "inspiration . . . restricted to the matters of faith and morals" (1967: 150). Newman's view, which is a variant of the theory of "non-textual inspiration" (Gnuse 1985: 44), does not require total inerrancy, and actually seems closer to that of Vatican II, whose proclamation on the topic offers itself as an explication of our text:

> Therefore, since everything asserted by the inspired authors or sacred writers must be held to be asserted by the Holy Spirit, it follows that the books of Scripture must be acknowledged as teaching solidly, faithfully and without error that truth which God wanted put into sacred writings for the sake of salvation. (in Flannery 1984: 757)

According to this understanding, the truth of scripture inheres not in every jot and tittle of the biblical text, as Gaussen insists (1841: 36), but in its much more generalizable soteriological meanings. We will return to Gaussen and Newman in the next chapter (at 2 Timothy 4:13).

Contemporary Christian fundamentalists clearly draw upon readings of this text which are akin to Gaussen's. From relatively moderate theological statements (such as that of J. I. Packer [1958]) to much more radical political positions (such as those espoused by Jerry Falwell), Christians who self-identify as fundamentalist have recourse to 2 Timothy 3:16 as one of their core supports. Just what biblical inerrancy can mean in practice varies from case to case, obviously, but in right-leaning circles the implications of this passage from the Pastorals are tied to everything from Creationism (Morris 2004: b) to anti-abortion politics (Cromartie 2003: 110) to the militancy of theonomist movements (Davis and Hankins 2003: 114).

All scripture inspires (v. 16)

Theopneustia is almost universally taken as a passive form (Knight 1992: 446): scripture is God-breathed, not God-breathing. Were it active it would mean that scripture inspires, and this is perhaps why Clement of Alexandria believes that the "sacred writings" Timothy has known from his infancy can "sanctify and deify," and are for that reason "truly holy" (*Protrep.* 9, ANF 2.196). The active sense of inspiration, although barely acknowledged in modern commentaries because so little used, plays an important role in Quakerism. The seventeenth century Quaker theologian, Robert Barclay, confronts accusations that the idea of an active, personal inspiration, that "inner light" so essential to Quaker spirituality, necessarily "renders the scriptures altogether uncertain, or useless." He does so, first of all, by acknowledging not only that the Bible is inspired, but also that whatever the Bible says of itself is true (*An Apology for the True Christian Divinity*, 1827: 83). However, scripture is accorded only second place behind God's spiritual guidance of believers. The Bible as the inspired word of God is simply one source of divine authority among many. If it has a place of particular importance for the community, it is in its ability to adjudicate, as "the only fit outward judge of controversies," between competing Christian messages. Barclay also notes that errors have slipped into the Bible "by the injury of times" (86), although not to a degree that might call into question the inspiration behind Bible as a whole. What matters most of all is that the spirit-guided, the God-breathed, life of believers be placed front and center in the community.

Another basic issue to consider involves the relationship between inspired scripture and interpretation. One of the problems is, as Elliott Johnson puts it in an introductory study of hermeneutics (after citing 2 Tim. 3:16): "if the goal of interpretation is to determine the author's intended meaning, the immediate question arises, Which author?" (1990: 51). Although Johnson insists, in answering this question, that the "shared single meaning of the text is the basis of" interpretation and meaning-making (53), nevertheless his response, like similar considerations throughout the tradition, emphasizes God's ultimate authority for biblical sense (see also Schneider 1999: 46–48). One can also ask whether or not inspired scripture can be understood without recourse to inspiration for the interpreter. Charles Hodge, the important nineteenth century American Calvinist theologian and expositor, argued that "the Scriptures are to be interpreted under the guidance of the Holy Spirit, which guidance is to be humbly and earnestly sought" (Hodge 1873: 1.187). Karl Barth, who saw himself as standing in a tradition which held to a theory of divine inspiration, provided a modified version of Hodge's answer. One seeks the inspired meaning of the biblical text not by adopting the position of a neutral, scientific, historical investigator, but rather though "the most intense form of participation and historical engagement" (Burnett 2004: 115; for Barth's view of scriptural inspiration, see his *Church Dogmatics* I/2 §19).

"Paul" concludes this letter with additional warnings about the opposition Timothy will face in Ephesus. He also reflects upon his own life as his death approaches, describing himself as one who has "fought the good fight" and "kept the faith." Despite his sense that he is "already" at death's door, however, he nevertheless expects Timothy to come visit him, and asks his protégé to bring along with him some possessions he misses in prison.

The Opponents: Entertaining Teachers (4:1–4)

As at 1 Timothy 5:21 and 6:13, the Pastor issues a solemn charge to Timothy, for which he calls upon both God and Christ as his witnesses. The language

The Pastoral Epistles Through the Centuries, First Edition. Jay Twomey.
© 2009 by Jay Twomey. Published 2020 by John Wiley & Sons Ltd.

recalls ancient installment formulae (Towner 2006: 595), and well suits the Pastor's purpose of establishing Timothy as Paul's official successor. Christ is further identified, in this oath, as he who "is to judge the living and the dead," or in the King James translation, "the quick and the dead." However, despite the way this language echoes through the centuries, in theological and literary texts, it is difficult to know when 2 Timothy 4:1 is being cited in later literature, as opposed to Acts 10:39–42, or 1 Peter 4:5–6, or liturgical services for the dead. Collins notes that whereas the Acts passage subordinates Christ to God, the Pastor "attributes the judiciary function to God alone" (2002: 267; one sees a similar subordinationist intention in 1 Peter, according to Davies 1996: 83, and in Paul, e.g., 1 Cor. 15:28). But we shall see that subordinationism or its absence cannot adequately be taken as a marker of the Pastor's influence when "the quick and the dead" is appropriated in later literature. Some modern readers, in fact, have taken their interpretations entirely in the other direction. Frances Young, for instance, understands 2 Timothy 4:1 unambiguously to mean that the "universal God" of the Pastorals "is not only Creator, but also Judge," perhaps because Christ is but a "manifestation" of God (1994: 50, 63–67; cf. Towner 2006: 596).

The charge of the oath itself is that Timothy should "be instant in season and out of season" (KJV) in preaching to, rebuking, and teaching the community. Ancient rhetoricians emphasized the importance of crafting one's message and tone to suit one's audience, in order to be effective and always to be "in season," as it were, as an orator. The Pastor tells Timothy to be "instant out of season" too, and some have taken this to mean that "Paul" is intentionally flaunting such rhetorical conventions, perhaps as would a Cynic philosopher (Malherbe 1984). Either way, the reason Timothy must be "instant" or "persistent" (NRSV) is that people soon will no longer "put up with sound doctrine." This comment helps to reinforce the motif of abandonment which the Pastor develops in his portrait of Paul (Bassler 1996: 170), and it continues the effort of these letters generally (with the brief exception of 2 Tim. 2) of disparaging opponents without engaging their ethical or theological positions critically.

To judge the living and the dead (v. 1)

Chrysostom, who is uncertain if the Pastor means "the living and the dead" figuratively or literally, reads this oath as an intensification of 1 Timothy 6:13: "[i]n the former Epistle he raised his fears, saying, 'I give thee charge in the sight of God, Who quickeneth all things': but here he sets before him what is more dreadful, 'Who shall judge the quick and the dead'" (*Hom. 2 Tim.*, NPNF1 13.510). The verse is indeed a powerful one, especially when paired with apocalyptic imagery, as here, or as in the sixteenth century Belgic Confession, which asserts as a tenet of belief that "when the time appointed by the Lord (which is unknown to all creatures) is come and the number of the elect complete ... our Lord Jesus Christ will come from heaven, corporally and visibly, as He ascended with great glory and majesty, to declare himself Judge of the quick and the dead, burning this old world with fire and flame to cleanse it" (Art. 37, in Melton 1988: 172).

But again it can be difficult to know for sure if any later usage has the Pastor's verse in mind. Taking Collins' suggestion (see above) regarding Christ's primary role in judgment may seem like a useful place to begin our study of the reception of 2 Timothy 4:1. Thus for example, the Nicene Creed, since it prefaces its reference to future judgment of the living and the dead with the statement that Christ "is seated at the right hand of the Father," feels slightly less allied with the Pastor's vision than with that of Acts. However, as a criterion for judging the provenance of "the quick and the dead," subordination is quite unreliable. Sometimes readers believe that Christ is subordinated to the Father in our verse. To Matthew Henry it seems requisite that this verse be read in terms both of Acts 10:42 and John 5:22 ("the Father judges no one but has given all judgment to the son") which would clearly limit Christ's authority to the powers deputed to him by God (1721–25: 324). And the opposite is also true: one simply cannot turn around and assume that assumptions about or suggestions of Christ's independent activity at the *eschaton* necessarily mean that a writer has 1 Timothy 4:1 in mind. John Donne, for instance, reads "the quick and the dead" literally, repudiating the figurative interpretations forwarded on the one hand by Chrysostom (*Hom 2 Tim.*, NPNF1 13.510) and Augustine (*Ench.* 55, NPNF1 3.255), both of whom suggest that the verse may refer to the righteous and the damned, and on the other by Rufinus, who thinks the "quick" are souls and the "dead" are bodies at judgment (*Commentary on The Apostle's Creed* 33, NPNF2 3.556). For Donne, as for the Paul of 1 Corinthians 15:51, people will still be alive when Christ returns as judge. Now, nothing in Donne's reading suggests that Christ will act on anything but his own authority on that day. Nevertheless, Donne cites not 2 Timothy, but Acts and the Apostle's Creed (*Sermon on Ps. 89.48*, 1963: 36). The Quaker George Fox declares, in striking language, that the resurrected Jesus is "God of the dead, and the living [contrast Mark 12:27 and parr.]," and in that sovereign capacity he will return "to judge the quick and the dead." Fox gives no specific biblical citation here, although he does place the apocalyptic language in a Pastoral context by saying that the judge he has in mind is "the man Christ Jesus," a reference to 1 Timothy 2:5 (*The Great Mystery of the Great Whore*, 1659: 99). Since that passage, however, portrays Jesus as a mediator, functioning in a differential relationship between God and humanity, it is unclear if even here we have an unambiguous affirmation of Christ's absolute independence in his role as judge.

So, which biblical text does Shakespeare's Hamlet have in mind when bantering with the gravedigger? The prince, before he finds out that it is Ophelia who has died, denies that the grave being dug belongs to the gravedigger, and accuses him of lying when he says so, because "[t]is for the dead, not for the quick, therefore thou liest"; to which the gravedigger replies: "[t]is a quick lie sir, 'twill away againe from me to you" (*Hamlet* 5.1.126, 1980: 1114). Whom is Louis L'Amour citing in the title of his Western *The Quick and The Dead*? One of the "many testimonies of the divine Scriptures" (Rufinus, *Commentary on The Apostle's Creed* 33, NPNF2 3.556), or 2 Timothy specifically?

Galway Kinnell, in his poem "The Quick and the Dead," may not have our text in mind either. Yet, this is a poem of judgment and resurrection, one requiring a form of mediation for which a subordinationist rhetoric is entirely lacking. The poet notices that a vole he had killed seems to be, although dead, pulsing with life. In fact, it is being transformed by insects into food and a nest for eggs and fertilizer for plants. The little creature is "dead, and yet he lives, / he jerks, he heaves, he shudders, / as if something quickens in him." A scene of decomposition like this may be unsettling, but for Kinnell it is instructive, especially when contrasted with the modern funerary practices of humans. Unlike dead creatures who settle into dust, awaiting their eventual transformation, the human body, when it:

> has been drained of its broths and filled
> again with formaldehyde and salts
> or unguents and aromatic oils, and pranked
> up in its holiday best and laid out
> in a satin-lined airtight stainless-steel
> coffin inside a leakproof concrete vault –
> I know that if no fellow creatures
> can force their way in to do the underdigging
> and jiggling and earthing over and mating
> and egg-laying and birthing forth, then for us
> the most that can come to pass
> will be a centuries-long withering down
> to a gowpen of dead dust, and never
> the crawling of new life out of the old,
> which is what we have for eternity on earth.
> (2006: 30–33)

The judgment in this case is already announced in our alienation from natural processes; and salvation comes only to those who are quickened in death by their vulnerability, their exposure to the remorseless hunger of the living.

The time is unfavorable (v. 2)

Most readers assume, correctly, that the Pastor simply means by this expression "whenever and wherever you can, no matter how you feel, no matter what the reception is likely to be." Theodoret seems only to have read the first portion of this exhortation because he, paraphrasing the Pastor, explains: "nothing that happens out of season wins compliments" (*Comm. 2 Tim.*, 2001: 246). "Paul" was always very good about judging his rhetorical situations and coming out on top, Theodoret writes, and thus is urging Timothy to hone his rhetorical skills.

Readers have been just as interested in what it means to "be instant out of season," however. As an expression of the "aggressive" and "ruthless persistence" (Calvin 1964: 333) which the Pastor expects of Timothy, "out of season" is perhaps echoed in the title of one of Nietzsche's early works, *Untimely [unzeit-gemasse] Meditations*, behind which one may hear Luther's translation of the phrase, "*zur Zeit oder zur Unzeit.*" Less philosophically, and certainly with less of a critical intent than Nietzsche would require, "instant out of season" can also mean, simply, childishly irascible. Nineteenth century Irish poet John Todhunter, in a long poem entitled *Laurella*, tells of a priest who, for the life of him, cannot imagine why a young girl would choose not to marry:

> The good man was perplexed. She would not wed,
> Nor take the veil! The thing was strange—what notion
> Had got into the little vixen's head?
> Most women have two poles—love and devotion . . .

When Laurella refuses to explain further, the priest loses all patience

> And, in pure zeal, grown 'instant out of season',
> For the girl's motives he began to teaze.
>   (1876: 14–15)

Laurella, however, cuts him short, and the priest, who soon realizes that the young woman is in love, must wait like an adolescent boy for his "confessional titbit" (15).

Itching ears (v. 3)

A key reason for the Pastor's charge to Timothy is that soon people will no longer "put up with sound doctrine." Instead, "having itching ears," they will "heap to themselves teachers" according to "their own lusts" (KJV) or "to suit their own desires" (NRSV). The scorn implied in these images is nearly palpable. The image of people hunting about, with itching ears, for a teaching they can accept calls to mind what we might think of as the "cafeteria religion" of the spiritual quester. Characterized negatively, of course, some such version of this questing has been the frequent target of readers in the tradition. People are too quick to seek out a certain intellectual stimulation at the expense of real "improvement" according to Theodoret. Just as "itching is productive of a certain aural satisfaction," so too the stimulation people discover, in the "myths" of v. 4, titillates without satisfying any real needs (*Comm. 2 Tim.*, 2001: 247). Augustine, ironically undermining the intellectual investments involved, reduces the satisfaction experienced by these questers to the unthinkingly carnal. Citing Proverbs 9:17, in which Lady Folly encourages the fool to "[p] artake with pleasure of hidden bread and the sweetness of stolen waters," Augustine considers the "itching" of v. 3 physiologically: it is not unlike "a kind of itching . . . in the flesh" by which "the soundness of chastity is corrupted" (*Jo. ev. tr.* 97.4, NPNF1 7.375). Taking the image in a similar direction, Puritan Thomas Watson considers the "itching" as a kind of sexual temptation. Rather than Proverbs, however, Watson turns to the story of Joseph and Potiphar's wife in Genesis 39 for intertextual inspiration:

> Had Joseph been familiar with his mistress in a wanton sporting manner, he might in time have been drawn to commit folly with her. Some out of novelty and curiosity have gone to hear mass, and afterwards have lent the idol not only their ear but their knee. In our times are there not many who have gone with itching ears into sectarian company and have come home with the plague in their head? (*The Beatitudes* 1660: 242–43)

The itchy-eared are also compared to Dinah, who is said to have "lost her chastity" when she was out "gadding [citing Gen. 34:2!]" (ibid.: 243). One suspects that Watson and Augustine are trying to link the "desires" the Pastor disparages to traditional representations of apostasy as fornication in the Hebrew Bible.

Taking the verse out of context, however, one could read the Pastor's own words in judgment against him. This is how the ninth century forgery of Pseudo-Isidore, "Epistle of Pope Anterus," engages our text. In the middle of a relatively disjointed passage about the righteous life, the writer declares: "[l]et each one take care that he have neither an itching tongue nor itching ears; that is to say, that he neither be a detractor of others himself, nor listen to others in their detractions" (ANF 8.628). If those of itching tongues and ears are those who vilify others, and if judgment awaits them, then certainly the Pastor has reason to fear for his immortal soul. By equating the desire to speak ill of others with the desire to listen to calumnious speech, "Pope Anterus" collapses the twin problems of the Pastor's community: the presence of false teachers on the one hand, and a willing audience for their heterodoxies on the other. An interesting literary, and entirely secularized, appropriation of v. 3 which does something quite similar is to be found in a poem by nineteenth century Irish poet William Allingham. Allingham's speaker laments, in the manner of a more likeable J. Alfred Prufrock, the emptiness of elite society, in which one is subjected to:

> Stir and change from morn till night,
> . . .
> Every topic its oration,
> Every mood its conversation,
> Clever men and lovely women,
> Tides of human life to swim in, –
> O the marvels of the town!
>
> Can I swim? or shall I drown?
> Heavenly bright the water-gleam,
> Cold and muddy proves the stream.
> Endless talk – but what is it?
> Insight, poetry, wisdom, wit?
> Or news and gossip, lies and sneers,
> Limber tongues and itching ears?

The speaker goes on to list the literary, musical, and artistic "distractions" which, at least in the circles in which he moves, serve no purpose other than to mark one's cultural status. He also, somewhat like the Pastor, longs to stop "wander[ing] away to [entertaining] myths" and instead wants to seek out "the truth" (v. 4):

> Rather, friend, O show me where
> In blessed silence and pure air,
> I may bury fathoms deep
> In the fountain of sweet sleep
> My wearied senses, wilder'd mind.
> No such place in Town I find.
>
> (1890: 163–65)

There is something of the Pastor's "Paul" in this closure as well, the long-wearied soldier of Christ looking forward to his final reward. Here, however, that reward is an earthly one, the spirit's rest in an unhurried and peaceful nature.

"Paul": The Good Fighter (4:6–8; cf. 1 Tim. 1:18; 6:12; 2 Tim. 2:5)

One of the most important passages in these letters, for many scholars, is this text which purports to capture Paul's mood on the eve of his execution. He is resigned to his fate ("I am already being poured out," v. 6), and yet confident in his future ("there is reserved for me the crown of righteousness," 8). As all commentators note, this image recalls classical offerings to the gods, ceremonies at which wine was poured out to honor a deity. Reprising metaphors found elsewhere in the Pastorals, "Paul" now reflects that he has "fought the good fight . . . finished the race . . . kept the faith." The King James translation at 1 Timothy 1:18 is "war a good warfare," as opposed to the NRSV's "fight the good fight." The Greek verbs for fight, here and at 2 Timothy 4:7, are, in fact, different, the former (*stratevo*) referring to military operations, and the latter (*agonizomai*) to athletic contests like wrestling. Towner sees the difference in terms of differences in "Paul's" hortatory intentions. In 1 Timothy 1:18, he is encouraging Timothy to ward off opponents, and so "battle terminology" is more appropriate. He speaks in terms of athletics when it is a matter of encouraging Timothy "to attend to his own contest of faith" (2006: 410; cf. Bassler 1996: 171). This is an interesting literary-critical response, but 1 Timothy 1:18 may also to refer to an inner struggle, maintaining one's own faith and conscience even when others don't, whereas 2 Timothy 4:7, following closely on the heels of the pejorative treatment of opponents and apostates in vv. 3–4, might easily suggest confrontation with others. Collins' reading is quite different. He suggests that all of this language derives primarily from the military (2002: 48, 273). Perhaps one should not try to reduce the range of available interpretations too hastily (cf. Knight 1992: 459), particularly because the two basic readings that emerge again and again in the tradition, of the "fight" as a confrontation with human or demonic others, and as a struggle within oneself, are commonly indistinguishable in their essentials.

The Pastor's "Paul" is an active figure, fighting to shape his community theologically and ethically as well as socially and politically. At the same time, he fully expects his life's work to culminate not in this world, but the next, the world to be inaugurated in the *eschaton*, "on that day," when he will receive his well-earned "crown of righteousness." Hanson is suspicious of this verse. Does it suggest, contrary to what one finds in the authentic letters (e.g., in Phil. 3:12–14), that as "Paul" neared his death he expected to be rewarded for his "righteous life on earth" (1982: 156)? Nevertheless, that "Paul" should speak here of a crown is not problematic in this regard, for it fits with the imagery of an athletic victory (cf. 1 Cor. 9:25).

I am being poured out (v. 6)

Traditional interpreters have often thought that the offering upon which "Paul" models his own sacrifice is specifically connected to Jewish Temple cult (cf. Chrysostom, *Hom. 2 Tim.*, NPNF1 13.511; Bunyan, "Paul's Departure and Crown," 1850: 383). In any case, that "Paul" has become an offering means that his life is a sacrifice to God. And this idea, taken up in later writers, has been articulated in two ways, either as a description of martyrdom, or as a way of speaking of the life and/or death of believers more generally. Theodoret addresses "Paul's" death as a martyr in the simplest terms, interpreting the "libation" imagery literally: this man's "blood was being shed for the sake of religion" (*Comm. 2 Tim.*, 2001: 247). Ellen White also reads the passage as an accurate depiction of Paul's death-by-bloodletting. He "poured out his blood as a witness for the word of God and a testimony of Jesus Christ" (1911: 513). Like some modern commentators (e.g., D-C 1972: 121), White also remarks upon, or rather she excitedly embraces, the triumphalism of "Paul's" final self-assessment. His statement that he is offering himself up in sacrifice "has rung out through all the ages since" (1911: 513). This triumphalist reading has deep roots, though, and can be found, for instance, in Joseph Mede's seventeenth century apocalypticism. Mede, in his *Key to The Apocalypse*, cites 2 Timothy 4:6 as part of his explication of Revelation's fifth seal (Rev. 6:9–11). Referring to the Diocletian persecution of the early fourth century, Mede writes:

> [t]his butchery is represented by the vision of "souls slain for the word of God, and for his testimony which they maintained, lying under the altar," that is, on the ground, at the foot of the altar, like victims recently slaughtered. For martyrdom is a certain species of sacrifice; whence that assertion of the apostle to Timothy, when his own martyrdom was near approaching: "I am now about to be offered, and the time of my departure is at hand." To which also applies that expression of the same apostle to the Philippians (Phil. 2:17): "If I am offered for the sacrifice and service of your faith." (1833: 95)

The authentic Pauline epistles, of course, do present an eschatology; but it is remarkably different from Revelation's globally destructive vision of the end times, and has little in common, we hasten to add, with the Pastor's vision of the end. Mede, by making "Paul's" sacrifice illustrative of an apocalyptic interpretation of martyrdom, transforms his "departure" into an instrument of the warrior lamb who will take "a remarkable vengeance . . . on the empire for the guilt of so much blood" (96; cf. Bunyan's "Paul's Crown and Departure," 1850: 385, for a similar treatment).

Other readers, while not ignoring "Paul's" martyrdom, focus rather on how the language of this passage can speak to any Christian. Chrysostom, for example, uses the Pastor's sacrificial imagery to speak of the process of self-purification. Paul, he writes, "was purer than any sacrifice . . . 'ready to be offered.'" As a way of understanding Romans 12:1, our verse from 2 Timothy, in Chrysostom's hands, becomes a promise that "if thou hast aught in thee relaxed and secular, and yet offerest the sacrifice with a good intention, the fire of the Spirit will come down, and both wear away that worldliness, and perfect the whole sacrifice" (*Hom. Rom.*, NPNF1 11.497). One needn't die in the process, however, for the sacrifice can consist of good works. On the other hand, v. 6 can and has been used often to reflect upon the death of Christians in funeral sermons and orations, comforting the bereaved by remembering how well "Paul" faced not his death but his "departure." Something of this attitude is captured by Athanasius, who comments upon "Paul's" courage in facing his death when it was time. In this case, however, one has to recognize that the Pastor's "Paul" plays an apologetic role for Athanasius, who must defend himself against charges of cowardice after having abandoned his episcopal duties and fled in the face of danger. He contrasts the Paul of Acts 9:25, who allowed himself to escape from enemies, with the Paul of Acts 23:11 and 25:10, who looks forward to preaching in Rome, despite the risks this entails. At each moment, Athanasius implies, Paul merely did what God wanted him to do. Finally, when death came, in other words, when the time for his dying had clearly arrived and he knew that death rather than flight was his duty, "he gloried in it, saying, 'For I am now ready to be offered, and the time of my departure is at hand'" (*Apol. de fuga* 18, NPNF2 4.261; see also the commentary at 3:12).

I have fought the good fight (v. 7)

We noted above that the nature of the "fight" in this verse is not entirely clear. Accordingly, readers in the tradition have opted to take v. 7 in either athletic or military terms. Ambrose of Milan is characteristic of those who conceive of the "fight" as kind of competition:

> For in a contest there is much labour needed—and after the contest victory falls to some, to others disgrace. Is the palm ever given or the crown granted before the course is finished? Paul writes well; He says: "I have fought a good fight, I have finished my course, I have kept the faith; henceforth there is laid up for me a crown of righteousness, which the Lord, the righteous judge, shall give me at

that day; and not to me only, but unto all them also that love His appearing."
(*Duties of the Clergy* 1.15, NPNF2 10.11)

Especially interesting here is the opposition between winning and losing "the
good fight." The loser is disgraced by the winner's victory. Some readers have
stressed the disgracefulness of defeat in often parodic terms. Origen mocks
Celsus and pagans generally as people "lame and mutilated in soul . . . who run
to the temples as to places having a real sacredness and who cannot see that
no mere mechanical work of man can be truly sacred" (*C. Cels* 7.52 ANF 4.632).
In this context, Origen also thinks of "Paul's" fight in athletic terms; he is
likened to the boxer mentioned in 1 Corinthians 9:26. William Henry Clarke,
in a nineteenth century sermon, seems attuned to the same dynamic of victory,
that it is the contrary of disgrace. Yet he sanitizes the entire contest, assuring
his hearers that "no notorious criminal, not even a near relation of one, was
allowed to contend [in the Greek games]; and any person convicted of unfair
or sinister conduct, was punished by a heavy fine" (1834: 259). Thus the
Christian athlete has, according to "Paul," a model of the strictest uprightness
to follow in the lists. Clarke's reading is ambiguous, though, as it shifts abruptly
from the language of a competitive games to that of mortal combat between
the Christian and Satan (259–60).

Other readings also blend the military and the athletic themes. Theodoret's
paraphrase takes "Paul" to say "in my battle with the devil's every column I
have raised the trophy" (*Comm. 2 Tim.*, 2001: 247, cf. 212). Chrysostom's "Paul"
similarly defeats enemies in battle and wins the trophy at sport at the same
time (*Hom. 2 Tim.*, NPNF1 13.511). This oscillation between combat and
contest, with the demons on the opposing team, is taken a step further by John
Cassian, who very nearly imagines the action from the other side. The struggle
is fierce, he writes, for both us and them, for the saints and the demons, "[f]or
in their conflict they themselves have some sort of anxiety and depression, and
especially when they are matched with stronger rivals, i.e., saints and perfect
men." This is an important consideration because:

> where it is spoken of as a fight, and conflict, and battle, there must be effort and
> exertion and anxiety on both sides, and equally there must either be in store for
> them chagrin and confusion for their failure, or delight consequent upon their
> victory. But where one fights with ease and security against another who struggles
> with great effort, and in order to overthrow his rival makes use of his will alone
> as his strength, there it ought not to be called a battle, struggle, or strife, but a
> sort of unfair and unreasonable assault and attack. (*Conf.* 7.21, NPNF2 11.369)

There is no "sympathy for the devil" implied here, of course, as diverting as it
might be to consider the possibility. Cassian, in the persona of one Abbot

Serenus, argues rather that demons have limited powers to attack their human targets the monks, thanks to the protection of God. But he also claims that they prefer to clash with those whose souls will prove equal to the struggle. This second point means that if a monk does not feel the presence of the demonic, he is not striving vigorously enough towards holiness. The inconsistency in this reasoning (on the one hand God, and on the other, the devil, is responsible for the fierceness of the attack) is explained by Cassian's evident purpose, which is both to solace and exhort monks who find themselves subject to all manner of temptations and distractions in their long hours of solitude.

Many other readings of 2 Timothy 4:7 and its parallels in the Pastorals simply assume that "fighting the good fight" means "warring the good warfare," that it is a militant image. Often, however, the outcome of the "good fight" is more clearly than it is in Cassian a foregone conclusion. In the second part of John Buynan's *The Pilgrim's Progress*, Mr. Great-heart sallies forth to confront Gyant-dispair. His companions tremble at the prospect of the battle, but Great-heart comforts them, saying "I have a Commandment to resist Sin, to overcome Evil, to fight the good Fight of Faith: and I pray, with whom should I fight this good Fight, if not with Gyant-dispair?" (2003: 261–62). The battle, once joined, is swiftly concluded: "Great-heart was his death, for he left him not till he had severed his head from his shoulders" (262). Similarly, Calvin, reading 1 Timothy 6:12, interprets the "goodness" of the "good fight" in terms of the undoubted success of the Christian combatant. And because the fight is good, it is "not to be shunned; for, if earthly soldiers do not hesitate to fight, when the result is doubtful, and when there is a risk of being killed, how much more bravely ought we to do battle under the guidance and banner of Christ, when we are certain of victory?" (1964: 276). The victory Michael achieves against Satan and his dark angels in Milton's *Paradise Lost* was always guaranteed. His forces are said by God to be "invincible," and he "stand[s] approved in the sight of God." Curiously, though, just when one would expect an absolute, Milton describes this good warfare in comparative terms as "the better fight" (6.29–30, 1981: 171), better than the one Satan chose to wage at any rate. The well-known hymn, "Fight the Good Fight," by John Monsell (not the 1981 song of the same name by the Canadian pop group Triumph), announces the same theme of triumphal assurance in its opening stanza:

> Fight the good fight with all thy might;
> Christ is thy Strength, and Christ thy Right;
> Lay hold on life, and it shall be
> Thy joy and crown eternally.
> (in Watson 2002: 323)

One must fight still, of course, but if one places ones total confidence in Christ, the battle cannot be lost. An unexpected variation, in a sermon of John Wesley, on this theme of victorious battle against the foes of the Christian life represents that foe, oddly, as heaven itself. Or almost. Wesley certainly recognizes that in the "good fight" the enemy is any temptation or fear that prevents one from achieving one's goal. There is no reason to worry, of course, since "[n]othing is impossible to him that believeth." But in Wesley's exuberant rhetoric, the battle for salvation is still waged, somehow, *against* heaven: "[f]rom the moment that you begin to experience this [inner conviction], fight the good fight of faith; take the kingdom of heaven by violence! Take it as it were by storm!" ("Spiritual Idolatry," *Works* 6.444).

In modern usage, "fight the good fight" often refers to struggles against immoral, corrupt, violent political systems and programs of any stripe. Theodore Roosevelt, for example, wrote to Stalin in a letter of December 1942 that he wished, on behalf of the American people, to extend holiday greetings to Soviet forces, as to all those who "fight the good fight in order that they may win victory which will bring the world peace, freedom, and the advancement of human welfare" (in Butler 2005: 106). Allies in one good fight, clearly, can become adversaries in another, as the history of the Cold War attests. On a more local level, politically active individuals can adopt this same language to press the religious dimension of larger social struggles. This is how James Harris reads the "good fight" imagery in the Pastorals:

> The black Christian's life, and especially the minister's life, is indeed a good fight. The layperson and the preacher are in a war. We are fighting a battle. There are some battles in the church and world worth waging. A good fight is a fight against oppression, evil, and apathy. A good fight is against unfairness, injustice, poverty, racism, sexism, militarism, and domination. It is against the forces of ignorance. (*Pastoral Theology*, 1991: 102)

While Harris goes on to characterize these problems as "the power of Satan," within and without the church, he places them squarely in their historical and political contexts and thinks it folly to wait for salvation in the next life, for "to be happy is to be Christian and free in this world, here and now" (13).

Some of the very many literary and pop-cultural citations of the Pastor's "good fight" imagery, far too numerous to survey with any comprehensiveness, have a political rather than strictly religious subject as well. Ambrose Bierce's poem "A Single Termer," for instance, imagines an early twentieth century Republican politician immediately after his death:

> When Senator Foraker came to die
> His features lit up with a glow,

> And he said: "I am going to dwell on high
> And the Democrats down below."

The dead senator then cites 2 Timothy 4:7, but alters the verse to match his political corruption, as a servant of the corporate elite rather than the constituency he had been elected to represent.

> "I have kept the faith, I have fought the fight,
> To the Trusts forever true.
> With Elkins to lead, I have followed the light—
> Saint Peter, it's up to you."
> (1909: 4.80 either 1)

Saint Peter then decides that even though Foraker is a man of sin, he'll lock him into heaven rather than risk having him escape from hell to do further harm on earth. Another poem, "it's strange," by Charles Bukowski, also evokes, in its reference to v. 7, the passing of public figures. Somehow in its muted sadness it calls to mind Chrysostom's sympathetic reading of our text. Chrysostom, whose own father died when he was young, writes that v. 7 had always puzzled him: "[b]ut now by the grace of God I seem to have found it out. . . . He is desirous to console the despondency of his disciple. . . . [a]s a father whose son was sitting by him, bewailing his orphan state, might console him, saying, Weep not, my son; we have lived a good life, we have arrived at old age, and now we leave thee" (*Hom. 2 Tim.*, NPNF1 13.511). The relationship between the speaker or reader of Bukowski's poem and its subject, the death of a famous person, is far more nebulous than that between Timothy and "Paul." Still, Bukowski nicely captures the empty-heartedness of Chrysostom's orphan, but without any solace, let alone moral certainty, with regard to the dead.

> it's strange when famous people die
> whether they have fought the good fight or
> the bad one.
> it's strange when famous people die
> whether we like them or not
> they are like old buildings old streets
> things and places that we are used to
> which we accept simply because they're
> there.
> it's strange when famous people die
> it's like the death of a father or
> a pet cat or dog.
> and it's strange when famous people are killed

> or when they kill themselves.
> the trouble with the famous is that they must
> be replaced and they can never quite be
> replaced, and that gives us this unique
> sadness.
> it's strange when famous people die
> the sidewalks look different and our
> children look different and our bedmates
> and our curtains and our automobiles.
> it's strange when famous people die:
>
> we become troubled.
>
> (1981: 168)

Crown of righteousness (v. 8)

After fighting the good fight, does "Paul" simply expect that he will win the crown, that he has earned it? Readers in the tradition have worried about this issue, perhaps none more so than Augustine. In references to "Paul's" confidence in 4:8, which seems to imply, contrary to the Augustinian theology of grace, that human beings can to some extent achieve salvation for themselves, Augustine is willing to admit that the "crown is recompensed to . . . ["Paul's"] merits," but only because those merits themselves "are the gifts of God" (*C. ep. Pelag.* 35, NPNF1 5.199). When God responds to "Paul's" demand for repayment, "He crowns His own gifts, not . . . ["Paul's"] merits" (*Jo. ev. tr.* 3.10, NPNF1 7.22; cf. *En. ps.* 84.16, NPNF1 8.404). Aquinas, too, though more flexible in his understanding of merit, argues, in conjunction with this verse, that "the worth of the work depends on the dignity of grace" (ST FS Q[114] A[3]). The Calvinist tradition agrees with this basic sense that "Paul" has not merited his crown, his reward, through anything he may have done. Of course, the verse goes on to say that not just "Paul," but in fact "all who have longed for . . . [Christ's] appearing" will be crowned as well. But for readers of this stripe, such as Jonathan Edwards, the Pastor's language is merely meant to be taken as an encouragement "to extraordinary labours for God, for no other reason, but that we should seek them" (*Works of President Edwards* 10.225). Moreover, even if God grants "Paul" and other "saints" a strong confidence in their own salvation, such as "Paul" manifests here and in 2 Timothy 1:12, "nothing [about their salvation] can be certainly argued from their confidence, how great and strong soever it seems to be" (*Works of Jonathan Edwards* 2.169, 170). In other words, some who long for Christ's appearing will not receive a crown of righteousness in that day, despite the Pastor's optimistic statement that they will.

Some, taking a different view, believe that the Pastor is referring to martyrs. Cyprian, whom we have seen to be an ardent advocate of martyrdom, waxes rhapsodic at the promise of this verse:

> Precious is the death which has bought immortality at the cost of its blood, which has received the crown from the consummation of its virtues. How did Christ rejoice therein! How willingly did He both fight and conquer in such servants of His, as the protector of their faith, and giving to believers as much as he who taketh believes that he receives! He was present at His own contest; He lifted up, strengthened, animated the champions and assertors of His name. And He who once conquered death on our behalf, always conquers it in us. (*Ep.* 8, ANF 5.288)

Cyprian would evidently support the general claim that one earns the crown only with the direct aid of Christ himself, even if he seems to have a more fluid sense of agency and merit than some of the figures mentioned above would allow for. Not so Hilary of Poitiers, for whom a sincere confession of faith is enough to secure salvation. In Hilary's view, the Pastor's "Paul" certainly earned his reward by virtue of his martyrdom. Indeed, there is no distinction between the worthy deed and its recompense: "[t]o Paul ... [the] sacrifice was the crown of righteousness" itself (*On the Trinity* 10.46, NPNF2 9.194). Reading this passage similarly, Jacob Arminius takes it as evidence that the doctrine of predestination is mistaken. If "the recompense of those who fight the good fight and who run well [is] a crown of righteousness," it is reasonable to conclude that "God ... has not, from his own absolute decree, without any consideration or regard whatever to faith and obedience, appointed to any man, or determined to appoint to him, life eternal" (*Writings* 1.226–27).

We have been assuming that "Paul's" crown will be given him in the eschatological kingdom, where he will reign with Christ (2:12). Others have held that the crown of righteousness may be worn in this life as well. Edward Taylor, in a poetic "Meditation" on this verse, prays God to give him his crown now.

> A Crown, Lord, yea, a Crown of Righteousness.
> Oh! what a Gift is this? Give Lord I pray
> An Holy Head, and Heart it to possess
> And I shall give thee glory for the pay.
> A Crown is brave, and Righteousness much more.
> The glory of them both will pay the score.

The gift is not the crown itself, certainly, but the worthiness of it, the very righteousness it stands for. It is for this he prays, and in the process laments his own wicked, or "naughty" state. What is fascinating is that Taylor bargains with God in this poem. If you, God, grant me my crown of righteousness, I'll return the favor "and thou / Shalt have my Songs to diadem thy brow":

> Oh! Happy me, if thou wilt Crown me thus.
> Oh! naughty heart! What swell with Sin? fy, fy.
> Oh! Gracious Lord, me pardon: do not Crush
> Me all to mammocks: Crown and not destroy.
> Ile tune thy Prayses while this Crown doth come.
> Thy Glory bring I tuckt up in my Songe.
>   (1960: 71–72)

The crown, if it is to be given in this life, need not be considered a religious reward, only, but like "the good fight" can be taken up politically by activists attuned to the power of religious language. One example of this kind is Frances Ellen Watkins Harper's 1893 speech at the World's Congress of Representative Women. In her contribution Harper, an African-American suffragist, speaks out on "woman's political future," arguing for the franchise in view of the qualitative change it will bring to America: "in the political future of our nation woman will not have done what she could if she does not endeavor to have our republic stand foremost among the nations of the earth, wearing sobriety as a crown and righteousness as a garment and a girdle" (in Logan 1995: 44). The nation is crowned here, not women or women voters. And it is the crown of sobriety, of course, not righteousness. But in light of 1 Timothy 2:9, which orders women to clothe themselves with "sobriety" (KJV) while remaining silent and subordinate to men, it is difficult not to hear in Harper's echoing of Isaiah's righteous garment language (e.g. Isa 11:5; 61:11) the subversive appropriation and extension of the Pastor's imagery. Women voters will reshape the nation and, in the process, will eliminate the institutionally maintained and religiously justified misogyny that limited their full political agency in the first place.

Conclusion and Greetings (4:9–22)

2 Timothy concludes with the most extensive greetings section in the Pastoral corpus. 1 Timothy, like Ephesians and 2 Thessalonians, also deutero-Pauline texts, leaves out the greeting section altogether. Galatians does as well but, as Collins notes, the absence of the greetings there is of a piece with the letter as a whole, which provides evidence of a "strained relationship" between Paul and the letter's recipients (2002: 174). Of the people mentioned by the Pastor at

the end of 2 Timothy, just over half are known from other sources, including most famously the missionary couple Prisca and Aquila, mentioned by Paul in the greetings sections of Romans and 1 Corinthians, and given some narrative space in Acts 18. Demas, who is mentioned in Colossians and Philemon positively, here becomes a deserter because of his love for "this present world" (v. 10). Demas is also a traitor to Paul, along with Hermogenes, in the *Acts of Paul and Thecla*. Dennis MacDonald surveys the scholarship on the relationship between the Pastorals and the *Acts*, and concludes that both had independent access to oral traditions about Paul and his associates (1983: 65), and that each draws upon that material in different ways to shape their particular portraits of Paul. In the *Acts of Paul and Thecla*, Paul is an ascetic who discourages marriage and actively encourages the intensive participation of women in his ministry. The Pastorals, of course, describe a Paul who is quite different, very nearly the opposite in fact. In both sources, Demas is described in fairly cursory terms. He betrays Paul in the *Acts* (3:12–14, ANF 8.488), and merely deserts him in the Pastorals, and yet it is this desertion which has earned him the opprobrium of the ages.

The Pastor complains that only Luke remained by "Paul's" side in his final imprisonment. Many commentators regard v. 21 as a contradiction of this statement. It does seem clear that "Paul" cannot be alone with Luke if he also shares the company of Eubulus, "Pudens and Linus and Claudia and all the brothers and sisters," although perhaps it depends upon how one defines "alone" (Towner 2006: 655 thinks that "Paul" is speaking only of his mission team, not of any and all contacts whatsoever). After implying his near total isolation, "Paul" urges Timothy to come to him as quickly as possible, and "to bring the cloak that I left with Carpus at Troas, and also the books, and above all the parchments" (v. 13). Those who assume Pauline authorship of the Pastorals point to this verse as a sure sign of authenticity (Guthrie 1990:184). Those who feel that these letters are pseudonymous argue that a creative writer can certainly make up these details as he goes along, as an effort "to impart verisimilitude" (Collins 2002: 283). As Donelson notes, "the [seemingly] careless references to mundane affairs of daily life, the specific requests for ordinary and seemingly insignificant objects to be delivered, and even the attempt to display personal feelings are all fully documented in other [pseudonymous] letters," and function as a careful literary strategy designed, among other reasons, to produce a sense of authenticity (1986: 25). Such details might serve other purposes as well (37). For instance, to the extent that the Pastor's purpose in these letters is to establish a particular genealogy of Pauline succession, perhaps "Paul" intends to hand this cloak on to Timothy because it somehow represents his ministry, as Elijah's mantle represented his prophetic office in 2 Kings 2:8–15 (cf. Hanson 1982: 158–59; Bassler 1996: 176).

Demas, in love with this present world (v. 10)

Readers do not entirely agree on just what Demas' desertion entails. For some, whose responses can be almost sympathetic, Demas is simply afraid – afraid of suffering with Paul. Calvin's reading is characteristic of these. He writes in his commentary on the Pastorals that "we are not to suppose that he [i.e., Demas] completely denied Christ and gave himself over again to ungodliness or the allurements of the world, but only that he cared more for his own convenience and safety than for the life of Paul." In the extraordinarily difficult circumstances of Paul's final ministry, Demas, "one of the most outstanding of Paul's companions," "was overcome by his dislike for the cross and decided to look to his own interests" (1964: 340). He is not acquitted for all that, but is understandable, indeed recognizable, as someone potentially like ourselves (see also Chrysostom, *Hom. 2 Tim.*, NPNF1 13.513). For many others, who focus on what Charlotte Brontë in *Jane Eyre* calls "the vice of Demas," that is, greed (2000: 403), Demas is rather a criminal character, despicable in every way. Many associate him with other biblical characters known for greed or treachery or both, like Ananias and Saphira, not to mention Judas (Flavel, *Fountain of Life*, 1701: 1.111). One of the most famous readings of this kind is John Bunyan's. In *The Pilgrim's Progress*, Christian and Hopeful meet Demas while on their way to the Celestial City. Demas tries to tempt the two wayfarers with promises of treasure by luring them into his dangerous "silver-mine," but Christian rebuffs him, charging:

> I know you, Gehazi [2 Kings 5:20–27] was your Great Grandfather, and Judas your Father, and you have trod in their steps. It is but a devilish prank that thou usest: Thy Father was hanged for a Traitor, and thou deservest no better reward. Assure thy self, that when we come to the King, we will do him word of this thy behavior. (2003: 104–05).

A recent work of Christian fiction, Shane Johnson's *The Demas Revelation*, takes the corruption of Demas to new extremes by casting him as a puppet of the devil who composes a set of hoax confessions in which Paul and the Twelve deny the veracity of the gospel. Jesus never rose from the dead, they admit, he was not the Messiah – they faked everything after his crucifixion "so that the hope that lived in the eyes of our brethren, his followers, would not be extinguished" (Johnson 2007: 105–06). These confessions, discovered at archaeological sites in Rome and Pompeii in the early twenty-first century, set off a fairly predictable storm of apostasy worldwide, and provide the novelist with a vehicle for perpetuating what is, by now, the standard self-understanding of the Christian right in America: the world hates Jesus, and believers are a persecuted minority who must fight for their very survival against the forces of a godless liberalism. Even the discovery of Demas' own, authentic, confession, in which he admits to faking the denials of Paul, Peter, and the others, can do little to restore the faith to its former, apparently quite precarious, glory (275–79; 283). Because Demas repents, however, the novel gives the impression that, as "Paul" prays at the end of 2 Timothy, it may "not have been counted against" him (4:15).

Bring the cloak, the books, the parchment (v. 13)

Readers throughout the tradition have been struck, as have modern commentators, by the triviality of this and similar details at the end of 2 Timothy. Chrysostom wants to know, "[b]ut what had he to do with books, who was about to depart and go to God?" (*Hom. 2 Tim.*, NPNF1 13.514). Matthew Henry asks an even sharper version of the same question: "Paul was guided by Divine Inspiration, and yet he would have his Books with him?" (1721: 325). Of course, readers who believe that Paul wrote these texts will provide reasonable answers to make sense of this passage. Calvin's explanations are typical. He says, along with Chrysostom, that the word translated here as "cloak" may actually refer to "a chest or box for books." It may simply be a cloak too, of course, and if it is it makes sense that Paul should want it "since from long use it would be more comfortable for him and he would want to avoid expense." As for the books, "it is obvious . . . that although the apostle was already preparing for death, he had not given up reading. . . . [Thus] this passage commends continual reading to all godly men" (1964: 340–01). For many, however, there is very little in this verse which is worthy of exegetical consideration. Jerome has to struggle to find a worthy justification for "Paul's" comments. Ultimately, for him, their very dullness may itself be the lesson:

> Such is the state of man; if we are a little careless we learn our weakness, and find that our power is limited. Do you suppose that the Apostle Paul, when he wrote "the coat (or cloak) that I left at Troas with Carpus, bring when thou comest, and the books, especially the parchments," was thinking of heavenly mysteries, and not of those things which are required for daily life and to satisfy our bodily necessities? Find me a man who is never hungry, thirsty, or cold, who knows nothing of pain, or fever, or the torture of strangury [i.e., a urinary tract infection], and I will grant you that a man can think of nothing but virtue. (*Against the Pelagians* 3.4, NPNF2 6.473–74)

Jerome is, in context, simply noting that even those biblical figures who should most be capable of doing God's will are subject to failure and weakness. That from among the Pauline corpus he chooses this text, as opposed to, say, one of Paul's more vitriolic outbursts (e.g., Gal. 5:12), is telling. Clearly it seem to Jerome a failure to live up to the New Testament's spiritual worth.

When it comes to the question of biblical inspiration, discussed at 3:16 (and recalled above by Matthew Henry), our verse becomes a defining text, precisely because of the very "weakness" Jerome observes. John Henry Newman considers this verse to be a classic *obiter dictum*, an incidental detail which has no bearing upon the lives of believers. He asks, with more than a little sarcasm, whether "Timothy . . . [would] think this an infallible utterance? And supposing it had been discovered, on most plausible evidence, that the Apostle left his cloak with Eutychus, not with Carpus, would Timothy, would Catholics now, make themselves unhappy, because St. Paul had committed . . . 'a falsehood'?" (*On Inspiration* 1967: 143–44). Surely, he adds, had Paul wanted to he could have indicated that this verse is truly a divine mandate by writing something along the lines of "Thus saith the Lord, Send the *penula* [from the Vulgate, 'cloak']" (144). The argument for a stricter sense of biblical inspiration, on the other hand, requires that every text be fraught with God's meaningful purpose. 2 Timothy 4:13 is no exception. Louis Gaussen's *Theopneustia* opens the discussion of this passage, after asserting once again that all scripture is holy and infallibly inspired, with a brilliant *non sequitur*: doesn't the gospel itself speak of Jesus' garment as he is expiring on the cross (e.g., John 19:24)? "Would you have this passage erased from the number of inspired words?" he asks (1841: 246). As for "Paul's" own cloak, Gaussen's point is that such authentic details are morally important, they present us with an essential window into the last days of the apostle, an affecting and spiritually effective experience of Paul's own suffering. Without them, the New Testament would be incomplete. Samuel Taylor Coleridge makes the same point, but for rather different reasons. He claims that if "some captious Litigator should lay hold of a text here or there, St. Paul's cloak left at Troas with Carpus, or a Verse from the Canticles, and ask – of what spiritual use is this? The answer is ready – It proves to us that nothing can be so trifling as not to supply an evil heart with a pretext for unbelief" (*Confessions of an Enquiring Spirit*, *Works* 11[2].1169). The problem, for Coleridge, has less to do with the doctrine of plenary inspiration, than with the sense of an illuminating spiritual communication between readers of the Bible and all aspects of scripture – from the theologically sublime to the mundane. Still, he is not that far removed from Gaussen's own quite romantic sensibility when it comes to the importance of passages such as this one.

Titus 1

Titus begins with a salutation, that opening element in ancient letters which identifies the sender and recipient. In this case the salutation also incorporates a brief theological overview of "Paul's" project. Titus, we soon learn, has been left in Crete to work with the nascent Christian community there. He must appoint bishops of a certain moral and social quality; but he must also stifle a troublesome (quite possibly Jewish-Christian) opposition. The chapter concludes with a scathing condemnation of these opponents.

The Pastoral Epistles Through the Centuries, First Edition. Jay Twomey.
© 2009 by Jay Twomey. Published 2020 by John Wiley & Sons Ltd.

The Salutation (1:1–4; 2 Tim. 1:9)

Titus begins with one of the longest, and most complex, salutations of the canonical Pauline corpus. Many of the terms and concepts have been encountered earlier in these letters, and this has led some to imagine that Titus may originally have been written as the first letter of this collection, so that its salutation could function as an introductory statement for the group as a whole (Bassler 1996: 181). Certainly the fact that Titus does not mention Paul's imprisonment has led many to the conclusion that Titus was written before, or at least was meant to precede, 2 Timothy (e.g., Chrysostom, *Hom. Tit.*, NPNF1 13.519; Erasmus *Paraphrases*, 1993: 56; Fee 1984: 12). Some common themes given voice here by the Pastor include: "the truth" as synonymous with the Christian teaching (1 Tim. 2:4; 3:15; 4:3; 6:5; 2 Tim. 2:15, 18; 2:25; 3:7–8; 4:4; Titus 1:14); "godliness" as a synonym for ideal Christian behavior (1 Tim. 2:2, 10; 4:7–8; 6:3–11; 2 Tim. 3:5, 12; Titus 2:12; cf. 1 Tim. 3:16); the "appearance" Christology as an indication of God's saving activity (1 Tim. 3:16; 6:14; 2 Tim. 1:10; 4:1, 8; Titus 2:13); and the use of the title "savior" to refer to God (1 Tim. 1:1; 2:3; 4:10; Titus 2:10; 3:4) or Christ (2 Tim. 1:10; Titus 3:6) or both (see at Titus 2:12). As is the case with much in Titus, because it is the shortest of the three letters, and more importantly because it can seem to be a mirror-image of 1 Timothy, readers in the tradition who have been drawn to these themes have frequently chosen to speak of them in terms of their articulation in the other two Pastorals, 1 Timothy especially. As Gordon Fee puts it, speaking of modern commentary, Titus "has been treated with benign neglect" (1984: 11).

However, Titus does have unique material as well, and certain readings of its particular expression of the material it shares with 1 and/or 2 Timothy are important. For example, the Pastor writes that salvation was promised by God "before the ages began" (cf. 2 Tim. 1:9). In Hanson's view, that the "hope of eternal life" has its origin in a promise God made "before the ages began" means that "salvation belongs to the timeless eternal world; only revelation belongs to time" (1982: 170).

Before the ages began (v. 2)

The precise meaning of this verse, however, is sometimes elusive. In the *City of God*, Augustine, whose Latin for this clause is *ante tempora aeterna* (cf. the Vulgate: *ante tempora saecularia*), says that he cannot understand what the text means by speaking of a promise made "before eternal times":

I own that I do not know what ages passed before the human race was created, yet I have no doubt that no created thing is co-eternal with the Creator. But even the apostle speaks of time as eternal, and this with reference, not to the future, but, which is more surprising, to the past. . . . But then, how did He promise; for the promise was made to men, and yet they had no existence before eternal times? (*De civ. Dei* 12.16; NPNF1 2.236–37)

Augustine's answer is that God made the promise to himself (cf. Wesley 1850: 556, "to Christ, our Head"). Seen in this light, our verse is therefore a biblical proof for the doctrine of predestination. But Calvin, working both with this verse and with this passage from Augustine, remarks that the latter "gets into difficulties" because he has misunderstood Titus 1:2. God did not promise an as-yet inexistent human race anything before the world began. Rather, the Pastor's "meaning is simply that the promise is more ancient than a long succession of ages, because it began immediately from the foundation of the world" (1964: 354). The difference between this verse and 2 Timothy 1:9, Calvin adds, is that here we are alerted to God's promise to humanity, and there we are made aware of God's eternal decision regarding salvation.

The Cambridge Platonist Henry More, on the other hand, takes what puzzles Augustine about this text rather more scientifically than theologically, using the idea of a time "before the ages began" to speak of worlds which preexisted our own. Titus 1:2, along with 2 Timothy 1:9, "doe most naturally imply . . . the Supposition of an antecedent State, and the Præexistency of Souls, a part of which, falln and decayd, God designed for the peopling of this dark Earth" (in Ward 2000: 272–73). What for the Pastor is the uniquely significant divine plan for humanity, and for Christians in particular (cf. 1 Tim. 4:10), is something of an afterthought in More. Moreover, Earth was not "created with the entire Universe; but arose out of the Rubbish . . . of a præexistant Chaos" (in Ward 2000: 270).

The Opponents: Cretan Liars (1:9–16)

After the salutation, the Pastor once again offers a virtue list like those we find in 1 Timothy 3 and 5. Titus has been left behind in, or perhaps sent on to, Crete (Towner 2006: 678) and is yet in the early stages of his work there. The church in Ephesus seems already to be well established, and Paul writes to Timothy that he must remain behind to supervise the teaching of right doctrine (1 Tim. 1:3). By contrast, the church in Crete is still lacking its basic leadership structure (v. 5). As we noted at 1 Timothy 3:1–13, the references to church leaders in the Pastorals are often ambiguous at best, and here the leadership positions seem entirely indistinguishable. Regardless of this ambiguity, the elders or bishops are to be worthy men of the community, "able both to preach with sound doctrine and to refute those who contradict it" (v. 9). The refutation in store for "gainsayers" (KJV), however, is much harsher than anything we have seen in the Pastorals. The Pastor tells Titus that troublemakers, and "especially those of the circumcision," need to have their "mouths stopped" (v. 11, KJV), and he goes on to denigrate the Cretans with a line of verse from a Cretan poet characterizing them as "liars, vicious brutes, lazy gluttons" (v. 12). The Pastor refers to this poet as a "prophet," an idea that makes Collins uncomfortable enough to translate prophet, here, as "spokesperson" (2002: 334). Even worse is the fact that the verse in question, which the Pastor calls a "true" "testimony" (v. 13), denigrates the Cretans as liars for saying that Zeus is dead (D-C 1972: 136–37). This verse, by the way, is often discussed in semantics and logic as "the Cretan paradox": if the writer of the verse is Cretan, and all Cretans are liars, then how can one judge the veracity of his claim?

The Greek verb used for stopping the mouth literally refers to bridling a horse, perhaps even to gagging (Collins 2002: 333; Towner 2006: 696). Some modern commentators are, of course, troubled by the violence implied here (especially in comparison with, say, Titus 3:2–3, 9–10). Hanson takes the low road in this regard, merely commenting that "it is quite impossible to imagine Paul doing anything so obtuse" as this in a letter that will be read to the whole community (1982: 177). But others, like Wolfgang Stegemann, are more seriously troubled by what they see in the letter as "an ancient form of racism." The usual anti-Jewish polemic is bad enough, but racism enters the picture, he argues, "in the dreadful proverb about the Cretans [since] their ethnic origins are linked with quasi-biological features" (ibid.). Since the Cretans in view are either Jewish or are cast, polemically, as Jews, the proverb is thus at least potentially anti-Semitic as well (2002: 293).

The Pastor continues his anti-Jewish, anti-ascetic polemic with a declaration that echoes throughout these letters (cf. 1 Tim. 4:4), and has analogues in other New Testament texts as well (Mark 7:14–15; Rom. 14:14): believers are not to make distinctions in God's creation between clean and unclean, or to invent spurious dichotomies of the spiritual versus the material, and so forth. As with the advocacy of a certain violence in v. 11 above, this passage has also found strangely divisive support in some modern commentaries. Dibelius and Conzelmann, for example, remark in passing that the purity idea raised in v. 15 is "a statement to which enlightened persons of all countries subscribe as against cultic asceticism regarding food" (1972: 137; cf. Hanson 1982: 178).

The response to this verse through the centuries, however, has been far more complex and interesting than the reactions to, and appropriations of, v. 11. Readers have wanted to know just what the Pastor may have meant by "all things." In other words, what restrictions still apply when purity is the prime consideration? On the other hand, if all things are indeed pure, then what do feelings of impurity tell us about ourselves?

Especially those of the circumcision (v. 10)

The fact that those who need to be silenced are Jewish, described as "those of the circumcision," those who are "paying attention to Jewish myths," seems evident from this passage (vv. 11, 14). Chrysostom, for instance, writes of the Jewish "old wives' tales" that they were fit only for the minds of children (*Hom. 1 Tim.*, NPNF1 13.445). The Jews toy with traditions for the sake of gaining a "reputation [for] historical knowledge and research." He also blames the Greeks for the same tendency, though, "for they enumerated their Gods" (410). Thomas Aquinas supposes that these verses refer to the Talmud which, in his view, does not provide the good sort of myths, those which "contain true sense and represent something useful," but rather those which are "vain" (Thomas Aquinas 2007: 168). And for Erasmus, the only possible response was exasperation, since "no nation rebels more stubbornly against the gospel than the Jews" (*Paraphrases*, 1993: 60). Luther actually considers the reference to circumcision an insult in itself (*Lectures on Titus, Works* 29.36).

Theodoret, however, provides an interesting alternative reading to this much more prevalent one. Because the Pastor goes on to quote a Greek poet, Theodoret writes that the opponents described here "were Gentiles, not Jews . . . Callimachus (whence comes the beginning of the proverb [in v. 12]) was not a prophet of the Jews; in fact, he was a poet of the Greeks." A few moments after this, he adds, as if in recognition of the way verses such as these can fuel anti-Jewish polemic: "for the present we have taken on the task of commentary, not of criticizing Jews" (*Comm. Tit.*, 2001: 254; Thodoret, however, also considered the Jews "obtuse" and is said to have written a book bearing the title "Against the Jews," no longer extant; see Theodoret 2006: 163, 6).

They must be silenced (v. 11)

The desire to silence alternative voices endures, as we have noted, through the centuries. Readings picking up the Pastor's specific language have sometimes a rather aggressive, and at other times a rather more nuanced, understanding about how, essentially, to effect unity in the faith. Jerome, in considering the responsibilities of priests, remarks while citing our text that "an innocent and unobtrusive conversation [aimed at influencing one's opponents] does as much harm by its silence as it does good by its example. If the ravening wolves are to be frightened away it must be by the barking of dogs and by the staff of the shepherd" (*Ep.* 69.8, NPNF2 6.147). Differences are to be treated as potential acts of violence, in this view. Later writers agreed, but are less certain on how to meet the threat. Calvin, who seems to have had the Jerome passage in mind at this point in his commentary, writes that "a good pastor" should not "by his silence . . . allow wicked and harmful doctrines to creep in." He would like to think that after "smiting' such people "by the sword of God's word . . . the Church can command them to be silent," but he knows very well that this is probably only wishful thinking. The most realistic way to shut the mouths of opponents is "to refute their vain talk even if they do not stop making a noise" (1964: 362). Luther's reading of this passage is more or less exactly the same, except insofar as he thinks that the Pastor really had theological debate in mind: "since Paul himself bids us silence empty talkers, let us go into the details of the case and deal with the subject" as the opponents present it, the better to convince them, once we've eviscerated their arguments, that their position is wrong (*Works* 33.102).

A remarkable combination of these readings and polemical tactics is to be found in the prison writings of Katharine Evans and Sarah Chevers, two Quaker women held by the Inquisition on Malta in the 1660s. The women, defending themselves under harsh conditions from Catholic authorities intent on converting them, wrote triumphantly that:

> [T]he Lord did work mightily for us, and we were kept by the Power of the Lord over our Enemies, and were bold for God's Truth, and did make war with them in righteousness, so that they could not gain-say us in the truth: So that Scripture was fulfilled, *The wicked mouths must be stopped*; and they were put to silence, praises be to our God, and were made to confess or say, *Of a truth God was in us*; our God was a consuming fire to them [Heb. 12:29], they were not able to stand in his presence, but they would howl and make a noise like Dogs, and cry, *Jesu, Maria*, and flye as people driven by a mighty rushing Wind; the Power of the Lord did pursue after them like a Sword. (*Short Relation*, 1662: 36)

The enemies here are dogs, not wolves, but the text nevertheless incorporates elements of Jerome's figurative use of "vicious brutes" (v. 12) while at the same time working under the assumption that mouths will be stopped only when the arguments they utter have been convincingly vanquished.

In the early twentieth century, Karl Barth acknowledges that part of the "fight of faith" is stopping the mouths of theological opponents. But unlike Evans and Chevers and the perspective on theological and doctrinal conflict they represent, Barth claims that "this is not a fight against, but for, these people." Reading 1 Timothy 2:1–4 ("prayers . . . for everyone") and 2 Timothy 2:24–25 ("God may perhaps grant that they will repent") alongside our verse, Barth argues that "[t]he ministry of the Word can in no wise be understood as a fight of one party against a counter party" (1936: 87–88).

Their very own prophet (v. 12)

The Cretan "prophet" quoted by the Pastor in v. 12 is variously identified as Epimenides (seventh century BCE) or Callimachus (third century BCE). To most readers, however, the origin of this verse is less important than the fact that a New Testament writer has, first, referred to a pagan author, and second, called that author a prophet.

This is not the first place in the New Testament where Paul or some Pauline persona has quoted from pagan writers (see also Acts 17:28, 1 Cor. 15:33). Chrysostom, playing the part of the horrified Christian encountering this text for the first time, asks: is Paul not saying, then, that Zeus is immortal? After all, if the prophet is a truth-teller, aren't his religious beliefs also true? Moreover, the verse in question seems to deny that Zeus is dead. Have no fear, he continues, for Paul is taking the verse out of context, and he means only to emphasize that Cretans are liars; he is saying nothing about their gods (*Hom. Tit.*, NPNF1 13.528). It may still be asked why this letter should cite a pagan at all, to which Chrysostom replies, brilliantly, that God speaks to people in terms they can understand. He directed the wise men to the place of Jesus' birth by means of a star, rather than a prophet or angel, because "their art made them conversant with these, [therefore] He made use of such means to guide them" (528–29). God is like "a father [who] considers not his own dignity, but talks lispingly with his children, and calls their meat and drink not by their Greek names, but by some childish and barbarous words" (529).

For Augustine, God is less directly involved in the utterances of this "obscure prophet of a foreign race" than Chrysostom imagines. In his conflict with Donatists who argued that baptisms performed by apostate priests were null and void, Augustine, for whom those same baptisms were valid, insists upon a distinction between the truth itself and its speakers. One does not shun the truth simply because it comes from someone normally considered false. The Pastor cites this poet's statement about the Cretans "because he found it to be true":

[therefore,] why do not we, when we find in any one what belongs to Christ, and is true even though the man with whom it may be found be deceitful and perverse, why do not we in such a case make a distinction between the fault which is found in the man, and the truth which he has not of his own but of God's? and why do we not say, This sacrament is true, as Paul said, "This witness is true"? (*Answer to the Letters of Petilian* 30, NPNF1 4.547)

For his part, Calvin is not sure why Paul "should call this man a prophet." He lists some possible reasons, including irony – perhaps Paul was merely mocking the Cretans with a prophet "worthy" of them. But he finally decides that the reason is pure literary convention, "since poets are sometimes called prophets in Greek." The truth is what matters, he says, echoing Augustine, and adds that "it is superstitious to refuse to make any use of secular authors" (1964: 363). Luther agrees, commenting that "the true sayings of the poets, when they show us our sins" are "especially" divine (*Works* 29.38). In each of these readings, however, the primary focus is on the availability of God's truth in even unexpected places.

Other readings of this text have tended to emphasize much more energetically the importance of non-scriptural authors to the life of the Christian mind. For instance, Clement of Alexandria comments, like Calvin and Luther after him, that "even to the prophets of the Greeks [Paul] . . . attributes something of the truth, and is not ashamed" (*Str.* 1.14, ANF 2.313). But Clement, for whom "the way of truth is . . . one" (*Str.* 1.5, ANF 2.305), is far more enthusiastic than they about the prospect of reading the Greek thinkers and poets alongside scripture. It is true that the Mosaic writings precede, and are superior to, those of the Greeks, in his version of intellectual history. Nonetheless, Clement remarks approvingly that the Greeks, in their philosophical style, "adopted brevity, as suited for exhortation, and most useful," and goes on to cite Plato to the effect that – contrary to what one would expect from Titus 1:12 – the "Cretans . . . enjoyed the best laws" (*Str.* 1.14, ANF 2.313). In seventeenth century Mexico, Sor Juana Inés de la Cruz found it useful to defend her own poetic work by referring to the Pastor's Cretan prophet, whom she thinks must be Parmenides. "Even Paul," she writes, "studied the poets." But not only Paul, Jerome also, she writes. David, of course wrote poetry, as did Mary herself, "the Queen of Wisdom," who "with her holy lips intoned the Canticle of the Magnificat" (2005: 285). And she concludes with another echo from the Pastorals (1 Tim. 3:7; 2 Tim. 2:26): "[w]hat harm then can there be in poetry? The ill use of something is not the fault of art, but of the bad practitioner who falsifies it and makes it a snare of the devil. This is true for all subjects and disciplines" (286).

To the pure, all things are pure (1:15)

This verse is among the most widely appropriated from the Pastorals. The extensive and diverse uses to which it has been necessitates breaking the remainder of this chapter into subsections on: 1) literature, the arts, and "illicit" culture; 2) religious practices; and 3) the body.

1.　Literature, the arts, and "illicit" culture
Sor Juana's question (cited just above), "what harm is there in poetry," is one with relevance for this verse as well. If all things are pure to the pure, if "Paul" can quote from a pagan poet (and prophet), then may not believers fully embrace secular aesthetic texts without risking their "consciences" (v. 15), without "denying God" (v. 16)? Jerome finds that he must struggle with this question quite literally. Giving advice on eloquence and self-presentation, he remarks that while pagan literature may be enticing and instructive, one should avoid it. "Although" as scripture says, "'unto the pure all things are pure' [KJV] . . . still we ought not to drink the cup of Christ, and, at the same time, the cup of devils [1 Cor. 10:21]." This is a position, however, at which he arrived only after serious difficulty. He explains that when he had at first devoted himself to a life of spiritual "warfare" he found it difficult to give up his love of literature: "I would fast only that I might afterwards read Cicero. After many nights spent in vigil, after floods of tears called from my inmost heart, after the recollection of my past sins, I would once more take up Plautus." Eventually he became deathly ill and, on the verge of expiration was swept up into the heavens:

> Suddenly I was caught up in the spirit and dragged before the judgment seat of the Judge. . . . Asked who and what I was I replied: "I am a Christian." But He who presided said: "Thou liest, thou art a follower of Cicero and not of Christ. For 'where thy treasure is, there will thy heart be also [Matt. 6:21].'" Instantly I became dumb, and amid the strokes of the lash—for He had ordered me to be scourged—I was tortured more severely still by the fire of conscience . . . May it never, hereafter, be my lot to fall under such an inquisition! I profess that my shoulders were black and blue, that I felt the bruises long after I awoke from my sleep, and that thenceforth I read the books of God with a zeal greater than I had previously given to the books of men. (*Ep.* 22.29–30, NPNF2 6.35–36).

One of the more curious things about Jerome is the fact that, despite this experience, he continued to be a devotee of pagan writing, citing Virgil a decade later, for example, in *Epistle* 54.5 (NPNF2 6.103). In any event, he does not go so far as to suggest that his favorite Latin literature is impure in itself. Rather, in the logic of our verse, it was the way his love for these works rendered his devotions less pure that matters.

We have seen, with regard to v. 12, that figures like Calvin and Luther feel one can take one's concern about the Christian use of non-Christian texts too far. But Luther's reading of 1:15 probably sums up how Jerome may have felt about his post-visionary appreciation of pagan authors: as long as one knows, in one's conscience, that whatever one is doing "is pleasing to God," then one is pure (*Works* 29.46). This is exactly how Milton understands "unto the pure all things are pure," but the way he deploys his interpretation is quite at odds with the conservative tradition. Contrary to the historicist reading of the verse, Milton feels that the Pastor is here speaking "not only [of] meats and drinks, but all kinds of knowledge, whether of good or evil." Taking the Pastor seriously, then, means accepting that "the knowledge cannot defile, nor consequently the books, if the will and conscience be not defiled. For books are as meats and viands are; some of good, some of evil substance; and yet God . . . said without exception, "Rise, Peter, kill and eat;" leaving the choice to each man's discretion." The analogy is not entirely apt, as he knows, but even as it breaks down it only serves further to justify his extrapolation: "Bad meats will scarce breed good nourishment in the healthiest concoction; but herein the difference is of bad books, that they to a discreet and judicious reader serve in many respects to discover, confute, to forewarn, and to illustrate" (*Areopagitica*, *Prose Works* 1959: 2.512). Milton's defense of a free press, and more generally his understanding of the Pastor's meaning, should encourage all Christians to resist efforts to ban religiously "illicit" books from libraries or school reading lists (for an effort of this sort, see Tippens, "Who's Afraid of Harry Potter," 2002). The source of purity is not, as in Tertullian (see below), found in the practices and beliefs of others, but rather in one's own intellectual being.

Such liberal readings, of course, will always be countered by more conservative responses to culture. The early twentieth century *Christian Worker's Commentary* is well aware of generalizing readings of v. 15, which, like Milton, assert that nothing, in itself, is spiritually bad for us so long as we ourselves are pure. It rejects this perspective by limiting the verse to historical matters – the Pastor has in mind Jewish dietary restrictions only. When used more generally, the commentary notes, our verse becomes "an aphorism greatly abused": "How monstrous in the light of the true meaning of the words for people to employ them as permission to look at obscene pictures in art galleries, and listen to lewd stories, and read impure books, and witness impure plays" (Gray 1915: 412). The *Worker's Commentary* thus endorses a position forwarded by Calvin and others. Especially since "Paul" was concerned with laws now obsolete for Christians, one must conclude that this verse pertains only to "things indifferent" (*Institutes* 3.19.9, 1960: 1.841; cf. Leo the Great, *Serm.* 42.4, NPNF2 12.157).

To raise "all things are pure" aloft as the banner of an unrestricted freedom is "perverse," merely "an excuse for . . . desires . . . [and] lust" (*Institutes* 3.19.9, 1960: 1.840).

A number of literary references further develop some of the tendencies explored above. In the conservative vein, v. 15 has sometimes been appropriated in support of an intellectual elitism, a certain variety of which once elicited from D. H. Lawrence the following witty apothegm: "To the Puritans all things are impure" (*Etruscan Places*, 1985: 2). It is difficult to consider Nietzsche's Zarathustra conservative, what with his exuberance and radical challenge to the moral and philosophical status quo. When he reinterprets "unto the pure, all things are pure" to mean "unto swine, all things become swine," however, his inversion falls into a rather easy mockery of traditional values as if from a less timorous, more expansive perspective. That the world has its dangers and its filth "does not mean that the world itself is a filthy monster" (*Thus Spoke Zarathustra* 2005: 178). At best one might consider this an inspiring *fin-de-siècle* romanticism, which genuinely encourages readers to abandon the limiting other-worldliness of stoicism and conventional piety. But at worst it may sound like the crowing of a cultural elite incapable of acknowledging the range of everyday human experience in those of a more customary stripe. The same might be said for Richard Howard's poem "Jacques Offenbach." Mocking the popular composer as a trivial sell-out, and thus mocking those who enjoy Offenbach's music, Howard, echoing Nietzsche, writes:

> . . . To the pure
> all things are rotten, and you
> have made music so profligate it is no
>
> wonder more Germans would come
> to Paris and suppress it with cannonballs.
> (1979: 33)

The ambiguity of Howard's use of v. 15 is intriguing. If Offenbach, and by extension, his appreciative audiences, are pure, then the rottenness of only a certain kind of cultural refinement is being exposed and mocked. On the other hand, it could be that Howard imagines as pure his own discerning tastes, in which case the "all things" of the next line would mean, essentially, "most of what passes for culture these days." Either way, the curmudgeonly Howard and the radical Nietzsche, in their relative binarisms, actually capture the Pastor's spirit quite effectively, even if the basic sentiments involved are worlds apart.

Jeanette Winterson's novel, *Oranges Are Not the Only Fruit*, which is organized biblically with chapter titles from the Christian Bible beginning with

Genesis and ending with Ruth, adapts Titus 1:15 more liberally, essentially as Milton does, this time to assert the viability of a queer religious life. The novel tells the story of a young, evangelical, lesbian named Jeanette who must come to grips with conflicts between her sexual identity and her religious faith, conflicts which she neither understands nor accepts. When her relationship with her first lover, Melanie, is discovered, she is hauled before the congregation. The pastor announces:

> 'I will read you the words of St Paul' . . . and he did [read them], and many more words besides about unnatural passions and the mark of the demon.
> 'To the pure all things are pure,' I yelled at him. 'It's you not us.'
> He turned to Melanie.
> 'Do you promise to give up this sin and beg the Lord to forgive you?'
> 'Yes.' She was trembling uncontrollably. I hardly heard what she said.
> 'Then go into the vestry with Mrs White and the elders will come and pray for you. It's not too late for those who truly repent.'
> He turned to me.
> 'I love her.'
> 'Then you do not love the Lord.'
> 'Yes, I love both of them.'
>
> (1985: 105)

In Winterson's novel, the idea of purity does not produce divisive options, but rather a relatively decentralized view of religious authority according to which the minister, and others like Jeanette's mother, who oppose the young love affair, and the two young women, could, ideally, coexist. The ideal is just an ideal, of course, and young Jeanette must eventually leave home to find or create the community she'd thought she'd belonged to already.

2. RELIGIOUS PRACTICES

Tertullian, voicing concerns about pagan religion, has to confront the argument of some that idols and other religious paraphernalia are not harmful to believers since they are made from wood and stone, i.e., from God's creation. He agrees with the Pastor's basic sentiment, but he still will claim that . . .

> nothing is more impure than idols. The substances are themselves as creatures of God without impurity, and in this their native state are free to the use of all; but the ministries to which in their use they are devoted, makes all the difference; for I, too, kill a cock for myself, just as Socrates did for Aesculapius [in the *Phaedo*]; and if the smell of some place or other offends me, I burn the Arabian product myself, but not with the same ceremony, nor in the same dress, nor with the same pomp, with which it is done to idols.

In Tertullian's view, then, the source of impurity is not so much the objects and items used in pagan religious practices, but rather "the dress, and rites, and pomp of what is offered to the gods" (*De cor.* 10, ANF 3.99; cf. *De cult. fem.* 1.8, ANF 4.17). These rites do certainly render contact with the objects in question an act of impurity, however, and he would forbid Christians from polluting themselves in this way.

Augustine argues that the religious affiliation of the individual is what ultimately matters most in deciding upon purity. The Pharisees of the gospels, for instance, because they "have not the faith of Christ" and are not "born again of water and of the Spirit" are only capable of impurity, even while engaging in activities, like almsgiving, that are for all intents and purposes indistinguishable from the same acts performed by Christians (*Ench.* 75, NPNF1 3.261–62). Interestingly, in this context Augustine is discussing Luke 11:41, which seems to hold out the hope that if the Pharisees were to give alms sincerely, "all things would be clean for them." This Augustine rejects out of hand, for the very simple reason that only the baptized believer, only the Christian, is capable of purity (cf. Calvin, 1964: 367). The importance of general religious affiliation is stressed less in Augustine's reflections upon baptism than the purity of the individual believer. In the fourth century Donatist crisis in the North African Church, for example, people who had been baptized by priests considered to be apostates were subsequently denied communion because the baptism itself was seen to have been impure, tainted, and thus null and void. Augustine mounts a vigorous defense of these baptisms. Citing our text, he argues that "if a bad man offer sacrifice to God, and a good man receive it at his hands, the sacrifice is to each man of such character as he himself has shown himself to be" (*Answer to Petilian* 2.52, NPNF1 4.561).

Purity has its limits too for Aquinas. In general the Pastor's claim is entirely valid, but there are possible exceptions. To return to the discussion of almsgiving, Aquinas says that in the "new law" nothing is considered unclean. Therefore, in theory anyway, one may offer anything as an "oblation." But say the offering is harmful to others, "as in the case of a son who offers to God the means of supporting his father . . . or if it give rise to scandal or contempt, or the like." In such cases, even though the thing offered is, in itself, pure, the offering will be considered, if not impure, then certainly unacceptable. (ST SS Q[86] A[3]).

3.   THE BODY

One area of serious concern for readers of this verse through the centuries has been the human body in all its materiality. Athanasius reports on monks who are susceptible to the demonically inspired worry that people are inherently unclean by virtue of their excretions. He asks in response to these fears, "what sin or uncleanness there is in any natural secretion, – as though a man were minded to make a culpable matter of the cleanings of the nose or the sputa from the mouth? And we may add also the secretions of the belly, such as are a physical necessity of animal life" (*Ep*. 48, NPNF2 4.556).

And if the body in general is a source of pollution, what about certain bodies in particular? Cyprian has to cite v. 15 to encourage the baptism of newborn infants whose bodies are deemed so impure, by many, as to be nearly untouchable (*Ep*. 58.4, ANF 5.354). Criticizing a theological position of the Manicheans, Augustine comments that some people think Christ's divinity would be impure if he came from a woman's womb. While he has nothing very affirmative to say about the female body, nonetheless Augustine uses v. 15 to show that what matters is one's perspective. If the perspective is pure, then all things can be understood in purity. To help make his point, he draws an analogy between Christ's birth and the sun.

> [T]he rays of this sun, which indeed they [i.e., the Manicheans] do not praise as a creature of God, but adore as God, are diffused all the world over, through the noisomenesses of sewers and every kind of horrible thing, and that they operate in these according to their nature, and yet never become debased by any defilement thence contracted, albeit that the visible light is by nature in closer conjunction with visible pollutions. How much less, therefore, could the Word of God, who is neither corporeal nor visible, sustain defilement from the female body, wherein He assumed human flesh together with soul and spirit, through the incoming of which the majesty of the Word dwells in a less immediate conjunction with the frailty of a human body! (*De fide et sym*. 4.10, NPNF1 3.325–26)

Bede's *Ecclesiastical History of the English People* preserves the correspondence between another Augustine and Gregory the Great, again on the matter of women's bodies. Augustine of Canterbury had written to Gregory asking his advice on a number of points important to the nascent English Christian community. One such question was in regard to whether pregnant women, or women who have just given birth, or women during their period, may enter a church and participate in worship, receive sacraments, and so on. Gregory's reply is, given the very real attitudes behind the questions themselves, remarkable. He cites v. 15, which he takes to refer to dietary restrictions, and then asks "[i]f, therefore, meat is not unclean to him whose mind is not unclean, why shall that which a woman suffers according to nature, with a clean mind, be imputed to her as uncleanness?" (1.27, 1999: 50). He goes on to warn men, however, that they are not to enter a church after sexual intercourse with a woman, nor even immediately after having purified themselves, for they are still likely to be guilty of concupiscence.

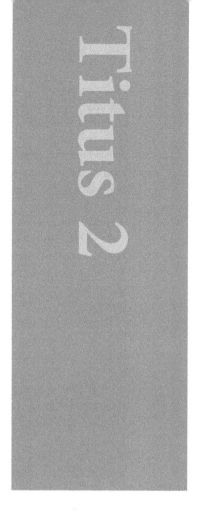

The second chapter of the letter explains that all members – older and younger men and women, slaves – of the Christian community are to behave with gravity, decency, solicitousness, and self-control. The reason is that Christ has come, and believers have learned from him to await their salvation, a salvation granted to all, with a pious propriety.

The Church: A Household Code (2:2–10)

Titus 2 begins with another of the Pastorals' household codes (see D-C 1972: 5; Verner 1983: 13–25), counseling old and young, men and women, free and

The Pastoral Epistles Through the Centuries, First Edition. Jay Twomey.
© 2009 by Jay Twomey. Published 2020 by John Wiley & Sons Ltd.

enslaved, on how to behave in the household of God. We have treated similar material elsewhere in the commentary (see at 2 Tim. 2:9–15; 5; 6:1–2). Modern commentators, especially those who detect actual social and theological conflicts behind these letters, will explain the Pastor's advice to Titus here as an attempt to circumvent those problems. According to some, it is possible that wealthy older women are signaling their status by their drunken, irreverent behavior (v. 3; Collins 2002: 321; Towner 2006: 723–24). Perhaps the Pastor is all too aware of social stereotypes and is urging the members of Titus' communities "to avoid behavior that would cause them to be so typed" (Towner 1989: 193). Slaves and women were likely, given their disempowerment, to cast about in the "marketplace" for alternative religions and philosophies, and well-off younger women were probably trying to achieve some social standing for themselves by imitating the lax sexual morals of their husbands (Towner 2006: 725).

The Pastor's advice to Titus that older women should teach (v. 3), however, does lead to questions about a potential contradiction with 1 Timothy 2:12, where women are forbidden from teaching. The fact that older women are urged to be not just decent and sober, but "reverent," and that they are "to teach what is good" seems to indicate a certain freedom to participate more actively in the religious life of Crete's nascent Christian community. Hanson goes so far as to propose that we have here an early "hint" of the priesthood of all believers (1982: 180). At any rate, the elder women are to teach the younger women to be "good managers of the household." In the King James translation women are not managers, but "keepers at home," which is probably more accurate as *oikourgous* does not imply active participation in decisions concerning the household economy but rather the simple fact that one works in the house (Bassler 1996: 196; Knight 1992: 308).

They are to teach (v. 3)

Most readers have accepted v. 3 by restricting women's teaching to the domestic sphere. The absence of any reference to male pupils is taken as a sign that the teaching here is simply not what the Pastor has in mind in 1 Timothy. Origen, however, can read Titus 2:3, in conjunction with a symbolic interpretation of foot-washing (required of widows at 1 Tim. 5:10) as teaching, to grant women the same teaching responsibilities enjoyed by male elders in the community (*Commentary on John* 32.132, in Origen 1998: 231, 373 n. 28). One could extrapolate on this basis to consider the office of deacones (1 Tim. 3:11) as a teaching role too, although some, like Matthew Henry, explicitly deny the connection between the two passages (Henry 1721–25: 333).

Others feel that our text is unambiguous: "Paul" here grants women the right to teach, plain and simple. Anne Hutchinson, at her trial in seventeenth century Massachusetts, defended her teaching practices by citing Titus 2:3 as "a clear rule" in her favor. When asked by Governor Winthrop whether she would refuse to instruct a man if he sought her out as his teacher, Hutchinson replies that she would only if she knew of a biblical rule against doing so. 1 Timothy 2:12 is apparently not sufficiently "clear" for her in this regard. Moreover, she says, the very court trying her seems to allow women to teach men since, as she says, they have called her in to teach them! (in Kerber and De Hart 2003: 81–82).

Good managers (v. 5)

We noted above the difference between the NRSV and the KJV translations of this verse. As "good managers" (NRSV; compare Wycliffe: "hauynge cure of the hous"), women would seem to have a certain authority, at least at home. But given its cultural significance, not to mention its historical priority, the KJV's "keepers at home," a much more restrictive (if accurate) rendering, is the most widely accepted version of our text. A number of seventeenth century household manuals take the restrictiveness of this reading for granted. One, by William Gouge, draws upon the Pastorals in a variety of ways, claiming for instance that the "particular calling" of a woman "is *subiection*" (*Of Domesticall Duties*, 1622: 312; cf. 1 Tim. 2:11; Titus 2:5). Gouge lambastes women who cannot stand merely to be "keepers at home," who must circulate in public, "[s]uch as thinke their houses a prison unto them, that cannot long tarrie at home: they thinke they haue power to goe when and whither they will, and to tarrie out as long as they list, thinke their husbands of it what they will." Such women, he continues, ought to take a lesson from "*the Leuites adulterous wife* [!], whose fearefull end was a stampe of Gods iudgement on such loose lewdnesse" (314). In the nineteenth century, such household manuals become less vicious and even consider certain limitations to v. 5. For example, one insists, first of all, that "if anything there demands her presence," then a woman "*must be a keeper at home*"; when nothing presses at home, however, she ought to be free "to assist the noble [philanthropic] societies which solicit her patronage" (James 1829: 57). This manual, entitled *The Family Monitor: Or A Help to Domestic Happiness*, also concedes that women might take the time to read, occasionally, when there is little work to be done. Yet, "her taste for literature," like her desire to socialize with friends, "must be kept within due bounds" (56).

It will come as no surprise that many women in the tradition have, like Anne Hutchinson, been troubled by attitudes such as these whenever they have arisen. In the sixteenth century, Teresa of Avila had worried about the appropriateness of her very active religious life. Reflecting upon those concerns, she writes in her *Spiritual Relations* that perhaps "the people were right who disapproved of my going out to make foundations . . . considering what Saint Paul says about women keeping at home." But such is not, in any simple way, "God's will," she adds; and Christ himself, in an audition, dispels her concerns by advising that Teresa tell her opponents "they are not to be guided by one part of Scripture alone, but to look at others; ask them if they suppose they will be able to tie My hands" (6.19, 1957: 1.344). Teresa does not discuss what other verse might take precedence over Titus 2:5, although v. 3, not to mention Paul's implicit support for women prophets at 1 Corinthians 11:5, is as good a candidate as any.

An early twentieth century Ulster columnist writing under the pseudonym Charity Hope, like many other early feminists critical of biblical restrictions on women's agency, attacks the logic of our verse from within. She does not question that women have their place in the home. Rather she praises the extensive number of women "who sacrifice home and comfort and ease in their work for humanity," noting also that very few men slander these women for the work they do. Women are labeled "unwomanly," criticized for failing to be "keepers of the home," only when they agitate for political reform on behalf of their "oppressed sisters" (in Broczyna 1999: 137–38). By pointing out the "fallacy" of assuming that the culture at large does not already sanction women's work outside the home (ibid.), Hope exposes the hypocrisy of the selective application of biblical texts like ours.

Theological Speculation: Christ the God (2:11–14)

The chapter closes with a striking theological flourish. Once again (as at 1 Tim. 2:4; 4:10; 2 Tim. 4:8) the universalist note is sounded as the Pastor announces that "the grace of God has appeared, bringing salvation to all" (v. 11). This past epiphany will lead to a final appearance, for which "we wait" and hope, that "of the glory of our great God and Savior, Jesus Christ" (v. 13). One of the more intriguing passages in the Pastorals, v. 13 is among the very few New Testament texts in which Jesus is, in the words of the Geneva Bible's note, "most plainly called" God (cf. 2 Pet. 1:1; others would cite additional texts, e.g., Rom. 9:5 and John 1:1, as proof of a broader theological tendency in the New Testament; see Knight 1992: 321–26 for his excellent discussion of the relevant linguistic, literary, and theological concerns). In part because ascribing the title God to Jesus strikes many readers as un-Pauline, or ahistorical, or possibly even heretically ditheistic (Hanson 1982: 39–40, 184–85), in part because to do so would seem quite simply to contradict the Pastor's Christology elsewhere, at 1 Timothy 2:5 and 2 Timothy 4:1 for instance (D-C 1972: 143; Davies 1996: 103), translators frequently opt for alternative renderings. The Pastor may have meant "the epiphany of our great God and savior's glory – Jesus Christ" (Towner 2006: 758), according to which reading Jesus is a certain manifestation of God the Father (cf. Young 1994: 73). He may also have intended, as he does elsewhere (e.g., Titus 1:4), to distinguish clearly between the two persons, as in the King James Version: "the glorious appearing of the great God and [of] our Saviour Jesus Christ" (cf. Erasmus, *Paraphrases* 1993: 63; Calvin, *Institutes* 3.25.1, 1960: 2.988). It seems most likely that Hanson and Knight are correct in their assessment that the verse ought to be read as it is translated in the NRSV. Whether or not the Pastor understands the implications of v. 13 is uncertain; one can only assume that he did not notice the potential for conflict with his other theological and/or Christological claims (Bassler 1996: 201).

The grace of God has appeared, bringing salvation to all (v. 11)

Certain passages from Titus play a significant role in the worship services of the church as well. Language evoking the appearance of Jesus as God's grace (and glory; see below) is found in liturgies throughout all periods of Christian history. The ancient Ambrosian, or Milan, liturgy cites v. 11 for the Feast of Epiphany, January 6, while the Roman and other liturgies reserve this verse for Christmas – an indication of the similarity of these feasts, certainly, as well as of the relatively broad understanding of epiphany, a concept which can refer to Christ's incarnation, his manifestation to the Gentiles (in the form of the Magi), his baptism by John, and more (Martimort 1986: 79–82).

The blessed hope and the manifestation of the glory (v. 13a)

The Pastor remarks that Christians are waiting, although readers in the tradition are not in full agreement on what they are waiting for. That v. 13 refers to the second coming of Christ is the general consensus of the tradition as a whole. Beyond that generality, there are two relatively distinct tendencies in the history of this passage's interpretation.

The first involves mildly eschatological readings concerned with the salvation of individual souls. Augustine reflects this tendency nicely in an aside to his exposition of John 5:5, where a man who has been ill for 38 years is said to symbolize a certain imperfection, coming just short of the perfection of 40.

> In this world, then, we celebrate, as it were, the forty days' abstinence, when we
> live aright, and abstain from iniquities and from unlawful pleasures. But because
> this abstinence shall not be without reward, we look for 'that blessed hope, and
> the revelation of the glory of the great God, and of our Saviour Jesus Christ.' In
> that hope, when the reality of the hope shall have come to pass, we shall receive
> our wages . . . (*Jo. ev. tr.*17.4, NPNF1 7.112)

The "glory of the great God" is the afterlife for believers, the goal toward which
all those who renounce the City of Men strive. Chrysostom's reading is much
the same. "Holding fast" to the hope of the next life is akin, he writes, to making
"provision for the future" in this one: "Let us be careful of our salvation, let us
in all things call upon God, that He may stretch forth His hand to us" (*Hom.
Tit.*, NPNF1 13.540). God's coming glory is to be, for Calvin as well, an eschatological event. He has no doubt that on the last day there will be a final judgment. Still, he mutes the violent potential of the text by understanding "the
glory of God" not only as that which "He shall have in Himself, but also the
glory which He will then diffuse everywhere so that all His elect shall be given
a share in it" (1964: 374). The Anglican *Book of Common Prayer* has included,
in various editions from the mid-sixteenth century to the early twentieth, and
in the still official 1662 edition of the Church of England, a prayer for the
second Sunday of Advent, which bears witness to this interpretive tradition:

> Blessed lord, which hast caused all holy Scriptures to be written for our learning:
> Grant us that we may in such wise hear them, read, mark, learn, and inwardly
> digest them, that by patience, and comfort of thy holy Word, we may embrace,
> and ever hold fast the blessed hope of everlasting life, which thou hast given us
> in our Saviour Jesus Christ. (1662 edn, Anglican Church website)

The "blessed hope of everlasting life" in this prayer involves, like similar echoes
of Titus 2:13 in funeral sermons and catechisms (i.e., the *Catechism of the
Catholic Church*, US Catholic Church 1995: 320), the life of the church broadly,
as well as an expectation of the last day. But it is also easily construed in terms
of individual believers and their hope for their own eternal salvation.

A fascinating variant of this traditional reading raises expectations for personal development analogous, but frequently without reference, to the reward
of eternal life. Maximus the Confessor, contesting the Christology of the
seventh century Monothelites, who held that Jesus had only a divine, and no
human will, writes, as perhaps the Pastor himself could, that those who are on
the true path know how to avoid "the gulfs of confusion or the chasms of division," characteristic of this heresy. The ability to skirt such difficulties is given
"by the leading and guiding of the grace of the all-holy Spirit to those who
press on in prayer through a pure and orthodox faith to the perfect face-to-face

[1 Cor. 13:12] knowledge of the great God and Saviour of all, Christ . . . and initiation into him" (1996: 182). The blessed hope is still here, but it is implicit in a striving for union with the divine by means of reflection and religious practice. Bonaventure's appropriation of this passage bears some resemblance to Maximus' in that its language has less to do with death and eternal reward than with learning to find one's way toward holiness. In this case, though, the holiness is that of St. Francis. Bonaventure begins the poetic prologue to his *Life of St. Francis* by asserting that "[i]n these last days the grace of God our Savior has appeared in his servant Francis." This is a remarkable transference to Francis of the theological content of the remainder of Titus 2:11, "bringing salvation to all." Without going so far as to suggest that Francis actually stands in for Christ, Bonaventure grants him a significant religious function, for "[i]n him . . . [believers] can venerate God's superabundant mercy and be taught by his example . . . to thirst after blessed hope with unflagging desire" (1978: 179). Still, later in the poem, Francis becomes that hope, at least obliquely, when Bonaventure says "he is considered to be symbolized by the image of the Angel who ascends from the sunrise bearing the seal of the living God [Rev. 7:2]" (181).

John Ruskin's citation of v. 13 as evidence for the religious quality of rhyme, which he associates with Christian poetry, takes us much further afield. The eschatological dimension of "the blessed hope and the glorious appearing" is transmuted from the second coming to the nature and structure of verse. Ruskin argues that, as opposed to the unrhymed verse of the classical poets, rhyme carries with it a religious, specifically Christian, hope:

> The 'Ryme,' you may at first fancy, is the especially childish part of the work. Not so. It is the especially chivalric and Christian part of it. It characterises the Christian chant or canticle, as a higher thing than a Greek ode, *melos*, or *hymnos*, or than a Latin *carmen*. Think of it; for this again is wonderful! . . . You have to understand this most deeply of all Christian minstrels, from first to last; that they are more musical, because more joyful, than any others on earth: ethereal minstrels, pilgrims of the sky, true to the kindred points of heaven and home; their joy essentially the sky-lark's, in light, in purity; but, with their human eyes, looking for the glorious appearing of something in the sky, which the bird cannot. This it is that changes Etruscan murmur into *Terza rima* – Horatian Latin into Provençal troubadour's melody . . . (1880–81: 198)

A few pages later, Ruskin indicates that he understands fully the eschatological context from which he has taken his "glorious appearing," when he explains that he is speaking of "a new power of music and song given to the humanity which has hope of the Resurrection" (201). The special quality of rhyme, however, remains for the most part something almost natural, that experience of the poet who, like a bird, looks skyward for meaning, and puts that meaning into his or her song. And at any rate, whatever the religious significance of rhyme, Ruskin's interest here is more fully poetic than spiritual.

These readings are to be contrasted with a more apocalyptic strand of interpretation, one which seems to have its roots in the Reformation period. Erasmus, in his paraphrase of Titus, casts this passage in an intensely apocalyptic light. The "manifestation of the glory" (NRSV), which believers patiently await, becomes the expectation that "God the Father will crush all evil and will reveal his glory and greatness before his worshippers" (1993: 63; interestingly, Erasmus is also one of the few pre-modern readers to distinguish between Christ and God in his rendering of v. 13). Published nearly 50 years later, the Heidelberg Catechism includes an echo of Titus 2:13 in its statement of apocalyptic hope: "[i]n all my sorrow and persecution I lift up my head and eagerly await as judge from heaven the very same person who before has submitted Himself to the judgment of God for my sake, and has removed all the curse from me [Luke 21:28; Rom. 8:22–25; Phil. 3:20, 21; Titus 2:13, 14]. He will cast all His and my enemies into everlasting condemnation, but He will take me and all His chosen ones to Himself into heavenly joy and glory [Matt. 25:31–46; 1 Thess. 4:16, 17; 2 Thess. 1:6–10]" (Westminster Theological Seminary/Heidelberg Catechism website). Joseph Mede, in his *Key to the Apocalypse*, imagines "the glorious appearance of our Lord in a flame of fire" (1833: 435). The writings of Jonathan Edwards are shot through with apocalyptic appropriations of v. 13. For example, in a sermon entitled "The End of the Wicked Contemplated by the Righteous," Edwards speaks of "[t]he power of God," noting that it "is sometimes spoken of as very glorious, as appearing in the temporal destruction of his enemies; 'Thy right hand, O Lord, is become glorious in power; thy right hand, O Lord, hath dashed in pieces the enemy [Exod. 15:6].'" He goes on to posit our verse as an intensification of the one just cited from Exodus: "[b]ut how much more glorious will it appear in his triumphing over, and dashing in pieces at once, all his enemies, wicked men and devils together, all his haughty foes! The power of God will gloriously appear in dashing to pieces his enemies as a potter's vessel [cf. Rom. 9:20–22]" (*Works of President Edwards* 4.511).

This sort of reading has clearly had an impact upon Dispensationalist thinking, as inaugurated by John Nelson Darby in the nineteenth century. In Darby's apocalyptic musings, Christ would return in the end time twice, "the first [time] in secret to rapture the church out of the world and up to heaven. He would then return after seven years of worldwide tribulation to establish a dominion on earth based in Jerusalem. Darby coordinate[s] this latter event with the discussion of the 'glorious appearing' referred to in" our text (Witherington 2005: 94). In the United States, Darby's Dispensationalist vision has come to have an astonishingly widespread influence, thanks in part to the early twentieth century Scofield Reference Bible, and more recently to the wildly successful bestselling *Left Behind* series of novels by Tim LaHaye and Jerry Jenkins. One of the last books in this series even takes its title from v. 13: *Glorious Appearing: The End of Days* (2004).

Our great God and Savior, Jesus Christ (v. 13b)

The hope and glory for which believers await is not that of Christ the mediator "between God and humankind" (1 Tim. 2:5–6), but that of Christ "the great God and Savior." Most readers in the tradition believe that the Pastor is truly ascribing the title God to Jesus. The language of the verse accounts for this ascription to a great extent, but in this case the (likely accurate) interpretation of v. 13 gets its initial and enduring impetus from the Arian controversy. The Arians held that Christ was created by God; he is prior to the world but is himself an intermediate creature, something of an angelic being, and not of one substance with the Father. Athanasius, one of the major early opponents of Arianism, feels that the Arian position also threatens the doctrine of the incarnation, presumably because the being who takes on flesh in Arius' view is "other than the Word and Wisdom who is an uncreated eternal attribute of God" (Anatolios 2004: 235). Titus 2:13–14 is for Athanasius proof both that Christ is God and that he became man (*Ep.* 60.6, NPNF2 4.577). Theodoret asserts that the Pastor "called Christ mighty God to refute the heretical blasphemy" (*Comm. Tit.*, 2001: 256) and Chrysostom, reading this verse, asks simply, if pointedly: "[w]here are those who say that the Son is inferior to the Father?" (*Hom. Tit.*, NPNF1 13.537). Even as late as the Reformation interpretations of this verse target the Arian heresy. Calvin, for example, noting the translation alternatives, writes that "the Arians seized on" a version of v. 13 in which Christ is not identified as God, "to prove from it that the Son is less than the Father, holding that Paul calls the Father 'the great God' in order to distinguish Him from the Son" (1964: 374). One can refute this "error" by insisting that the titles belong to Christ, he continues. It is even easier to deny the Arian position if one takes Paul to mean "that when Christ appears, the greatness of God's glory shall be revealed to us" (375), proving that the two share an essential identity.

And purify for himself a people of his own (2:14)

The Christ-God, whose glory will be manifest at his second coming, is said to have "trained" the Christian community in piety (v. 12). His self-sacrifice on the cross similarly had as its goal, in the Pastor's view, the purification of a "peculiar people, zealous of good works" (KJV). The Quakers saw themselves as this "peculiar people" separated out from the world. Indeed, their early practices came to be called "the peculiarities" precisely because of this self-identification (see Pink Dandelion 2007: 62). In Ralph Waldo Emerson's hands, this verse becomes an inspirational text, encouraging people toward their own "self-cultivation" (Sermon 146, 4.83). God's gift to his peculiar people is the gift of a virtuous principle, imparted to humanity both collectively and individually. However, unlike the Pastor, who grants to Christ the power of "purifying his own people," Emerson's divinity can only help those who help themselves: unless you enhance "your own disposition and effort" in self-redemption, God's grace is but in "vain" (88).

Titus 3

"Paul" concludes this letter, and thus the canonical Pastoral corpus, with additional ethical instructions: the church is to obey imperial and local political authorities while maintaining, in general, a civil attitude toward all people. He reminds Titus that those who are now Christians, himself included, used to be just as morally suspect as the contemporary non-Christian world. They were saved, however, through baptism. The Pastor goes on, one last time, to criticize his opponents, and to advise Titus simply to ignore those who will not cease and desist their theological speculations. Finally, Titus is asked to make the appropriate arrangements to pay a visit to "Paul" as soon as possible.

The Pastoral Epistles Through the Centuries, First Edition. Jay Twomey.
© 2009 by Jay Twomey. Published 2020 by John Wiley & Sons Ltd.

The Church: Baptism (3:1–11)

Chapter 3 begins with material similar to the virtue and vice lists found else-where in the Pastorals. Moreover, the Cretan congregation is told here, as the Ephesians are in 1 Timothy, to pray for those in positions of authority. Much of the Pastor's energy in these letters is consumed with concerns for church order in the face of internal opposition; but aside from desiring to avoid con-spicuous differences with the world outside, especially with regard to the social dynamics of the community, the Pastor envisions little in the way of external conflict. As Bassler rightly notes, "the external situation seems to be free of tensions; it simply defines the parameters of behavior, while the internal situ-ation shapes the argument" (1996: 206). We have explored something of the variety of interpretive responses to this attitude toward secular power earlier in the commentary (see at 1 Tim. 2:1).

Modern commentators usually take vv. 4–7 to be a baptismal formula of some kind. In Collins' assessment it is a hymn, and "contains one of the most important statements on the nature of baptism to be found in the New Testa-ment" (2002: 360). Even if water baptism is not in view, the passage certainly considers the Spirit, mentioned rarely in the Pastoral Epistles (see also 1 Tim. 4:1; 2 Tim. 1:14), to be an agent of a figurative washing and renewal (Towner 2006: 781). The theology implicit in this text's understanding of works ("not because of any works of righteousness that we had done," v. 5) and justification by grace (v. 7) seems to derive from, or to reflect, a more authen-tically Pauline tradition, even for those who deny Pauline authorship (Bassler 1996: 207–08). At the same time, the idea that the rite of baptism itself can save has worried many commentators. Hanson, however, feels that this worry is anachronistic; such critics seem to be complaining that the Pastor had not read his Luther carefully enough (Hanson 1982: 192). Indeed, scholars and theolo-gians such as Bultmann have remarked upon the mystical element in this passage from Titus. The "water of rebirth" [or: "the laver of regeneration" (Douay-Rheims), "the washing of regeneration" (KJV)] can quite easily be understood as a form of mystical participation in the dying and rising of Christ (1955: 1.140).

Be gentle (v. 2)

With regard to the Pastor's attitude toward pagan political power (see at 1 Tim. 2:1), we need only add here a fascinating commentary of Luther's which per-tains less to church–state relations than to the nature of politics itself: "whoever does not know how to dissemble does not know how to rule" (*Lectures on Titus, Works* 29.75). In context, Luther is considering the importance of *epieikeia*, or gentleness, equity, as an important Christian concept adapted from legal theory. Laws are general, he writes, and their strict application to everyone, no matter the circumstance, is tantamount to violence. Instead laws should be applied whenever possible with gentleness, and with regard to the specifics of particular cases. With this as the basis for his comments on Titus 3:2, Luther goes on to argue that such gentleness is, in effect, a form of dissembling. And Christians must dissemble in this way whenever they see something in the political arena which puts them ill at ease. Possibly because the Pastor is seen to be countering a certain Christian rebelliousness against ungodly authority, in Luther's reading the virtue of gentleness is transmuted into *Realpolitik*: "[t]his is dissembling, not only to bear with something but to put the best construction on it as though I did not see it. . . . it is a patience toward public evils as well as a patience and tolerance toward private evils. . . . this is a necessary virtue for those who want to live either in the midst of public affairs or among those who administer public affairs" (76). Luther also uses the idea of a dissembling gentleness to counsel patience toward bad rulers. Merging vv. 2 and 3, he remarks that if you "have *epieikeia*" you can "think to yourself: 'that prince is crazy. I remember the time when I was crazy too'" (77), and so look the other way to avoid unnecessary, unfruitful and ultimately un-Christian conflict.

Saved through the water of rebirth (v. 5)

Although the World Council of Churches' statement on the biblical bases of baptism limits Titus' contribution to "renewal by the Spirit" (World Council of Churches website), readers of our text have taken it to represent a variety of traditional ways of thinking about the ritual. Tertullian, whose fourfold view of baptism as "remission from sin, delivery from death, regeneration and bestowing of the Holy Spirit" characterizes much of the Church's teaching on baptism (Urban 1995: 269), considers "the laver of regeneration" also to be the source of "Christian modesty" (*On Modesty* 1, ANF 4.74). Augustine, in an important innovation, also claims for baptism the power to eliminate not only sins, but in fact the stain of original sin, and this position becomes dominant in the western church until the Reformation: "[b]aptism, therefore, washes away indeed all sins – absolutely all sins, whether of deeds or words or thoughts, whether original or added, whether such as are committed in ignorance or allowed in knowledge." He adds the following essential caveat, however: "[B]ut it does not take away the weakness which the regenerate man resists when he fights the good fight, but to which he consents when as man he is overtaken in any fault" (*C. ep. Pelag.* 3.5, NPNF1 5.404; cf. *C. Faust.* 11.7, NPNF1 4.181). This understanding of baptism's limited power to regenerate the soul is expressed also by Ambrose in his allegorical reading of the Song of Songs. Ambrose takes the beloved's self-description ("I am black but beautiful" [1:5]) as a comment on life after regeneration: she is "black because of the frailty of the human condition, beautiful because of grace; black because the offspring of sinners, beautiful because of the sacrament of faith" (in Norris 2003: 156; cf. Gregory of Nyssa's similar conjunction of texts and interpretations, 40).

Despite this attempt at a careful balancing of baptism's powers with the limitations of a fallen humanity, within the tradition there is often a tendency to stress the powers over the limitations. Thus Aquinas claims, citing our verse, that both "the grace of the Holy Ghost and the fullness of virtues are given in baptism" (ST TP Q[1] A[4]). Even though Aquinas knows very well that the believer after baptism is bound to sin, he still wants to claim that the rite does not concern past sin only, but future moral worth as well. Some readers even believe that the body can also be transformed in baptism. Augustine relates an anecdote, in the *City of God*, about a gouty doctor who was "relieved . . . not only of the extraordinary pain he was tortured with, but also of the disease itself" after being "washed in the laver of regeneration" (22.8, 2000: 824). Such readings are not entirely distinguishable from a more mystical strain of inter-pretation. Among the most fascinating of speculative readings is that of Origen, according to whom the regeneration experienced in baptism has something to do with the angelic guardianship of believers. He applies Jesus' remark in Matthew that the "little ones" have "angels" (18:10) to his understanding of our text: in the renewal of baptism, believers become "little ones," and are either assigned beneficent, protecting angels at that moment, or perhaps they develop the power to influence the (Satanic) angelic beings which had followed them from birth (*Commentary on Matthew* 3.26, ANF 9.491; cf. Symeon the New Theologian, 1980: 369).

Other readings with a mystical flair emphasize baptism as illumination, especially when Titus 3:5f. is read alongside texts like John 3:5–8 (e.g., Augustine, *An. et or.* 3.18, NPNF1 5.350). Gregory of Nazianzen, in his *Oration on Holy Baptism*, speaks of the "laver of regeneration" which contributes to the believer's spiritual development, and leads him or her to a new level of religious identity. Being illuminated, made Christ-like, in baptism, which Gregory also calls the Seal, will in fact enable believers to repulse even Satan. Imagining that the devil might come to tempt the newly baptized as he had tempted Jesus in the wilderness, Gregory gives the following advice:

Say to him relying on the Seal, "I am myself the Image of God; I have not yet been cast down from the heavenly Glory, as thou wast through thy pride; I have put on Christ; I have been transformed into Christ by Baptism; worship thou me." Well do I know that he will depart, defeated and put to shame by this; as he did from Christ the first Light, so he will from those who are illumined by Christ. Such blessings does the laver bestow on those who apprehend it; such is the rich feast which it provides for those who hunger aright. (10, NPNF2 7.363)

A rather more realist trajectory of readings has ancient roots as well. Cyprian, for instance, commenting on baptismal rites explains that, in his view, baptized heretics wishing to leave their heretical sects for the true church cannot immediately be recognized by the orthodox, because the water of baptism itself is not the washing of regeneration. If it were true that the rite channeled divine power in some way, then baptism, on its own, would be efficacious always. But as the power of baptism derives from the presence of the Holy Spirit (*Ep.* 73.5, ANF 5.387), and as those without the church are without the Spirit, people who have been baptized by heretics have never really been baptized. The claim is not, however, that believers who come to the church from a heretical sect cannot be received into communion. They can be so received, but first they must be baptized anew (*Ep.* 73.12, ANF 5.389; cf. Augustine's different approach to baptismal purity at Titus 1:15).

In the Reformation, interpreters begin to insist upon this distinction between the baptismal rites and the actual, divinely authorized process of spiritual regeneration. Luther, for instance, in the Shorter Catechism, writes: "[c]learly the water does not do it, but the Word of God, which is with, in, and among the water, and faith, which trusts this Word of God in the water. For without the Word of God the water is plain water and not a baptism, but with the Word of God it is a baptism, that is, a grace-filled water of life and a 'bath of the new birth in the Holy Spirit'" (Luther 2001: 47). We hear in this echoes of Cyprian, certainly. But the Reformers take the issue further by displacing regeneration entirely from the baptismal rite. Luther accordingly explains that "[t]hese words [about baptism, in Titus] are directed against the righteousness of works" (*Lectures on Titus, Works* 29.84). Calvin actually refers to any such close association of the washing and the renewal as a form of "self-deception," for "Christ's blood is our true and only laver" (*Institutes* 4.15.2, 1960: 2.1305). One must learn to see past "the visible element" of the water, and past "all other means" as well, and to recognize that they merely provide "the knowledge and certainty" of gifts previously given, indeed granted from all eternity, to the saved (1304–05). Wesley, similarly, considers baptism to be merely "the outward sign" of "the thing signified," which is, in his note on this text, "sanctification" (*Explanatory Notes* 1850: 559). The terms used, of course (e.g., regeneration, sanctification), are not equivalent, but the Protestant readings of this passage remain consistently distinguishable from interpretations (as in the Catholic tradition) which link the activity of the Spirit in the believer's life very closely to the "washing" of the baptismal rite.

The Opponents: And Also Some Friends (3:10–11, 13)

For the final time in these letters, the Pastor characterizes his opponents, vaguely, as people engaged in "stupid controversies, genealogies, dissentions, and quarrels about the law" (v. 9; see at 1 Tim. 1:3–4), before adding something new: such people are "hereticks" (KJV; "cause [...] divisions" NRSV). The Greek word for heretic, in v. 10, is *airetikon*, and originally meant "one who chooses" or even "one with a discriminating mind." Modern commentators tend to shy away from using "heretic" because it is uncertain "whether [the term] . . . indicates membership in sects" here (D-C 1972: 151; they prefer "factious person" to "heretic"). Hanson, however, feels that "heretic" in this sense is more or less appropriate to the Pastor's intentions (1982: 194). Titus is to "have nothing more to do with" heretics who, "after a first and second admonition," refuse to return to the theological fold. The NRSV is rather mild compared to other renderings. Towner feels that the translation needs to reflect the severity of the Pastor's tone, and offers "drive out, dismiss, discharge" as possibilities (2006: 797). Many take this passage, along with 1 Timothy 1:20, as an early reference to excommunication, with some commenting that Titus 3:10 is even more worrisome than the prior text. Although the handing of offenders "over to Satan" seems, on the face of it, more violent, less forgiving, it "was intended to have a corrective, pedagogical effect . . . whereas here [in Titus] the offender's status seems irremedial" (Bassler 1996: 211; cf. Hanson, who finds this text "a sinister omen for the ages to come," 1982: 195).

Most commentaries have very little to say about Zenas. He is mentioned nowhere else in the New Testament, and the reference to his profession, while indicating to some in the tradition that he was a "scribe" (e.g., Calvin 1964: 389; the Pastor uses a term, *nomikos*, found also in Matthew and Luke for one versed in Torah), is now usually understood simply to mean that Zenas practiced law (Hanson 1982: 196; Towner 2006: 801–02).

Have nothing more to do with them (vv. 10–11)

The refusal to engage with theological opponents is sometimes, as we have noted before, taken as a sign by readers that the Pastorals are not authentically

Pauline. As Samuel Taylor Coleridge puts it, our verse "would be among my minor arguments for doubting the Paulinity of the Ep. to Titus. It seems to me to breathe the spirit of a later age, & a more established Church *power*" (1969: 12[6].55). However, few readers through the centuries have ever questioned the Pastor's motivations behind, or the correctness of, the term "heretic." There have been striking differences of opinion, though, with regard to the treatment of these potentially divisive sectarians. A majority of interpreters seem disconcertingly enthusiastic, at first blush, about taking a hard line on heresy; but many actually mitigate the text's harshest implications, while others try to eliminate them altogether. We will begin our survey with most recalcitrant anti-heretics, and thus the most punitive over-readers of vv. 10–11, before exploring the large interpretive middle-ground of those who treat the Pastor's advice more cautiously. Finally we will conclude with a look at a few interesting repudiations of, if not the text itself, then its less appealing appropriations.

Leo the Great, in a rhetorical tour de force, identifies heretics with rebels against established order. Writing to the emperor Flavius Valerius Leo against Eutyches, who had blurred the boundaries, somewhat, between Christ's two natures, Pope Leo argues that Eutyches is an "unholy parricide" whose arguments are "weapons of discord" wielded "against the triumphs of the Almighty's right hand." Following the Pastor's lead, Leo warns against debating with theological opponents, because:

> by admitting the discussions of such men the authority of the divinely inspired decrees [is] . . . diminished, when in all parts of your kingdom and in all borders of the earth that Faith which was confirmed at Chalcedon is being established on the surest basis of peace, nor is any one worthy of the name of Christian who cuts himself off from communion with us. Of whom the Apostle says, 'a man that is heretical after a first and a second admonition, avoid, knowing that such a one is perverse and condemned by his own judgment.' (*Ep.* 146, NPNF2 12.106–07)

Theology becomes a form of political warfare, and conversation with one's opponents is tantamount to yielding them the battlefield, which eventuality the orthodox must resist with all vigor. Tertullian had also, earlier, claimed that one must not enter into discussions with one's theological opponents. The Pastor, he notes, says "admonish" heretics, and not "discuss" with them. The consequences of debate, in Tertullian's view, are far less damning than they are for Leo: "a controversy over the Scriptures can, clearly, produce no other effect than help to upset either the stomach or the brain." Nevertheless, Tertullian recognizes that elsewhere in the New Testament Christians are enjoined to reach out to their disputatious brethren (e.g., Matt. 18:16–17). Thus, if one prefers the Pastor's tactics, one must deny to one's opponents the name of Christians, and this is exactly what Tertulian does (*Praescr.* 16, ANF 3.261). Leo simply builds upon this logic. The punishment for heresy Leo envisions, though, is exile, and he recognizes ultimately that Christ "alone can rightly punish such things" (*Ep.* 146, NPNF2 12.107), even if, by referring to heretics as parricides, he opens the door to capital punishment. By the time of Thomas Aquinas, however, the stakes are incomparably higher: heretics can, and should, be murdered for their views. Thomas reads Titus 3:10–11 as the definitive word on dealing with opponents. This text trumps the more lenient perspectives of 2 Timothy 2:24–25, and contributes to Thomas' conclusion that heretics:

> deserve not only to be separated from the Church by excommunication, but also to be severed from the world by death. For it is a much graver matter to corrupt the faith which quickens the soul, than to forge money, which supports temporal life. Wherefore if forgers of money and other evil-doers are forthwith condemned to death by the secular authority, much more reason is there for heretics, as soon as they are convicted of heresy, to be not only excommunicated but even put to death.

Aquinas is fully aware that the Pastor does not encourage the Church to condemn an opponent without first trying, by admonishments, to change him. But "after that, if he is yet stubborn, the Church no longer hoping for his conversion, looks to the salvation of others, by excommunicating him and separating him from the Church, and furthermore delivers him to the secular tribunal to be exterminated thereby from the world by death" (ST SS Q[11] A[3]). This is a rather dramatic change, incidentally, from Thomas' earlier commentary on Titus, which restricts itself to the position that the unrepentant heretic is merely to be "sent away" (2007: 193).

So starkly violent a response to heterodox perspectives is countered by a body of more ambiguous readings. Origen, for instance, writes that "if those who hold different opinions will not be convinced, we observe the injunction laid down for the treatment of such: 'A man that is a heretic, after the first and second admonition, reject, knowing that he that is such is subverted, and sinneth, being condemned of himself.'" Yet he immediately subjoins "the maxim, '[b]lessed are the peacemakers, and this also, '[b]lessed are the meek,'" in order to insist that Christians "would not regard with hatred the corrupters of Christianity, nor [slander] . . . those who had fallen into error" (*C. Cels.* 5.63, ANF 4.571). If Origen's goal is to insist upon kindness and humility as characteristic of Christians even in the face of dissent, Augustine's interest seems actually to involve coming to some understanding of what motivates one's theological opponents. He writes that:

> [t]he Apostle Paul hath said: 'A man that is an heretic after the first and second admonition reject, knowing that he that is such is subverted and sinneth, being condemned of himself.' But though the doctrine which men hold be false and perverse, if they do not maintain it with passionate obstinacy, especially when they have not devised it by the rashness of their own presumption, but have accepted it from parents who had been misguided and had fallen into error, and if they are with anxiety seeking the truth, and are prepared to be set right when they have found it, such men are not to be counted heretics.

Certainly, there is ample space in this reading for actual heretics to be denounced and treated violently. But Augustine still considers "admonition" to include an effort, at least, at reconciliation, even with some of his chief opponents (*Ep.* 43.1–2 NPNF1 1.276). Later, Erasmus will speak, in a seemingly Thomistic mode, of the need for "eradication"; but he intends the eradication of the opponent's questions rather than the opponents themselves. He can imagine them perishing, certainly, and if they do it is their own fault. Yet at the same time he leaves open the possibility that, once excluded from the community, such people will "come to [their] . . . senses" (*Paraphrases* 1993: 67). Calvin knows that some "infer from this passage [in Titus] that the originators of pernicious doctrines are to be restrained by excommunication alone, and [that] no further measures of greater rigor" should be "taken against them." This is a mistaken view, he argues, implying that magistrates have the rightful authority to control dissent "by force and violence" (1964: 388). Calvin's role in the execution of a contemporary "anti-Trinitarian" named Servetus (see Naphy 2004: 32–33) probably ought to disqualify his reading of Titus 3:10 from being placed among the more moderate voices of the tradition. Still, he does conclude this section of his commentary by urging that "moderation" be shown in cracking down on dissent, as one hopes first of all to "cure" one's opponents, rather than simply destroy them (1964: 388). The Anabaptists are in accord with many when they, citing Titus 3:10 along with other texts in the early seventeenth century Dordrecht Confession, declare that a heretic is not to be tolerated. But they also feel that "as well in shunning as in reproving such an offender, such moderation and Christian discretion be used, that such shunning and reproof may not be conducive to his ruin, but be serviceable to his amendment. For should he be in need, hungry, thirsty, naked, sick or visited by some other affliction, we are in duty bound, according to the doctrine and practice of Christ and his apostles, to render him aid and assistance, as necessity may require" (in Leith 1982: 307).

The final kind of interpretive response to Titus 3:10–11 which we will consider involves something of a repudiation of the most conservative readings of this text. Some readings, such as Hobbes', focus on the passage's language. In *Leviathan*, Hobbes denies that excommunication for differences in non-essential matters (i.e., anything other than the foundational belief "that Jesus was the Christ") has any basis in the New Testament. Reading Titus 3:10 alongside 2 Timothy 2:23, he notes that that while each verse counsels the avoidance of controversy, neither of them advocates expelling troublemakers from the community: "There is no other place that can so much as colourably be drawn to countenance the casting out of the Church faithful men, such as believed the foundation, only for a singular superstructure of their own, proceeding perhaps from a good and pious conscience." More than that, Hobbes adds, these letters were written to Timothy and Titus as representative pastors, and were never meant "to make new articles of faith by determining every small controversy, which oblige men to a needless burden of conscience, or provoke them to break the union of the Church" (1994: 3[2].505). This reading would serve as a total renunciation of Leo's response to Eutyches, for example, since both, clearly, believed Jesus to be the Messiah, even as they differ on finer Christological distinctions.

John Milton, returning to the basic meaning of heresy as the "choise . . . of one opinion before another, which may bee without discord" (*A Treatise of Civil Power in Ecclesiastical Causes, Complete Prose* 7.247), claims not that excommunication is not countenanced by the New Testament documents, but rather, and more basically, that every interpretation is heretical, since every interpretation is at some level a matter of choice. And if this is true of Christian readers of the Bible generally, it is even truer of Protestants. Since Protestants have scripture as their:

> common rule and touchstone . . . nothing can with more conscience, more equitie, nothing more protestantly can be permitted then a free and lawful debate at all times by writing, conference or disputation of what opinion soever, disputable by scripture. (7.249)

In fact, he continues, there are no heretics except for those who hold opinions that absolutely have no warrant in scripture at all. Such, he quips, are the "Papists," and even they deserve opprobrium simply because they consider heretical everyone besides themselves. This kind of heretic is punished by death in the Hebrew Bible.

> [B]ut in the gospel such are punishd by excommunion only [citing Titus 3:10]. But they who think not this heavie anough and understand not that dreadfull

aw and spiritual efficacie which the apostle hath expressd so highly to be in church-discipline . . . and think weakly that the church of God cannot long subsist but in a bodilie fear, for want of other prooff will needs wrest that place of S. Paul Rom. 13. to set up civil inquisition, and give power to the magistrate both of civil judgment and punishment in causes ecclesiastical. (7.249–50)

It is this, precisely, that has no warrant, Milton goes on to argue. Civil magistrates enter into the affairs of religion only as "tyrants and persecutors" (7.250). Their sole function is to ensure social stability and peace, as we learned earlier at 1 Timothy 2:2; and Christians may be punished by the civil authority only if they infringe upon civil laws.

In the eighteenth century Wesley takes matters a step further. Not even Hobbes' sole allowance for excommunication, i.e., as a response to one who rejects the fundamentals of the faith, is acceptable. Wesley notes that "this is the only place, in the whole scripture, where the word heretic occurs [without noting that 'heresy' in one form or another is not uncommon]; and here it evidently means" a schismatic. "This, and this alone, is an heretic . . . and his punishment is likewise here fixed. *Shun, avoid him, leave him to himself*" (*Explanatory Notes* 1850: 560). Unlike Towner's translation, which focuses on the punishment due the troublemaker, Wesley's draws attention back to those in the community, to the way they need to behave.

Zenas the lawyer (v. 13)

The letter concludes with further mission instructions. Titus is to "make every effort to send Zenas the lawyer and Apollos on their way" (v. 13). Apollos plays a significant, if secondary, role elsewhere in the New Testament (Acts 18:24; 19:1; 1 Cor. 1:12; 3:4–6, 22; 4:6; 16:12) but Zenas is otherwise unknown. Judging by the amount of space devoted to him, Zenas is also certainly less than interesting to most academic exegetes and commentators. He is the purported author of an apocryphal *Acts of Titus* (fifth–seventh century), but he plays no role in that narrative (see Pervo 1996).

Christian lawyers, on the other hand, have found in Zenas a fellow traveler, a model whose brief appearance can be amplified for any number of inspirational homiletic purposes. The Reverend Henry C. Potter, preaching to the new lawyers of Columbia's 1871 graduating class, begins with a portrait of Zenas' function in the early church. As the "young faith was perpetually crossing the lines of the elder religions, and confronting the hereditary rights of a traditional heathenism," it needed lawyers like Zenas to help negotiate those boundaries peacefully while maintaining the truly "revolutionary" character of the new religion (1872: 6). Potter reflects that Zenas was probably a lawyer before his conversion; following the urging of the same Paul who tells the Corinthians to remain in their callings (1 Cor. 7:20), Zenas simply turned his legal mind to the problems facing the church. Alexander the coppersmith (2 Tim. 4:14; see the commentary at 1 Tim. 1:18–20) has a walk-on role in this sermon as well; he is a foil for Zenas: the former uses what skills he has at his disposal for harm, the latter for good (1872: 7–8). The most fascinating moment in the sermon comes, however, when Potter turns to the sacred character of the lawyer's social function:

> Indeed, what could be more sacred or godlike than the mission of the principles and practice of the law? I mean the production and preservation of order? Looking backward to the infancy of things, we perceive that whatever is, rose out of some dead ground work of confusion and nothingness, and incessantly gravitates thitherwards again; nay, that, without a positive energy of God, no universe could have emerged from the void, or be suspended out of it for an hour. And seeing this, we feel that there is no task more indubitably divine than the creation of beauty out of the chaos, the imposition of law upon the lawless, and the setting forth of times and seasons from the stagnant and eternal night. (10–11)

Potter concludes by indicating that lawyers in particular face many temptations, but that they must resist the desire to sell their souls and their sense of justice for money or power. A more recent sermon, also given before lawyers, warns of other dangers inherent to a life at the bar. Justice Peter Young, of the Supreme Court of New South Wales, Australia, in his sermon delivered at the start of the 2006 law term, takes Zenas as his point of departure. He comments: "[i]t is comforting that right from the beginning of the church, lawyers are there in leadership roles, being involved in the church's mission not just in administration. This is a role that lawyers have adopted throughout the ages and still is the case today. Lawyers should be, and I'm pleased to say, often are, the mainstay of churches of almost all descriptions" (NSW Supreme Court website). In an unexpected twist, Young then goes on to discuss Zenas in terms of what appears initially to be an inverted reading of Titus 3:9 – lawyers should be troublemakers, advocating change in their religious communities. Of course, the verse in question, aimed at Gnostic controversies, he says, does not limit the critical role muckraking religious lawyers can play for the good of their churches. The active Christian lawyer who bothers fellow congregants by agitating for justice when they would rather stick to the status quo is often thought to be "stirring up dissention . . . undermining the peace of the congregation or the pastor's ministry." Really, though, he just carries on in Zenas' footsteps. The temptations lawyers face today, Young says, involve complacency, seeing the world as too corrupt already for change. One also runs the risk of sympathizing with one's criminal clients, thus hampering one's ability to function as a social reformer. He concludes with a pragmatic vision of the lawyer's call. It is less expansive than Potter's cosmic vocation, but it invokes a grand theme nonetheless: "we must use what God has given to us both of skills and funds to bring about the coming of the kingdom. May the Lord give us the strength to do so."

Conclusion

[I]nterpretation comes first, indeed interpretation overwhelms my text, as if to demonstrate how it also overwhelms, eclipses, *and always precedes* the biblical 'original.' (Sherwood 2000: 2)

As I noted in the introduction, until the nineteenth century, the Pastoral Epistles were considered authentically Pauline writings, while scholarship today largely assumes a post-Pauline origin for these texts. Nevertheless, one of the more interesting findings of this commentary is that most recent readers are simply unaware of, or uninterested in, the scholarly consensus. That is, just when one might expect to find a greater number of critical responses to these letters, or perhaps fewer references to them altogether, one finds a steadily continuing history of complex and contradictory readings not at all unlike the reception of the Pastorals in earlier centuries. Yet such continuities are perhaps

The Pastoral Epistles Through the Centuries, First Edition. Jay Twomey.
© 2009 by Jay Twomey. Published 2020 by John Wiley & Sons Ltd.

only surprising when authenticity is our privileged frame of reference. Most readers, simply continue to invest authority in the canonical Pauline corpus (i.e., all 13 letters) as a source of, and support for, faith commitments. Certain one may be that 2 Thessalonians is not Paul's own, but that assessment is neither here nor there when one reflects upon the significance of the letter for contemporary "Rapturology."

Interpretations do not need to be as thrilling as those involving the development of an end-time scenario, though. In fact, the point I'd like to insist upon here is that the thrill, or more accurately, the engaging richness, of texts like the Pastorals is fully informed by the canonical authority of all of the letters for readers well beyond the pseudepigraphal divide. It is perhaps this above all else that accounts for some of the striking interpretive continuities one finds through the centuries. The negative theologian's reflections upon 1 Timothy 6:16 (God "dwells in unapproachable light") may be quite independent of the scientific reader's appreciation of the same verse. Still, both the fifth century Pseudo-Dionysius and the twenty-first century composer Stephen Taylor use the Pastor's language as a resource for conceiving of the ethereal, impossible space of divinity. Characters named by the Pastor, figures like Alexander the coppersmith (2 Tim. 4:14), have likewise been given a consistent (and consistently negative) hearing over the course of their long existence. Theodoret of Cyrus considers the artisan to be, by virtue of his craft and class status, despicable, lowly, a natural-born opponent of Paul. In the nineteenth century, Thomas Hardy, a novelist well acquainted with the higher criticism, updates without significantly changing Theodoret's slanderous portrait: Tess D'Urberville, his eponymous heroine, falls at the hands of an unscrupulous scoundrel and religious fraud named after the Pastor's Alexander. And certainly, although women have had far greater access, as readers and authors, to print media over the last two centuries – and although contemporary New Testament studies owes a tremendous debt to feminist theory and interpretation – critical readers still work to undermine the Pastor's restrictions on women's religious agency in ways similar to those of Jerome (see at 1 Tim. 2:11–12), Chaucer's Wife of Bath, Sor Juana Inez de la Cruz, and Jeanette Winterson.

Such continuities clearly suggest that key ideas, expressions, and images from the Pastorals have had a relatively consistent and powerful presence in the Christian imagination through the centuries. But even if they frame a majority of the readings cited in this commentary, continuities are only part of the story. To some extent, a commentary such as this is about reception study in general (in addition to the reception of certain sets of texts). It must often work with the assumption that any instance of reception may not have traceable origins in earlier or traditional interpretations, even when similarities in interpretations strongly suggest continuities of tradition. It must also accept that certain echoes and uses of language from the texts studied 'may not be connected to an awareness of those texts at all. In other words, it must theorize the nature and outer limits of reception in the very act of constructing the specifics of a history of readings. But perhaps this is simply what reception study is all about in the first place. Yvonne Sherwood, in the introduction to her study of the Book of Jonah and its "afterlives," explains that her work, unlike much traditional biblical scholarship, does not seek only to understand Jonah in its original setting, but rather through its history of interpretation. I am tempted to write "histories" of interpretation, but the plural would only reinforce the apparently subsidiary status of non-scholarly, non-theological interpretation; and one of Sherwood's central purposes is to show that the biblical text is a fabric of interpretation (Jewish, Christian, literary, philosophical, pop-cultural, theological, etc.), always and only. Possibly it is too easy to make the same point in a commentary like this one, which gathers the material of 18 centuries of interpretation and appropriation, and uses biblical texts, strung out in single italicized verses here and there, to stitch together the whole. For in the end the biblical texts are still the *raison d'être* of this whole project, of course, and when the texts end, when we arrive at the last verse (or thereabouts) of the last chapter of Titus, the reception history is over. Certainly, my biblical text, the text of the Pastorals, is "overwhelmed," as Sherwood says, by interpretation. But, given my interest in positing certain readings of the original material over others, given the constraints of sequential and chronological ordering (always moving forward through the canonical letters as if they were communicating with us, always tracing a history with a definite origin of which we never lose sight), given the fact that many of the readers surveyed in this book take it for granted that they are somehow trying to understand and communicate an authoritative message . . . well, it is hard to know, eventually, just who's in charge: the Bible, or its readers, or their commentator. And yet, quite frankly, this is an uncertainty with which I am perfectly comfortable. So much so that, rather than decide the question in concluding, rather than outline further continuities and celebrate idiosyncratic discontinuities, I would prefer to end by beginning again – this time without the constraints of sequence or chronology, with an interest only in the mutuality of biblical meaning-making.

At various moments, this commentary has teased at the possibilities of a more ambiguous, tangential, even retrograde or reverse reception study. Uses of "the quick and the dead" are examined as highly ambiguous citations of 2 Timothy 4:1 – or possibly they are not citations from the Pastorals at all. The language of the Bible, like that of other foundational texts, circulates far from its original home, its origins forgotten, its return all but foreclosed by significant, perhaps inevitable, changes in cultural emphases. When return is possible, it is often critical, a return of the repressed. Jeanette Winterson's citation of "to the pure all things are pure" (Titus 1:15) is also a de facto rejection of the Pastor's restrictions on women's religious agency, and of his scandalization of (albeit male) homosexuality (at 1 Tim. 1:10). Other readers, some much more traditional, have also exploited apparent contradictions in the Pastorals, and this commentary treats them all as opportunities for alternative readings, for critical interventions into what are, at times, harmful texts.

Yet there are so many other readings one could discuss along these lines. Take Paul Muldoon's poem, "Third Epistle to Timothy" (2001: 451–55), which perplexes the student of reception history by not citing the Pastoral Epistles at all. How does a work such as this, which concerns the origins of the Troubles, and blends a father's childhood experiences with those both of his son and his own adult self, comment on, respond to, the Pastor? Or consider Gore Vidal's 1992 novel, *Live From Golgotha*, a farcical gospel rewrite featuring Timothy and Paul as religious entrepreneurs, and occasional gay lovers. Is it a reply to the Pastor, an attempt to jolt the Moral Majority and its friends in the Reagan administration, both, neither? And what of the group of mutual funds named The Timothy Plan (http://www.timothyplan.com/), whose current total assets of over $500 million are dedicated to "investing with biblical principles." The Plan's website references 1 Timothy 5:8 and 5:22 which, combined, assert the necessity of supporting one's family while not sharing "in the sins of others." Yet The Timothy Plan invests in the oil industry and supports defense contractors. Would the Pastor? Is that a legitimate question to ask of an ancient text? And just how would one include financial ledgers in a reception study of these epistles?

Were there time enough and space, this commentary could go further and further afield, exploring by indirection, or direct but critical citation, the historical, cultural, intellectual, and linguistic effects of the Pastoral Epistles. Ironically, such work necessarily repudiates the Pastor's aim of sealing the Pauline tradition as a "deposit." But, as Jouette Bassler rightly points out, the Pastor himself "has already modified the entrusted material in ways that he either does not recognize or does not acknowledge. His own handling of the Pauline deposit thus reveals a clear truth that stands in conflict with his words: The traditions must be interpreted for subsequent generations or become a lifeless fossil" (Bassler 1996: 123). The same is true of the Pastor's writings themselves, which can remain vibrant and relevant documents precisely because new generations of readers – whether they know it or not – continue to receive these letters with all the critical and creative acuity, all the slapdash and off-handed indirection, that has marked the history of their reception so far.

Ambrose (c. 333–97). Bishop of Milan and teacher of Augustine.

Allingham, William (1824–89). Irish poet.

Arminius, Jacobus (1560–1609). Dutch Reformed theologian.

Arnold, Matthew (1822–88). English poet and critic.

Astell, Mary (1666–1731). Early English feminist and intellectual, promoter of women's education.

Athanasius (295–373). Bishop of Alexandria, who wrote against the Arians.

Augustine of Hippo (354–430). Bishop of Hippo, the most influential theologian of western Christianity and an early proponent of the Christian (later Calvinist) doctrine of predestination. Author of the *Confessions* and *City of God*.

Balthasar, Hans Urs von (1905–88). Roman Catholic theologian.

Baraka, Amiri (1934–). Controversial African American poet and activist.

Barclay, Robert (1648–1690). Quaker theologian and theorist of the "inner light."

The Pastoral Epistles Through the Centuries, First Edition. Jay Twomey.
© 2009 by Jay Twomey. Published 2020 by John Wiley & Sons Ltd.

Barlow, George (1847–1914). English poet.

Barnett, Anthony (1941–). English poet.

Barth, Karl (1886–1968). Swiss Reform, existentialist theologian.

Basil of Caesaria (c. 329–79). Bishop of Caesaria and anti-Arian theologian.

Bede (c. 672–735). Benedictine monk, author of the *Ecclesiastical History of the English People*.

Bernard of Claivaux (1090–1153). Monastic reformer and abbot of one of the chief centers of the Cistercian order.

Bierce, Ambrose (1842–1913). American short-story writer.

Blake, William (1757–1827). English poet, artist and visionary.

Blondel, David (1591–1655). French Calvinist.

Bonaventure (1221–74). Italian Franciscan and scholastic theologian.

Brontë, Charlotte (1816–55). English novelist.

Bukowski, Charles (1920–94). American (Beat) poet.

Bultmann, Rudolf (1884–1976). German Lutheran theologian.

Bunyan, John (1628–88). Preacher, allegorist, author of *The Pilgrim's Progress*.

Bushnell, Horace (1802–76). American Congregationalist minister and theologian.

Calvin, John (1509–64). Theologian, exegete and reformer, whose pioneering theological polity paved the way for Reformed Christianity. Calvin's thoughts on God's sovereignty, human depravity, and double-predestination were a major influence on early American theologians such as Jonathan Edwards.

Cassiodorus (c.490–c.583). Roman statesman and Christian monk.

Catherine of Siena (1347–80). Italian Dominican mystic.

Celsus (second century). Early philosophical opponent of Christianity.

Cervantes Saavedra, Miguel de (1547–1616). Spanish writer, author of the comic masterpiece *Don Quixote*.

Chamberlaine, James (d. 1699). English poet.

Chaucer, Geoffrey (1343–1400). English poet, among the earliest to write in the vernacular, author of *The Canterbury Tales*.

Chivers, Thomas H. (1807–58). American poet, associate of Edgar Allen Poe.

Clarke, William H. (nineteenth century). Anglican clergyman.

Clement of Alexandria (c. 150–c. 215). Early theologian and philosopher.

Coleman, Wanda (1946–). African-American poet.

Coleridge, Samuel Taylor (1772–1834). English Romantic poet and theorist.

Cone, James (b. 1938). African-American Methodist theologian.

Coven, Stephen (d. 1692). English nonconformist.

Chrysostom, John (c. 347–407). Bishop of Constantinople, often referred to as the greatest preacher of the patristic era.

Cyprian (d.258). Latin church father.

Cuyler, Theodore L. (1822–1909). American Presbyterian minister.

Dante, Alighieri (1265–1321). Italian poet, author of the *Divine Comedy*.

Darby, John Nelson (1800–82). Anglican priest, dispensationalist theologian.

Dickens, Charles (1812–70). English novelist, author of *Great Expectations* and *Bleak House*.

Donne, John (1571–1631). English priest and metaphysical poet.

Meister Eckhart (1260–1328). German Dominican mystic and theologian.

Edwards, Jonathan (1703–58). American Congregationalist minister and revivalist.

Edwards, Thomas (1599–1648). English heresiologist.

Elliott, Charlotte (1789–1871). English hymnist and poet.

Emerson, Ralph Waldo (1803–82). American Unitarian minister and Transcendentalist.

Erasmus, Desiderius (1466–1536). Dutch humanist and Roman Catholic.

Evans, Katherine (d. 1692) **and Sarah Chevers** (d. 1644). English Quakers.

Fell, Margaret (1614–1702). Early English Quaker and proto-feminist.

Flavel, John (1627–91). English Presbyterian minister, and Nonconformist.

Fox, George (1624–91). Founder of Quakerism.

Francis of Assisi (1182–1226). Founder of the Franciscan order.

Francis de Sales (1567–1622). Roman Catholic bishop of Geneva, leader in the Counter-Reformation.

Francisco de Osuna (1492–1540). Spanish Franciscan and ascetic.

Fuller, Thomas (1608–61). Anglican clergyman and historian.

Gaussen, Louis (1790–1863). Swiss Reformed minister and theologian.

Gouge, William (1575–1653). English Puritan.

Greene, Graham (1904–91). English novelist.

Gregory of Nazianzus (329–89). Early Trinitarian theologian.

Gregory of Nyssa (335–95). Bishop and early Trinitarian theologian.

Guigo de Ponte (d. 1296). Carthusian monk.

Gutiérrez, Gustavo (b. 1928). Peruvian Dominican priest and liberation theologian.

Hamilton, Richard Winter (1794–1848). English Congregationalist minister.

Hardy, Thomas (1840–1928). English novelist and poet.

Harper, Frances Ellen Watkins (1825–1911). African-American abolitionist and suffragist.

Harris, James H. (b. 1952). African-American Baptist minister and theologian.

Harsent, David (b. 1942). English poet.

Henry, Matthew (1662–1714). English Presbyterian minister, author of influential *Exposition on the Old and New Testament*.

Hippolytus (d. 235). Leader, and later schismatic bishop, of the Church in Rome.

Hobbes, Thomas (1588–1679). English philosopher and political theorist, author of *Leviathan*.

Hope, Charity (nineteenth century). Pseudonym of Mrs. William L. Coade, Ulster feminist and editorialist.

Hopkins, Gerard Manley (1844–89). English poet and Jesuit priest.

Howard, Richard (b. 1929). American poet.

Hugh of Balma (d. 1439). Carthusian monk.

Hutchinson, Anne (1591–1643). American Puritan preacher and advocate of religious freedom.

Irenaeus of Lyon (late second century). Early bishop and major anti-Gnostic apologist.

Irving, Washington (1783–1859). American short-story writer.

Sor Juana Inés de la Cruz (1651–95). Mexican Catholic nun, poet and proto-feminist.

Jefferson, Thomas (1743–1826). Third US president, primary author of Declaration of Independence.

Jerome (c. 340–420). Biblical scholar responsible for the Vulgate, the Latin translation of the Bible.

Joachim of Fiore (c. 1135–1202). Mystic and one of the most influential interpreters of the Book of Revelation.

John Cassian (c. 360–443). Monastic founder, compiled the teachings and wisdom of the Desert Fathers.

John of Damascus (c. 650–750). Also known as John Damascene. Syrian theologian and monk.

Jordan, Thomas (1614–85). English actor, poet and playwright.

Joyce, James (1882–1941). Irish novelist, author of *Ulysses* and *Finnegan's Wake*.

Justin Martyr (mid-second century). Early theologian and apologist.

Kierkegaard, Søren (1813–55). Danish philosopher and Lutheran teacher.

King, Martin Luther (1929–68). African-American Baptist minister, leader of the civil rights movement.

Kinnell, Galway (1927–). American poet.

Knox, John (1514–72). Scottish Calvinist, leading figure in Scottish Reformation.

LaHaye, Tim (1926–) and **Jenkins, Jerry** (1949–). Authors of the apocalyptic *Left Behind* novels.

Langland, William (c. 1330–1400). Visionary and author of *Piers Plowman*.

Lawrence, D. H. (1885–1930). English novelist and poet.

Leo the Great (d. 461). Fifth century pope.

Lewis, C. S. (1898–1963). Irish Anglican novelist and scholar.

Locke, John (1632–1704). English philosopher and political theorist.

Luther, Martin (1483–1546). Augustinian monk who became the leader of the Reformation in Germany.

Marcion (second century). Christian heretic who disavowed the Hebrew Bible and portions of the New Testament.

Mason, Arthur (1851–1928). English hymn writer and translator.

Mather, Cotton (1663–1728). Boston minister and millennial preacher, influential for the Salem witch trials of the 1690s.

Maximus the Confessor (580–662). Monk and theologian.

Mede, Joseph (1586–1638). Fellow of Christ's College, Cambridge, and influential interpreter of the Book of Revelation.

Melville, Herman (1819–91). American novelist, author of *Moby Dick*.

Methodius of Olympus (d. 311). Anti-Origenist bishop.

Milton, John (1608–74). Poet, nonconformist, anti-monarchist, and apologist for the Commonwealth in England from 1649 to 1660, author of *Paradise Lost*.

More, Henry (1614–87). English philosopher.

Nicolas of Cusa (c. 1400–64). Medieval mystic and negative theologian.

Newman, John Henry (1801–90). English Catholic cardinal, founding figure of the Oxford Movement.

Nietzsche, Friedrich (1844–1900). German philosopher and critic.

Novatian (d. 258). Roman priest and "anti-pope," refused to readmit to full communion those who had lapsed during persecution.

Oecumenius of Tricca (tenth century). Biblical commentator.

Origen (c. 185–235). Theologian and allegorical exegete, based in Alexandria and later in Caesarea.

Owen, James (1654–1706). English nonconformist.

Pope John Paul II (1920–2005). Roman Catholic Pontiff from 1978 to 2005.

Pope Leo XIII (1810–1903). Roman Catholic Pontiff from 1878 to 1903.

Potter, Henry C. (1835–1908). American Episcopal bishop.

Prynne, William (1600–69). Puritan polemicist.

Pseudo-Dionysius (fifth century). Mystic and Neoplatonic theologian.

Rahner, Karl (1904–84). German Catholic theologian.

Ross, Frederick A. (1796–1883). American Presbyterian minister and anti-abolitionist.

Rossetti, Christina (1830–94). Victorian poet, social activist, and author of devotional works.

Rufinus (c. 345–410). Monk and theologian.

Ruskin, John (1819–1900). English art critic and social commentator.

Salvian the Presbyter (fifth century). Author of a treatise, *To the Church*, written under the pseudonym Timothy.

Schleiermacher, Friedrich (1768–1834). German theologian and philosopher.

Scofield, Cyrus (1843–1941). American minister and theological entrepreneur, editor of the *Scofield Reference Bible*.

Shakespeare, William (c. 1564–1616). Most significant Elizabethan playwright.

Shannon, James (1799–1859). American Restorationist minister and anti-abolitionist.

Spenser, Edmund (1552–1599). English poet, author of *The Faerie Queene*.

Stowe, Harriet Beecher (1811–96). American novelist and abolitionist.

Suso, Henry (1300–66). German mystic.

Symeon the New Theologian (949–1022). Eastern Orthodox theologian.

Taylor, Edward (1642–1729). American Puritan minister and poet.

Tertullian (c. 160–220). Early Christian theologian later a member of the Montanist apocalyptic sect.

Theodoret of Cyrus (c. 393–c. 457). Theologian of the Antioch school, deeply involved in early Christological controversies.

Thom, David (1795–1862). English Universalist.

Thomas Aquinas (c. 1225–74). Medieval scholastic theologian whose systematic exposition of Christian thought and scriptures provided the Catholic Church with its intellectual architecture.

Todhunter, John (1839–1916). Irish poet and playwright.

Tyndale, William (c. 1492–1536). English reformer and biblical translator, burned at the stake for his efforts.

Wang Ping (1957–). Chinese-American poet and novelist.

Watson, Thomas (1620–86). English Puritan theologian.

Watts, Isaac (1674–1748). English hymn writer.

Wesley, Charles (1707–88). English Methodist minister, and hymn writer.

Wesley, John (1707–88). Anglican priest, evangelist, founder of Methodism.

White, Ellen (1827–1915). Prophetic writer and founding figure of Adventism.

Whitefield, George (1714–71). English Methodist minister who also preached widely in North America.

Winchester, Elhanan (1751–97). American Universalist.

Winterson, Jeanette (1959–). English novelist.

Woolf, Virginia (1882–1941). English novelist and essayist.

Wycliffe, John (1324–84). English theologian and forerunner of the Reformation, who promoted the translation of the Bible into English.

Bibliography

ABBREVIATIONS

ANF	Ante-Nicene Fathers
APS	American Periodicals Series
D-C	Dibelius and Conzelmann, *The Pastoral Epistles*
EAI (1 & 2)	Early American Imprints (Series I and II).
ECCO	Eighteenth Century Collections Online
FC	Fathers of the Church
LION	Literature Online
MOA	Making of America
NPNF(1 & 2)	Select Library of Nicene- and Post-Nicene Fathers (First and Second Series)

The Pastoral Epistles Through the Centuries, First Edition. Jay Twomey.
© 2009 by Jay Twomey. Published 2020 by John Wiley & Sons Ltd.

PG	Patrologiae Cursus Completus (Series Graeca)	
ST FP Q[1] A[1]	Summa Theologica, First Part, Question 1, Answer 1 (see Websites, below)	
ST FS	Summa Theologica, First Part of the Second Part	
ST SS	Summa Theologica, Second Part of the Second Part	
ST TP	Summa Theologica, Third Part	
XP [Sup. TP]	Supplement to Summa Theologica, Third Part	

Ambrose	*De spir. sanct.*	*On The Holy Spirit*
Athanasius	*Apol. ad Const.*	*Apology to Constantius*
	Ep.	*Epistles*
	Hist. Ar.	*Arian History*
	Orat. cont. Ar.	*Orations Against the Arians*
Augustine	*An. et or.*	*On the Soul and its Origin*
	C. ep. Pelag.	*Against Two Letters of the Pelagians*
	C. Faust.	*Reply to Faustus*
	Conf.	*Confessions*
	Corrept.	*On Rebuke and Grace*
	De bapt.	*On Baptism*
	De bono conjug.	*On the Good of Marriage*
	De bono vid.	*On the Good of Widowhood*
	De civ. Dei	*City of God*
	De doc. Chr.	*On Christian Doctrine*
	De fide et sym.	*On Faith and the Creed*
	De gest. Pel.	*On The Proceedings of Pelagius*
	De gr. et lib. arb.	*On Grace and Free Will*
	De nat. boni	*On the Good of Nature*
	De nat. et grat.	*On Nature and Grace*
	De op. mon.	*On the Work of Monks*
	De praed. sanct.	*On the Predestination of the Saints*
	De spir. et litt.	*On the Spirit and the Letter*
	De Trin.	*On the Trinity*
	De virg.	*On Holy Virginity*
	En. ps.	*Commentary on the Psalms*
	Ench.	*Enchiridion*
	Ep. Jo.	*Homilies on the First Epistle of John*
	Jo. ev. tr.	*Tractates on the Gospel of John*
	Serm.	*Sermon(s)*

	Serm. Dom. mon.	On the Sermon on the Mount
Basil of Caesaria	*De spir. sanct.*	On The Holy Spirit
Cassian	*Conf.*	Conferences
	Inst.	Institutes
Cassiodorus	*Ex. ps.*	Explanation of the Psalms
Clement of Alexandria	*Exc. Theod.*	Excerpts of Theodotus
	Str.	Stromateis
	Paed.	Paedagogus
	Protrep.	Exhortation to the Heathen
Eusebius	*Eccl. Hist.*	History of the Church
Gregory of Nyssa	*C. Eun.*	Against Eunomius
Jerome	*C. Jov.*	Against Jovinian
	Ep.	Epistles
John Chrysostom	*De Sac.*	On the Priesthood
	Hom. 1 Tim.	Homilies on 1 Timothy
	Hom. 2 Tim.	Homilies on 2 Timothy
	Hom. stat.	Homilies on the Statues
	Hom. Tit.	Homilies on Titus
Nicolas of Cusa	*De doct. ign.*	On Learned Ignorance
Novatian	*De Trin.*	On the Trinity
Origen	*C. Cels.*	Against Celsus
	Cant.	Commentary on the Song of Songs
	De orat.	On Prayer
	De prin.	On First Principles
	Hom. Gen.	Homilies on Genesis
Pseudo-Dionysius	*De div. nom.*	On the Divine Names
Salvian the Presbyter	*Ad ecclesiam*	The Four Books of Timothy to the Church
Tertullian	*Ad ux.*	To His Wife
	Apol.	Apology
	De cor.	On the Crown
	De cult. fem.	On the Apparel of Women
	De fuga	De Fuga in Persecutione
	De idol.	On Idolatry
	De jejun.	On Fasting
	Praescr.	Prescription Against Heretics
	Virg.	On the Veiling of Virgins
Theodoret	*Comm. 1 Tim.*	Commentary on 1 Timothy
	Ecc. hist.	Ecclesiastical History
Thomas Aquinas	*Comm. super I Tim.*	Commentary on 1 Timothy

PRIMARY AND SECONDARY SOURCES

Abbott, W. M. 1966. *The Documents of Vatican II*. New York: Herder and Herder.

Allingham, W. 1890. *Blackberries*. London: Reeves and Turner. (LION)

Anatolios, K. 2004. *Athanasius*. New York: Routledge.

Anonymous. 1869. *A Collection of Temperance Dialogues*. Ottawa: S. T. Hammond. (LION)

Arminius, J. 1956. *The Writings of James Arminius*, ed. James Nichols and W. R. Bagnall, 3 vols. Grand Rapids, MI: Baker Book House.

Arnold, M. 1968. *Dogma and Dissent*, ed. R. H. Super. Ann Arbor, MI: University of Michigan Press.

Astell, M. 2002. *A Serious Proposal to the Ladies*, ed. Patricia Springborg. Orchard Park, NY: Broadview Press.

Augustine. 2000. *The City of God*, tr. Marcus Dods. New York: Modern Library.

Babcock, H. 1983. "Origen's Anti-Gnostic Polemic and the Doctrine of Universalism." *The Unitarian Universalist Christian*, 38.3–4: 53–59.

Balthasar, Hans Urs von. 1989. *The Glory of the Lord*, tr. Brian McNeil, 7 vols. San Francisco: Ignatius Press.

Baraka, I. A. 1973. *Afrikan Revolution*. Newark, NJ: Jihad Press. (LION)

Barclay, R. 1827. *An Apology for the True Christian Divinity*. New York: Samuel Wood and Sons. (CCEL)

Barlow, G. 1902–14. *The Poetical Works of George Barlow*, 11 vols. London: Henry J. Glaisher. (LION)

Barnes, A. 1835. *The Scriptural Argument for Episcopacy Examined*. New York: Leavitt, Lord & Co.

Barth, K. 1936. *God in Action: Theological Addresses*, tr. E. G. Homrighausen and Karl J. Ernst. New York: Round Table Press.

Barth, K. 2004. *Church Dogmatics*, I/2. New York: T & T Clark.

Barthelme, D. 2004. *The Dead Father*. New York: Farrar, Straus and Giroux.

Bassler, J. 1996a. *1 Timothy, 2 Timothy, Titus*. Nashville, TN: Abingdon Press.

Bauer, L. and Bauer, G. 1984. "The *Winter Landscape with Skaters and Bird Trap* by Pieter Bruegel the Elder." *The Art Bulletin*, 66.1 (March): 145–50.

Bauer, W. 1971. *Orthodoxy and Heresy in Earliest Christianity*, tr. Philadelphia Seminar on Christian Origins, ed. Robert A. Kraft and Gerhard Krodel. Philadelphia, PA: Fortress Press.

Bay, M. 2000. *The White Image in the Black Mind: African-American Ideas About White People*. New York: Oxford University Press.

Beal, J. P., Coriden, J. A. and Green, T. J. ed. 2000. *New Commentary on the Code of Canon Law*. New York: Paulist Press.

Beattie, G. 2005. *Women and Marriage in Paul and his Early Interpreters*. New York: T & T Clark International.

Bede. 1999. *Ecclesiastical History of the English People*, ed. Judith McClure and Roger Collins. New York: Oxford University Press.

Bereit, R. 2002. *In His Service: A Guide To Christian Living in the Military*. Colorado Springs, CO: Dawson Media.

Bernard of Clairvaux. 1904. *Some Letters of Saint Bernard, Abbot of Clairvaux*, tr. Samuel Eales, ed. Francis Gasquet. London: John Hodges. (CCEL)

Bernard of Clairvaux. 1987. *Bernard of Clairvaux: Selected Works*, tr. G. R. Evans. New York: Paulist Press.

Bierce, A. 1909. *The Collected Works of Ambrose Bierce*, 12 vols. New York: The Neale Publishing Company. (LION)

Blake, W. 1965. *The Poetry and Prose of William Blake*, ed. D. Erdman. Garden City, NY: Doubleday. (LION)

Blondel, D. 1661. *A Treatise of The Sibyls so Highly Celebrated*, tr. J. D. London: Printed by T. R. (EEBO)

Bonaventure. 1978. *Bonaventure: The Soul's Journey into God, The Tree of Life, The Life of St. Francis*, tr. Ewart Cousins. New York: Paulist Press.

Brontë, C. 1979. *Shirley*, ed. Herbert Rosengarten and Margaret Smith. New York: Oxford University Press.

Brontë, C. 2000. *Jane Eyre*, ed. Margaret Smith. New York: Oxford University Press.

Brown, D. 2003. *The Da Vinci Code: A Novel*. New York: Doubleday.

Brozyna, A. E. 1999. *Labour, Love and Prayer: Female Piety in Ulster Religious Literature, 1850–1914*. Montreal: McGill-Queen's University Press.

Bukowski, C. 1981. *Dangling in the Tournefortia*. Santa Barbara, CA: Black Sparrow Press.

Bultmann, R. 1955. *Theology of the New Testament*, tr. Kendrick Grobel, 2 vols. New York: Scribner.

Bunyan, J. 1850. *Bunyan's Devotional Works*, ed. John Newton Brown. Philadelphia, PA: American Baptist publication society. (MOA)

Bunyan, J. 2003. *The Pilgrim's Progress*, ed. W. R. Owens. New York: Oxford University Press.

Burnett, R. 2004. *Karl Barth's Theological Exegesis: The Hermeneutical Principles of the Römerbrief Period*. Grand Rapids, MI: Eerdmans.

Bushnell, H. 1864. *Christ and His Salvation*. New York: Charles Scribner. (MOA)

Bushnell, H. 1876. *Christian Nurture*. New York: Scribner, Armstrong & Co. (MOA)

Butler, S., ed. 2005. *My Dear Mr. Stalin: The Complete Correspondence of Franklin D. Roosevelt and Joseph V. Stalin*. New Haven, CT: Yale University Press.

Carey, P. 1998. *Pastoral Letters and Statements of the United States Catholic Bishops, Volume 6: 1989–1997*. Washington, DC: United Catholic Bishops Conference.

Calvin, J. 1856. *Commentaries on the Epistles to Timothy, Titus, and Philemon*, tr. W. Pringle. Edinburgh: Calvin Translation Society.

Calvin, J. 1960. *Institutes of The Christian Religion*, ed. John T. McNeil, tr. Ford Lewis Battles, 2 vols. Philadelphia, PA: Westminster Press.

Calvin, J. 1964. *The Second Epistle of Paul the Apostle to the Corinthians and the Epistles to Timothy, Titus and Philemon*, tr. T. A. Smail. Grand Rapids, MI: Eerdmans.

Calvin, J. 1983. *Sermons on the Epistles to Timothy and Titus* [1579], tr. [L. T.]. Carlisle, PA: Banner of Truth Trust.

Calvin, J. 1999. *Mystery of Godliness and Other Sermons.* Morgan, PA: Soli Deo Gloria Publications.

Carlen, C., ed. 1981. *The Papal Encyclicals.* Ann Arbor, MI: Pierian Press.

Carleton, K. 2001. *Bishops and Reform in the English Church, 1520–1559.* Rochester, NY: Boydell Press.

Cassiodorus. 1991. *Explanation of the Psalms,* tr. and ed. P. G. Walsh, 3 vols. New York: Paulist Press.

Catherine of Siena. 1980. *The Dialogue,* tr. S. Noffke. New York: Paulist Press.

Cervantes Saavedra, Miguel de. 1981. *Don Quixote,* ed. Joseph R. Jones and Kenneth Douglass, tr. John Ormsby. New York: Norton.

Cervantes Saavedra, Miguel de. 1998. *Exemplary Stories,* tr. Lesley Lipson. New York: Oxford University Press.

Chadwick, H. 2001. *The Church in Ancient Society: From Galilee to Gregory the Great.* New York: Oxford University Press.

Chamberlaine, J. 1680. *A Sacred Poem.* London: Printed by R. E. for R. Bentley, and M. Magnes [etc.]. (LION)

Chaucer, Geoffrey. 1987. *The Riverside Chaucer,* gen. ed. L. Benson. Boston, MA: Houghton Mifflin.

Chivers, T. H. 1845. *The Lost Pleiad and Other Poems.* New York: Edward O. Jenkins. (LION).

Clancy, F. 1993. "St. Augustine, His Predecessors and Contemporaries, and the Exegesis of 2 Tim. 2.20." *Studia Patristica* 27: 242–48.

Clark, E. 1977. *Women and Religion: A Feminist Sourcebook of Christian Thought.* New York: Harper & Row.

Clarke, E. 2005. *Dwelling Place: A Plantation Epic.* New Haven, CT: Yale University Press.

Clarke, W. H. 1834. *Sermons.* London: J. G. and F. Rivington.

Clement of Alexandria. 1970. *Extraits de Théodote,* tr. and ed. F. Sagnard. Paris: Éditions du Cerf.

Coleman, W. 1983. *Imagoes.* Santa Barbara, CA: Black Sparrow Press. (LION)

Coleridge, S. T. 1969–. *Collected Works of Samuel Taylor Coleridge,* ed. Kathleen Coburn et al., 16 vols. Princeton, NJ: Princeton University Press.

Collins, R. 2002. *1 & 2 Timothy and Titus: A Commentary.* Louisville, KY: Westminster John Knox Press.

Collins, V. T. 1996. "Walking in Light, Walking in Darkness: The Story of Women's Changing Rhetorical Space in Early Methodism." *Rhetoric Review* 14.2: 336–54.

Cone, J. 1993. *Black Theology: A Documentary History,* 2 vols. Maryknoll, NY: Orbis Books.

Coven, S. 1669. *The Militant Christian; or, The Good Soldier of Jesus Christ.* London: [no pub.]. (EEBO)

Cromartie, M., ed. 2003. *A Public Faith: Evangelicals and Civic Engagement.* Oxford: Rowman and Littlefield.

Crown, C., ed. 2004. *Coming Home! Self-Taught Artists, the Bible and the American South.* Jackson, MS: University Press of Mississippi.

Cunningham, A. 1985. *The Bishop in the Church: Patristic Texts on the Role of the Episkopos.* Wilmington, DE: Michael Glazier.

Cuyler, T. L. 1898. "Brave Onesiphorus – A Talk for The Times." *New York Evangelist* 69.6: 4. (APS)

D'Angelo, M. R. 2003. "'Knowing How to Preside over His Own Household': Imperial Masculinity and Christian Asceticism in the Pastorals, Hermas, and Luke-Acts." In *New Testament Masculinities*, ed. Stephen D. Moore and Janice Capel Anderson, 265–95. Atlanta, GA: Society of Biblical Literature.

Dante Alighieri. 1984. *The Paradiso*, tr. Allen Mandelbaum. New York: Bantam.

Davids, P. 1990. *First Epistle of Peter* (NINCT Commentary). Grand Rapids, MI: Eerdmans.

Davies, M. 1996. *The Pastoral Epistles.* Sheffield: Sheffield Academic.

Davis, D. H. and Hankins, B. ed. 2003. *New Religious Movements and Religious Liberty in America*, 2nd edn. Waco, TX: Baylor University Press.

Dewey, J. 1998. "1 Timothy." In *The Women's Bible Commentary*, ed. Carol A. Newsom and Sharon H. Ringe, 444–49. Louisville: Westminster John Knox Press.

Dibelius, M. and Conzelmann, H. 1972. *The Pastoral Epistles*, ed. Helmut Koester, tr. Philip Buttolph and Adela Yarbro. Philadelphia, PA: Fortress Press.

Dickens, C. 1857. *Little Dorrit.* London: Bradbury and Evans. (LION)

Doddridge, P. 1739–56. *The Family Expositor: Or, a Paraphrase and Version of the New Testament*, 6 vols. London: John Wilson. (ECCO)

Donelson, L. 1986. *Pseudepigraphy and Ethical Argument in the Pastoral Epistles.* Tübingen, Germany: Mohr.

Donne, J. 1624. *Devotions Upon Emergent Occasions.* London: Printed by Thomas Jones (EEBO)

Donne, J. 1963. *John Donne's Sermons on the Psalms and Gospels: With a Selection of Prayers and Meditations*, ed. Evelyn M. Simpson. Berkeley, CA: University of California Press.

Douglass, F. 2005. *Narrative of the Life of Frederick Douglass.* New York: Signet Classics.

Dunn, J. D. G. 1998. *The Theology of Paul the Apostle.* Grand Rapids, MI: Eerdmans.

Easton, B. S. 1947. *The Pastoral Epistles.* New York: Scribner.

Easton, B. S. 1948. *The Pastoral Epistles.* London: SCM Press.

Eckhart, M. 1980. *Breakthrough: Meister Eckhart's Creation Spirituality*, tr. M. Fox. Garden City, NY: Doubleday.

Edwards, J. 1957–. *The Works of Jonathan Edwards*, ed. Perry Miller et al., 25 vols. to date. New Haven, CT: Yale University Press.

Edwards, J. 1968. *The Works of President Edwards*, ed. Edward Williams and Edward Parsons, 10 vols. New York: B. Franklin.

Edwards, T. 1646. *Gangraena.* London: Printed by T.R. and E.M. for Ralph Smith. (EEBO)

Elliott, C. 1871. *Thoughts in Verse, on Sacred Subjects*, 2nd edn. London: William Hunt and Company, 1871. (LION)

Emerson, R. W. 1989–. *The Complete Sermons of Ralph Waldo Emerson*, ed. Albert J. von Frank, 4 vols. Columbia, MO: University of Missouri Press.

Erasmus, D. 1963. *The Enchiridion*, tr. and ed. R. Himelick. Bloomington, IN: Indiana University Press.

Erasmus, D. 1993. *Paraphrases on the Epistles to Timothy, Titus, and Philemon, the Epistles of Peter and Jude, the Epistle of James, the Epistle of John, the Epistle to the Hebrews*, tr. J. Bateman. Toronto: University of Toronto Press.

Erasmus, D. 2003. *The Praise of Folly*, tr. C. Miller. New Haven, CT: Yale University Press.

Evans, K. and Chevers, S. 1662. *This Is a Short Relation of Some of the Cruel Sufferings (For the Truths Sake) of Katharine Evans & Sarah Chevers . . .* London: Printed for Robert Wilson. (EEBO)

Fee, G. 1984. *1 and 2 Timothy, Titus*. San Francisco: Harper & Row.

Fee, G. 1995. *1 And 2 Timothy, Titus*. Peabody, MA: Hendrickson.

Fell, M. 1989. *"Women's Speaking,"* ed. Christine Rhone. London: Pythia Press.

Fendt, G. 2001. "Between a Pelagian Rock and a Hard Predestinarianism: The Currents of Controversy in *City of God* 11 and 12." *Journal of Religion* 81.2: 211–27.

Finley, J. 1854. *Sketches of Western Methodism: Biographical, Historical, and Miscellaneous. Illustrative of Pioneer Life*, ed. W. P. Strickland, D.D. Cincinnati, OH: Methodist Book Concern. (MOA)

Flannery, A., ed. 1984. *Documents of Vatican II*. Grand Rapids, MI: Eerdmans.

Flavel, J. 1701. *The Whole Works of the Reverend Mr. John Flavel*, 2 vols. London: [R. J.]. (ECCO)

Fox, G. 1659. *The Great Mystery of the Great Whore Unfolded*. London: Printed for Tho. Simmons. (EEBO)

Francis of Assisi. 1982. *Francis and Clare: The Complete Works*, tr. R. Armstrong and I. Brady. New York: Paulist Press.

Francis de Sales. 1971. *Treatise on the love of God*, tr. Henry Benedict Mackey. Westport, CT: Greenwood Press.

Francisco de Osuna. 1981. *The Third Spiritual Alphabet*, tr. M. Giles. New York: Paulist Press.

Fuller, T. 1640. *Joseph's Partie-Colored Coat*. London: Printed by John Dawson. (EEBO)

Gamble, H. 2006. "Marcion and the 'canon.'" In *The Cambridge History of Christianity*, 1, ed. Margaret M. Mitchell and Frances M. Young, 195–213. New York: Cambridge University Press.

Gaussen, L. 1841. *Theopneustia: The Plenary Inspiration of Scripture*. London: Samuel Bagster and Sons.

Glancy, J. 2003. "The Protocols of Masculinity in the Pastoral Epistles." In *New Testament Masculinities*, ed. S. Moore and J. Capel Anderson, 235–64. Atlanta, GA: Society of Biblical Literature.

Gnuse, R. 1985. *The Authority of the Bible: Theories of Inspiration, Revelation, and the Canon of Scripture*. New York: Paulist Press.

Gouge, W. 1622. *Of Domesticall Duties*. London: Printed by Iohn Haviland for William Bladen. (EEBO)

Graham, B. 1977. *How To Be Born Again*. Waco, TX: Word Books.

Grant, R. M. 1948. "More Fragments of Origen?" *Vigiliae Christianae* 2.4: 243–47.

Gray, J. 1915. *Christian Worker's Commentary on the Old and New Testaments*. New York: Fleming H. Revell Company.

Greene, G. 1973. "The Root of All Evil." In *Collected Stories*. New York: Viking Press.

Guigo de Ponte. 1997. *Carthusian Spirituality: The Writings of Hugh of Balma and Guigo de Ponte*, tr. D. Martin. New York: Paulist Press.

Guthrie, D. 1990. *The Pastoral Epistles*. Grand Rapids, MI: Eerdmans.

Gutierrez, G. 1991. *The God of Life*, tr. M. O'Connell. Maryknoll, NY: Orbis Books.

Hall, S. G. 2006. "Institutions in the Pre-Constantinian ecclesia." In *The Cambridge History of Christianity*, 1, ed. Margaret M. Mitchell and Frances M. Young, 415–33. New York: Cambridge University Press.

Hamilton, R. W. 1864. *Sermons*, 2nd edn. London: Hamilton, Adams & Co.

Hanson, A. T. 1968. *Studies in the Pastoral Epistles*. London: SPCK.

Hanson, A. T. 1982. *The Pastoral Epistles*. Grand Rapids, MI: Eerdmans.

Hardy, T. 1998. *Tess of the d'Urbervilles*, ed. Juliet Grindle and Simon Gatrell. New York: Oxford University Press.

Harnack, A. 1981. *Militia Christi: The Christian Religion and the Military in The First Three Centuries*, tr. David McInnes Gracie. Philadelphia, PA: Fortress Press.

Harper, S. "The Ordination of Women." <archives.umc.org/interior.asp?mid=1088>

Harrill, J. A. 2000. "The Use of the New Testament in the American Slave Controversy: A Case History in the Hermeneutical Tension between Biblical Criticism and Christian Moral Debate." *Religion and American Culture* 10.2: 149–86.

Harris, J. 1991. *Pastoral Theology: A Black-Church Perspective*. Minneapolis, MN: Fortress Press.

Harsent, D. 1984. *Mister Punch*. Oxford: Oxford University Press. (LION)

Hayden, R. 1975. *Angle of Ascent: New and Selected Poems*. New York: Liveright Publishing Corporation.

Helgeland, J. 1974. "Christians and the Roman Army A.D. 173–337." *Church History* 43.2: 149–163+200.

Henry, M. 1721–25. *An Exposition of the Several Epistoles Contained in the New Testament*. London: [Clark et al.]. (ECCO)

Hesselink, I. J. 2004. "Calvin's Theology." In *The Cambridge Companion to John Calvin*, ed. Donald K. McKim, 74–92. Cambridge: Cambridge University Press.

Hill, C. 1977. *Milton and The English Revolution*. New York: Viking Press.

Hobbes, T. 1994. *The Collected Writings of Thomas Hobbes*, ed. Sir William Molesworth, 11 vols. London: Routledge/Thoemmes Press.

Hodge, C. 1873. *Systematic Theology*, 1. New York: Scribner, Armstrong and Co.

Hodges, C. 2007. "Financial Strains and the Embezzlement Problem," *The Salt Lake Tribune*, March 2. <www.religionandsocialpolicy.org/news/article.cfm?id=6110>

Hopkins, D. 1999. *Introducing Black Theology of Liberation*. Maryknoll, NY: Orbis Books.

Hopkins, G. M. 1986. *Selections*, ed. Catherine Phillips. New York: Oxford University Press.

Howard, R. 1979. *Misgivings*. New York: Athenaeum.

Hughes, A. 2004. *Gangraena and the Struggle for the English Revolution*. Oxford: Oxford University Press.

Hymns Ancient and Modern For Use in the Services of the Church. 1904. London: William Clowes and Sons.

Irenaeus. 1987. *The Preaching of the Apostles*, ed. Jack N. Sparks. Brookline, MA: Holy Cross Orthodox Press.

Jackson, T. P. 1998. "Arminian Edification: Kierkegaard on Grace and Free Will." In *The Cambridge Companion to Kierkegaard*, ed. Alastair Hannay and Gordon D. Marino, 235–56. New York: Cambridge University Press.

James, J. A. 1829. *The Family Monitor: Or A Help to Domestic Happiness*. Concord, NH: Charles Hoag.

Jefferson, T. 1893. *The Writings of Thomas Jefferson*, 2. New York: G. P. Putnam's Sons.

Jenson, R. 1992. *America's Theologian: A Recommendation of Jonathan Edwards*. New York: Oxford University Press.

Johnson, E. 1990. *Expository Hermeneutics: An Introduction*. Grand Rapids, MI: Zondervan.

Johnson, L. T. 2001. *The First and Second Letters to Timothy: A New Translation with Introduction and Commentary*. New York: Doubleday.

Johnson, S. 2007. *The Demas Revelation*. Colorado Springs, CO: RiverOak.

Jordan, T. 1680. *The Muses Melody in a Consort of Poetry*. London: Printed by J. C. (LION)

Joyce, J. 1986. *Ulysses*, ed. Hans Walter Gabler. New York: Vintage Books.

Juana Inés de la Cruz, Sor. 2005. *Sor Juana Inés de la Cruz: Selected Writings*, tr. Pamela Kirk Rappaport. New York: Paulist Press.

Karris, R. J. 1973. "Background and Significance of the Polemic of the PE." *Journal of Biblical Literature* 92.4: 549–64.

Kelly, J. N. D. 1981. *A Commentary on the Pastoral Epistles*. Grand Rapids, MI: Baker Book House.

Keck, L. and Furnish, V. 1984. *The Pauline Letters*. Nashville, TN: Abingdon Press.

Kerber, L. K. and De Hart, J. S. 2003. *Women's America: Refocusing the Past*. New York: Oxford University Press.

Kierkegaard, S. 1961. *Christian Discourses*, tr. Walter Lowrie. New York: Oxford University Press.

Kierkegaard, S. 1971. *Either/Or*, tr. David F. Swenson and Lillian Marvin Swenson. Princeton, NJ: Princeton University Press [1971, c.1959]

Kierkegaard, S. 1978–. *Kierkegaard's Writings*, ed. and tr. Howard V. Hong and Edna H. Hong, 26 vols. Princeton, NJ: Princeton University Press.

Kidd, R. 1990. *Wealth and Beneficence in the Pastoral Epistles*. Atlanta, GA: Society of Biblical Literature.

King, M. L, Jr. 1992–. *The Papers of Martin Luther King, Jr.*, gen. ed. C. Carson, 5 vols. to date. Berkeley, CA: University of California Press.

Kinnell, G. 2006. *Strong Is Your Hold*. Boston, MA: Houghton Mifflin.

Knight, G. 1992. *The Pastoral Epistles: A Commentary on the Greek Text*. Grand Rapids, MI: Eerdmans.

Knowles, E., ed. 2005. *The Oxford Dictionary of Phrase and Fable*, 2nd edn. New York: Oxford University Press.

Knox, J. 1994. *On Rebellion*, ed. Roger Mason. Cambridge: Cambridge University Press.

LaHaye, T. and Jenkins, J. 2004. *Glorious Appearing: The End of Days*. Carol Wheaton, IL: Tyndale House.

Langland, W. 1954. *The Vision of William Concerning Piers the Plowman*, ed. Walter W. Skeat. London: Oxford University Press.

Lawrence, D. H. 1985. *D. H. Lawrence and Italy: Twilight in Italy; Sea and Sardinia; Etruscan Places*. New York: Penguin Travel Library.

Lawrence, D. H. 1993. *Complete Poems*. New York: Penguin. (LION)

Lees, F. R. and Burns, D. 1870. *The Temperance Bible Commentary*. New York: National Temperance Society and Publication House.

Leith, J., ed. 1982. *Creeds of the Churches: A Reader in Christian Doctrine from the Bible to the Present*. Louisville, KY: John Knox Press.

Lewis, C. S. 1961. *Perelandra*. New York: Macmillan.

Locke, J. 1966. *The Second Treatise of Government*, ed. J. W. Gough. Oxford: Blackwell.

Logan, S., ed. 1995. *With Pen and Voice: A Critical Anthology of Nineteenth-Century African-American Women*. Carbondale, IL: Southern Illinois University Press.

Luther, M. 1955–76. *Luther's Works*, ed. J. Pelikan et al., 55 vols. Saint Louis, MO: Concordia Publishing House.

Luther, M. 2000. *Complete Sermons of Martin Luther*, ed. John Nicholas Lenker, 7 vols. Grand Rapids, MI: Baker Books.

Luther, M. 2001. *Luther's Small Catechism*, tr. Timothy Wengert. Minneapolis, MN: Augsberg Fortress.

MacDonald, D. 1983. *The Legend and the Apostle: The Battle for Paul in Story and Canon*. Philadelphia, PA: Westminster.

MacDonald, M. 1988. *The Pauline Churches*. Cambridge: Cambridge University Press.

MacDonald, M. 1996. *Early Christian Women and Pagan Opinion: The Power of the Hysterical Woman*. Cambridge: Cambridge University Press.

McMillan, D. and Fladenmuller, K., ed. 1997. *Regular Life: Monastic, Canonical, and Mendicant Rules*. Kalamazoo, MI: Medieval Institute Publications.

Malherbe, A. 1984. "In Season and Out of Season: 2 Tim. 4:2." *Journal of Biblical Literature* 103.2: 235–43.

Marius, R. 1999. *Martin Luther: The Christian Between God and Death*. Cambridge, MA: Belknap Press.

Martimort, A., ed. 1986. *The Church at Prayer: An Introduction to the Liturgy*, 4, tr. Matthew J. O'Connell. Collegeville, MN: Liturgical Press.

Martin, D. 1995. *The Corinthian Body*. New Haven, CT: Yale University Press.

Martin, S. C. 1997. *Pauli Testamentum: 2 Timothy and the Last Words of Moses*. Rome: Editrice Pontifica Università Gregoriana.

Mather, C. 1693. *The Wonders of the Invisible World*. Boston, MA: Benjamin Harris [for Samuel Phillips]. (ECCO)

Mather, C. 1699. *A Family Well-Ordered, or, An Essay to Render Parents and Children Happy in One Another*. Boston, MA: Printed by B. Green & J. Allen, for Michael Perry and Benjamin Eliot. (EEBO)

Matthews, D. 1993. " 'Spiritual Warfare': Cultural Fundamentalism and the Equal Rights Amendment." *Religion and American Culture* 3.2: 129–54.

Maximus the Confessor. 1996. *Maximus the Confessor*, ed. Andrew Louth. New York: Routledge.

Mayer, W. and Allen, 2000. *John Chyrsostom*. New York: Routledge.

McGinn, B. 1979. *Apocalyptic Spirituality: Treatises and Letters of Lactantius, Adso of Montier-en-Der, Joachim of Fiore, the Franciscan Spirituals, Savonarola*. New York: Paulist Press.

Mede, J. 1833. *Key to the Apocalypse*, tr. R. Bransby Cooper. London: Printed for J. G. & F. Rivington. (CCEL)

Melton, J. G., ed. 1988. *The Encyclopedia of American Religions: Religious Creeds*. Detroit, MI: Gale Research.

Melville, H. 1846. *Typee: A Peep at Polynesian Life*, 2 vols. New York: Wiley & Putnam. (LION)

Merrill, J. L. 1988. "The Bible and the American Temperance Movement: Text, Context and Pretext." *Harvard Theological Review* 81.2: 145–70.

"Methodist Hymnal Committee Blasted." UPI, Thursday, May 22, 1986.

Methodius of Olympus. 1958. *The Symposium: A Treatise on Chastity*, tr. H. Musurillo. Westminster, MD: Newman Press.

Milton, J. 1953–82. *Complete Prose Works of John Milton*, ed. Don M. Wolf et al., 8 vols. New Haven, CT: Yale University Press.

Milton, J. 1991. *Political Writings*, tr. Claire Gruzelier, ed. Martin Dzelzainis. New York: Cambridge University Press.

Minns, D. 2006. "Truth and Tradition: Irenaeus." In *The Cambridge History of Christianity*, 1, ed. Margaret M. Mitchell and Frances M. Young, 261–73. New York: Cambridge University Press.

Modleski, T. 1998. *Old Wives' Tales: And Other Women's Stories*. New York: New York University Press.

Montelaro, J. 1991. The Pardoner's Self-Reflexive Peyne: Textual Abuse of The First Epistle to Timothy. *South Central Review*, 8.4: 6–16.

Morris, H. M. 2004. "Dr. Luke." *Back to Genesis* [published by the Institute for Creation Research], 189 (Sept. 2004): a–d.

Muldoon, P. 2001. *Poems, 1968–1998*. New York: Farrar, Straus and Giroux.

Naphy, W. 2004. "Calvin's Geneva." In *The Cambridge Companion to John Calvin*, ed. Donald McKim, 25–37. New York: Cambridge University Press.

Newman, J. H. 1967. *On The Inspiration of Scripture*, ed J. Derek Holmes and Robert Murray. Washington, DC: Corpus Books.

Nelson, T. 2005. *The 12 Essentials of Godly Success: Biblical Essentials to a Life Well Lived*. Nashville, TN: Broadman & Holman.

Nicolas of Cusa. 1997. *Nicolas of Cusa: Selected Spiritual Writings*, tr. H. Bond. New York: Paulist Press.

Nietzsche, F. 2005. *Thus Spoke Zarathustra: A Book for Everyone and Nobody*, tr. Graham Parkes. Oxford: Oxford University Press.

Noll, M. 1976. "Ebenezer Devotion: Religion and Society in Revolutionary Connecticut." *Church History*, 45.3: 293–307.

Norris, R. tr. and ed. 2003. *The Song of Songs: Interpreted by Early Christian and Medieval Commentators*. Grand Rapids, MI: Eerdmans.

Ott, J. and Jones, A., ed. 2007. *The Bishop Reformed: Studies of Episcopal Power and Culture in the Central Middle Ages*. Burlington VT: Ashgate.

Origen. 1979. *Origen: An Exhortation to Martyrdom, Prayer and Selected Works*, tr. R. Greer. New York: Paulist Press.

Origen. 1998. *Origen*, ed. and tr. Joseph W. Trigg. New York: Routledge.

Owen, J. 1694. *A Plea for Scripture Ordination*. London: Printed for A. Salusbury. (EEBO)

Packer, J. I. 1958. *Fundamentalism and The Word of God*. Leicester: Inter-Varsity Fellowship.

Pelikan, J. 1971–89. *The Christian Tradition*, 5 vols. Chicago: University of Chicago Press.

Pellerin, D. 2003. "Calvin: Militant or Man of Peace." *Review of Politics*, 65.1: 35–59.

Penn, M. 2001. "'Bold and Having No Shame:' Ambiguous Widows, Controlling Clergy, and Early Syrian Communities." *Hugoye: Journal of Syriac Studies*, 4.2: 1–22.

Pervo, R. 1996. "The *Acts of Titus*: A Preliminary Translation." *Society of Biblical Literature Seminar Papers* 35: 455–482.

Pink Dandelion, B. 2007. *An Introduction to Quakerism*. New York: Cambridge University Press.

Potter, H. 1872. "Zenas: The Lawyer." New York: D. Van Nostrand.

"The Power of Contrary Choice." Review of Jonathan Edwards, *Freedom of the Will* (1840 edition). *Princeton Review* 12.4 (1840): 532–49. (MOA)

Prynne, W. 1633. *Histrio-Mastix. The Players Scovrge, or Actors Tragœdie*. London: Printed by E. A. and W. I. for Michael Sparke. (EEBO)

Pseudo-Dionysius. 1987. *Pseudo-Dionysius: The Complete Works*, tr. C. Luibheid, ed. P. Rorem. New York: Paulist Press.

Rahner, K. 1973. *On the Theology of Death*. New York: Seabury Press.

Ritter, A. M. 2006. "Church and State up to c. 300 CE." In *The Cambridge History of Christianity*, 1, ed. Margaret M. Mitchell and Frances M. Young, 524–37. New York: Cambridge University Press.

Robinson, I. S. 1991. "Church and Papacy." In *The Cambridge History of Medieval Political Thought c. 350–c.1450*, ed. J. H. Burns, 252–305. New York: Cambridge University Press.

Ross, F. 1857. "Slavery Ordained of God." Philadelphia, PA: J. B. Lippincott. (MOA)

Rossetti, C. 1979–90. *The Complete Poems of Christina Rossetti: A Variorum Edition*, ed. R. W. Crump, 3 vols. Baton Rouge, LA: Louisiana State University Press.

Ruether, R. 1990. "Prophets and Humanists: Types of Religious Feminism in Stuart England." *Journal of Religion*, 70.1: 1–18.

Ruskin, J. 1880–81. *Fiction – Fair and Foul*. London: C. Kegan Paul & Co.

Salvian the Presbyter. 1947. *The Writings of Salvian, The Presbyter*, tr. by Jeremiah F. O'Sullivan. New York: Cima Pub. Co.

Schleiermacher, F. 1963. *The Christian Faith*, ed. H. R. Mackintosh and J. S. Stewart, 2 vols. New York: Harper and Row.

Schneider, S. 1999. *The Revelatory Text: Interpreting the New Testament as Sacred Scripture*. Collegeville, MN: Liturgical Press.

Schüssler Fiorenza, E. 1992. *But She Said: Feminist Practices of Biblical Interpretation*. Boston, MA: Beacon Press.

Scofield, C. 1957. "Rightly Dividing the Word of Truth: Being Ten Outline Studies of the More Important Divisions of Scripture." Findlay, OH: Dunham Publishing.

Select Library of Nicene and Post-Nicene Fathers. 1994. ed. P. Schaff, series I: 14 vols; series II: 14 vols. Peabody, MA: Hendrickson.

Shakespeare, W. 1980. *The Complete Works of Shakespeare*, ed. David Bevington. Glenview, IL: Scott, Foresman.

Shannon, J. 1855. *An Address Delivered Before the Pro-Slavery Convention of the State of Missouri*. St. Louis, MO: Republican Book and Job Office. <dlxs.library.cornell.edu/m/mayantislavery/index.html>

Sherwood, Y. 2000. *A Biblical Text and Its Afterlives: The Survival of Jonah in Western Culture*. Cambridge: Cambridge University Press.

Shoukri, D. 1999. "The Wife of Bath's Parody of Scholasticism." *Alif: Journal of Comparative Poetics* 19: 97–112.

Spenser, E. 1981. *The Faerie Queene*, ed. Thomas P. Roche, Jr. New Haven, CT: Yale University Press.

Spicq, C. 1969. *Les Epitres Pastorales*, 2 vols. Paris: J. Gabalda et Cie.

Stegemann, W. 2002. "Anti-Semitic and Racist Prejudices in Titus 1:10–16." In *Ethnicity and The Bible*, ed. Mark G. Brett, 271–94. Boston, MA: Brill.

Stowe, H. B. 1856. *Dred: A Tale of the Great Dismal Swamp*, 2 vols. Boston, MA: Phillips, Sampson and Company. (LION)

Suso, H. 1994. *Wisdom's Watch Upon the Hours*, tr. E. Colledge. Washington, DC: Catholic University of America Press.

Symeon the New Theologian. 1980. *Discourses*, tr. C. J. de Catanzaro. New York: Paulist Press.

Taylor, E. 1960. *The Poems of Edward Taylor*, ed. Donald E. Stanford. New Haven, CT: Yale University Press. (LION)

Taylor, S. 1999. "Unapproachable Light," on *Music from Six Continents*. CD. Vienna Modern Masters. [VMM 3048].

Teresa of Avila. 1957. *The Complete Works of Saint Teresa of Jesus*, ed. and tr. E. Allison, 3 vols. New York: Sheed & Ward.

Tertullian. 2004. *Tertullian*, tr. and ed. Geoffrey Dunn. New York: Routledge.

Theodoret of Cyrus. 2001. *Theodoret of Cyrus: Commentary on The Letters of St. Paul*, tr. R. Hill,. 2 vols. Brookline, MA: Holy Cross Orthodox Press.

Theodoret of Cyrus. 2006. *Theodoret of Cyrus*, ed. István Pásztori-Kupán. New York: Routledge.

Thom, D. 1833. *The Assurance of Faith: Or Calvinism Identified with Universalism*, 2 vols. London: Simpkin and Marshall.

Thomas Aquinas. 2007. *Commentaries on St. Paul's Epistles to Timothy, Titus, and Philemon*, tr. Chyrsostom Baer. South Bend, IN: St. Augustine's Press.

Tippens, D. 2002. "Who's Afraid of Harry Potter?" *New Wineskins*, Jan–Feb, Zoe Group Ministries <wineskins.org/filter.asp?SID=2&fi_key=36&co_key=284>.

Todhunter, J. 1876. *Laurella And other Poems*. London: Henry S. King. (LION)

Towner, P. 1989. *The Goal of Our Instruction: The Structure of Theology and Ethics in the Pastoral Epistles*. Sheffield: JSOT Press.

Towner, P. 2006. *The Letters to Timothy and Titus*. Grand Rapids, MI: Eerdmans.

Tracts for The Times, 6 vols. 1969. New York: AMS Press.

Trask, R. 1997. *'The Devil Hath Been Raised': A Documentary History of the Salem Village Witchcraft Outbreak*. Danvers, MA: The Yeoman Press.

Turner, D. 1995. *The Darkness of God: Negativity in Christian Mysticism*. Cambridge: Cambridge University Press.

Tyndale, W. 2000. *The Obedience of a Christian Man*, ed. David Daniell. New York: Penguin.

Urban, L. 1995. *A Short History of Christian Thought*. New York: Oxford University Press.

US Catholic Church. 1995. *Catechism of the Catholic Church*. New York: Doubleday.

Verner, D. 1983. *The Household of God: The Social World of the Pastoral Epistles*. Chicago: Scholars Press.

Vidal, G. 1992. *Live From Golgotha*. New York: Random House.

Voltaire, F. 1843. *A Philosophical Dictionary*, tr. [?]. London: W. Dugdale.

Wang, P. 1998. *Of Flesh and Spirit*. Minneapolis, MN: Coffee House Press.

Ward, R. 2000. *The Life of Henry More, Parts 1 and 2*, ed. Sarah Hutton et al. Boston, MA: Kluwer Academic Publishers.

Warkentin, M. 1982. *Ordination: A Biblical-Historical View*. Grand Rapids, MI: Eerdmans.

Watson, J. ed. 2002. *An Annotated Anthology of Hymns*. Oxford: Oxford University Press.

Watson, T. 1660. *The Beatitudes: or A Discourse Upon Part of Christs Famous Sermon on the Mount*. London: printed for Ralph Smith. (EEBO)

Watts, I. 1856. *The Psalms, Hymns, and Spiritual Songs, of the Rev. Isaac Watts*, ed. Samuel Worcester. Boston, MA: Crocker & Brewster. (MOA)

Wesley, J. 1829–31. *The Works of the Rev. John Wesley*, 14 vols. London: John Mason.

Wesley, J. 1850. *Explanatory Notes Upon the New Testament*. New York: Lane and Scott.

Wesley, J and Wesley, C. 1868. *The Poetical Works*, 13 vols. London: The Wesleyan-Methodist Conference Office. (LION)

White, E. 1911. *The Acts of The Apostles in The Proclamation of the Gospel of Jesus Christ*. Mountain View, CA: Pacific Press.

White, E. 2005. *Desire of the Ages*. Mountain View, CA: Pacific Press.

Whitefield, G. 1741. *Persecution, The Christian's Lot. A sermon, Preached on Monday Afternoon. September 14th, 1741. In the High-Church-Yard of Glasgow*. Glasgow: The Gallowgate Printing-House, and Robert Smith. (EEBO)

Wiethoff, W. 2002. *The Insolent Slave*. Columbia, SC: University of South Carolina Press.

Wijngaards, J. 2002. *No Women in Holy Orders? The Women Deacons of the Early Church*. Norwich: Canterbury Press.

Winchester, E. 1819. *The Universal Restoration*. Bellows Falls, VT: Bill Blake & Co. (EAI 2)

Winterson, J. 1985. *Oranges Are Not the Only Fruit*. Boston, MA: Pandora Press.

Witherington, B. 2005. *The Problem With Evangelical Theology: Testing the Exegetical Foundations of Calvinism, Dispensationalism and Wesleyanism*. Waco, TX: Baylor University Press.

Woolf, Virginia 2006. *Three Guineas*. New York: Harcourt.

Young, F. M. 1994. *The Theology of the Pastoral Letters*. Cambridge: Cambridge University Press.

Young, F. M. 2006. "Towards a Christian *paideia*." In *The Cambridge History of Christianity*, 1, ed. Margaret M. Mitchell and Frances M. Young, 485–500. New York: Cambridge University Press.

WEBSITES

Note: Some of the following websites are accessible only via subscribing libraries.

APS: www.proquest.com/products_pq/descriptions/aps.shtml

Christian Classics Ethereal Library: www.ccel.org/

Corpus Thomisticum, Sancti Thomae de Aquino, Super I Epistolam B. Pauli ad Timotheum lectura: www.corpusthomisticum.org/ct1.html

Da Vinci Code Fraud: www.bringyou.to/apologetics/DaVinciCode.htm

ECCO: www.gale.com/EighteenthCentury/

EEBO: eebo.chadwyck.com/home

Hal Lindsey Report: hallindsey.org

Heidelberg Catechism: www.wts.edu/resources/heidelberg.html

Joseph Smith Translation: scriptures.lds.org/en/jst/contents

Ladies Against Feminism: www.ladiesagainstfeminism.com/artman/publish/rss.xml

LION: lion.chadwyck.com/

MOA: www.hti.umich.edu/m/moagrp/

NSW Supreme Court: www.lawlink.nsw.gov.au/lawlink/Supreme_Court/ll_sc.nsf/pages/SCO_young300106

Thomas Aquinas, *Summa Theologica*: www.ccel.org/a/aquinas/summa/home.html

Tyndale Bible: wesley.nnu.edu/biblical_studies/tyndale/

World Council of Churches: www.oikoumene.org/en/resources/documents/wcc-commissions/faith-and-order-commission/i-unity-the-church-and-its-mission/baptism-eucharist-and-ministry-faith-and-order-paper-no-111-the-lima-text/baptism-eucharist-and-ministry.html

Writings of J. N. Darby: www.stempublishing.com/authors/darby/index.html

Wycliffe Bible: wesley.nnu.edu/biblical_studies/wycliffe/

Index of Biblical References (canonical order)

Chapters and verses are in bold, while page numbers are not. Note that general citations to a book, where no specific chapter or verse is given, are listed first under the book's title. The Pastoral Epistles themselves have not been indexed. Please consult the table of contents for specific verses.

The Pastoral Epistles Through the Centuries, First Edition. Jay Twomey.
© 2009 by Jay Twomey. Published 2020 by John Wiley & Sons Ltd.

General Index

The Pastoral Epistles Through the Centuries, First Edition. Jay Twomey.
© 2009 by Jay Twomey. Published 2020 by John Wiley & Sons Ltd.

predestination 36, 38, 113, 120, 122–4, 147, 149–52, 183, 191
Prynne, William 137–8
Pseudo-Dionysius 56, 62, 107, 111, 131, 142

Ross, Fred 93
Rossetti, Christina 135
Ruskin, John 209–10

Salvian the Presbyter 103
Schleiermacher, Friedrich 34
Scofield, Cyrus (*Scofield Reference Bible*) 145–6, 211
Shakespeare, William 171
Shannon, James 93
Smith, Joseph 109
Spenser, Edmund 100
Stowe, Harriet Beecher 25
Suso, Henry 107
Symeon the New Theologian 39, 57, 156, 216

Taylor, Edward 62, 183–4
Taylor, Stephen 110
Temperance Bible Commentary 87
Teresa of Avila 206
Tertullian 31, 34–5, 41, 70, 78–9, 84, 97, 111–12, 120, 130–1, 133, 160, 164, 198, 200–1, 215, 219
Theodore of Mopsuestia 59

Theodoret of Cyrus 18, 29–30, 35, 39, 41, 54–5, 57, 60, 62, 76, 84, 86, 105, 108, 110, 115, 118, 126, 142, 158, 172–3, 176, 178, 193, 211
Thom, David 124
Thomas Aquinas 22, 43, 59, 72, 77–8, 84, 91, 97, 108, 118, 131–2, 136–7, 141, 146, 164, 182, 193, 201, 216, 220
Todhunter, John 172
Trinity (Trinitarianism) 28, 60, 107, 126–7, 221
Tyndale, William 57, 70, 109

Voltaire 53

Wang Ping 101
Watson, Thomas 173
Watts, Isaac 111, 123
Wesley, Charles 27, 38, 162
Wesley, John 25, 27, 38, 39, 41, 46, 58, 67, 85, 90, 96, 99, 122–3, 139, 162–3, 180, 191, 217, 223
White, Ellen 18, 67, 176
Whitefield, George 160
Winchester, Elhanan 148–9
Winterson, Jeanette 199–200
Woolf, Virginia 85
World Council of Churches 215
Wycliffe Bible 71, 88, 108–9, 205

Young, Peter 224–5